Managing for Outcomes

A Basic Guide to the Evaluation of Best
Practices in the Human Services

John B. Mordock

CWLA Press • Washington, DC

CWLA Press is an imprint of the Child Welfare League of America. The Child Welfare League of America is the nation's oldest and largest membership-based child welfare organization. We are committed to engaging people everywhere in promoting the well-being of children, youth, and their families, and protecting every child from harm.

CHILD WELFARE LEAGUE OF AMERICA, INC.
HEADQUARTERS
440 First Street, NW, Third Floor, Washington, DC 20001-2085
E-mail: books@cwla.org

CURRENT PRINTING (last digit)
10 9 8 7 6 5 4 3 2 1

Cover design by Amy Aalick
Text design by Kelly Mack and Peggy Porter Tierney

Printed in the United States of America
ISBN # 0−87868-814-5

Library of Congress Cataloging-in-Publication Data

Mordock, John B., 1938-
    Managing for outcomes : a basic guide to the evaluation of best practices in the human services / John B. Mordock.
        p. cm.
    Includes bibliographical references.
    ISBN 0-87868-814-5
        1. Human services--Evaluation--Methodology. 2. Evaluation research (Social action program) I. Title.

HV40 .M665 2001
    361'.0068'4--dc21

                                                                2001047299

Contents

Table

Contents (Cont'd)

Figures

Preface

●●●●●●●●●●●●●●●●●●●●●●●●●●●●●●●●●●●●●●

There are numerous books on program evaluation. Most are written by academics who consult with human service agencies. The readership is primarily other evaluators, students of program evaluation, and researchers who use these materials to guide their evaluation efforts. These books stress basic evaluation procedures rather than the management practices that are necessary to implement them correctly. In contrast, this book is written by a manager for managers in human service agencies. It stresses management's role in developing and implementing program evaluation procedures that will result in the establishment of best practices.

Unlike the authors of other books on evaluation, the majority of my evaluative experience was not obtained as a college professor who contracts with agencies to evaluate projects, nor as a research staff member at a nonprofit agency (although I did serve briefly in the latter position). Instead, I have functioned for most of my professional life as a mental health administrator in a large nonprofit, comprehensive child and family service agency—Astor Home for Children. My interest in program evaluation and outcome assessment is longstanding. It grew out of a desire both to deliver the most helpful services to clients and to ensure that services are cost-effective for clients (that is, they get "their money's worth"). This book is written in the spirit of ensuring that when a distraught parent reluctantly sends her child to a residential treatment center, the child receives the best treatment available and returns home as soon as possible. It is written in the spirit of making certain that when a mother who is severely depressed and suicidal is brought by her family to a mental health clinic, the benefits of the treatment will outweigh the financial and social costs that the family incurs.

In each of the leadership positions that I held during my 28-year tenure at Astor Home for Children, I, along with other staff, attempted to evaluate both programs and program components. It was not always easy, but the rewards always outweighed the difficulties. Although on one occasion the agency received foundation funds to evaluate the impact of its residential program, for the most part, program evaluations were funded with operating funds. In large projects, local university students occasionally assisted with data gathering and analysis, but, more often, agency staff did the work. Consequently, when I write this book on program evaluation for managers, I write it as a manager speaking to other managers and I embed it in a management context. I will not ask the reader to do what I could not do myself, although I will ask the reader to perform evaluations that, in hindsight, I should have done more thoroughly in several programs. I will also ask managers to use tools that did not exist when I was active as a manager. Because my managerial experience was obtained in child and family services, many (although not all) of my examples are drawn from this experience.

This book focuses on the steps that are necessary to develop best practices and evaluate the effects of these practices. Effective programs are those in which client gains can be directly attributed to the delivery of services. Consequently, the book emphasizes outcome assessment procedures; assessment tools (including questionnaire design); quality assurance practices that ensure program integrity; and determinations of cost-effectiveness. The book does not go into depth about the specific techniques that can be employed to help in this endeavor, such as how to conduct in-person or telephone interviews, follow up studies, or specific surveys, although it refers to these topics and presents the steps to follow in their implementation. There are many specific books on these and other program evaluation topics.

In my experience as a manager, program evaluation is most helpful when it is built into every program operated by an agency and when it is management's role to develop, evaluate, and maintain effective programs. All managers in human service agencies should be able to independently evaluate the effectiveness of their services. This book is designed to acquaint human service managers with program evaluation philosophies and procedures so that they can evaluate their services relying solely on outside consultants. Although human service providers may need assistance from consultants to perform complex statistical analyses of their outcome information, they should not need them to conduct evaluations or to make simple statistical comparisons between treated and untreated groups.

Many funding sources have stressed outcome assessment. More recently, however, managed care organizations have emphasized outcomes. In response, many human service organizations have made efforts to more systematically examine the results of their programs. Unfortunately, much of the rhetoric in the managed care literature ignores the difficulties associated with the performance of good outcome assessment and the interpretation of outcome findings. The loud call to employ only cost-effective interventions suggests that many human service interventions have been proven effective and that one only need to compare cost-effectiveness. This assumption is not well-founded, as the effectiveness of relatively few interventions has been demonstrated. At the same time, the costs of effective interventions can vary from setting to setting.

Managed care organizations also stress the development of specific intervention protocols, called "best practices," that can be easily replicated across settings. This book focuses on developing best practices and stresses, particularly in Chapters 1 and 3, that a chief task of management is to identify effective practices and streamline their delivery. Nevertheless, unlike managed care organizations, this book reminds readers that the effort to develop specific treatment protocols has its roots in the "scientific management" practices of Fredrick Taylor. Scientific management resulted in the assembly line approach to manufacturing popular in the early 1900s. Supporters of these practices were never able to successfully apply them to white collar work, and they now are seen as dehumanizing.

The current effort of managed care organizations to introduce newer versions of these practices stems more from a need to control costs than a desire to employ the most helpful interventions. The belief persists that with protocol development, workers can become interchangeable and cheaper labor can be substituted for more expensive labor. Although treatment protocols can and should be developed, there is overwhelming evidence that certain human qualities—particularly qualities emphasized in the selection, training, and ongoing supervision of human service workers—contribute more to changes in clients than do the actual protocols themselves. Managers will do well to keep this relationship in mind when helping staff to develop specific intervention practices.

The interpretation of outcome findings and the determination of cost-effectiveness, as Chapter 8 demonstrates, require much more than mathematical calculations. These processes require complex value judgments with human concerns at the core of the judgments. The recent emphasis on applying "business practices" in human service agencies boils down to more economical forms of financial supervision. In such an environment, financial systems can come to compete with helping others, which is the actual business of human service agencies.

The tendencies of financial accountings are stark. Costs are seen as negatives, including the costs of labor which are viewed as an area for potential savings. Costs are considered as investments only when they are linked to an expected return. If costs lead only to "nonquantifiable" goods of the kind common to human service agencies, it will be difficult from a strictly financial perspective to certify them as valuable investments. From this perspective, benefits that cannot be quantified may have less clout than benefits that can be quantified. Better means cheaper; growth means reduction; productivity means discipline; and knowledge means regulation. The most immediate casualties of such thinking are dreams of the new: new programs, new combinations of service, and new ideas supported by the agency. In this environment, the value of outcome assessment in attempting to quantify the results of human services should be recognized, but such efforts should proceed with caution. Not all outcomes can be quantified, and when they cannot, the conclusion should not necessarily be that the program is failing to provide a valuable service.

Managers continually must struggle to keep the agency mission clearly in mind and remind others about the purpose of human service activities. If the nonprofit agencies for which I worked had placed financial considerations over human service considerations, they would have closed their doors long ago. Helena Devereux, the founder of the Devereux Schools, a therapeutic treatment program located in a number of states, once said that, "If a program was operating within its state approved rates, it wasn't adequately serving children." For many years, the Daughters of Charity, who operated the Astor Home for Children, donated to the program their salaries as child care workers, nurses, and administrators to ensure that services would be enriched. These agencies recognized that a cost- effective service is not one where minor changes are reported on outcome measures, but is a service that efficiently and effectively decreases human suffering.

Throughout the book, a number of published studies are presented to illustrate particular points. To save space, the studies are not cited as they would be in a publication for an academic audience, although there are citations to reviews of the literature, methodological studies, and opinion pieces. The busy human services manager cannot be expected to seek out the original studies but should be rest assured that the findings are accurately reported.

John B. Mordock, Ph.D.

Chapter 1

An Overview of Program Evaluation and Management

Relatively few agencies regularly perform program evaluations. Robert McCall, of the University of Pittsburgh's Office of Child Development and Policy Evaluation Project, has observed that few of the more than 500 agencies he has reviewed had any understanding of research methodologies needed to assess service outcomes. Similarly, a nationwide survey revealed that of the 758 sexual abuse treatment agencies responding, only 43% regularly used any standardized instruments or program-specific tools to assess their clients; 38% used instruments to assess outcomes following treatments; and next to none performed studies to assess real intervention impact (Keller, Cicchinelli, & Gardner, 1989). In another survey, only approximately one-fifth of residential treatment centers for emotionally disturbed youth (62 of more than 300 agencies) responded to questions about their outcome measures. Although it is possible that nonrespondents were engaged in outcome evaluation, the low rate of return suggested that most were not.

In response to the lack of knowledge about program evaluation in human service agencies, the United Way recently developed a training program on outcome assessment that includes an accompanying manual (United Way, 1996). The United Way encourages, if not requires, employees of member agencies to complete the training program. Program topics include an introduction to outcome measurement, preparation, choice of outcomes to be measured, identification of indicators for the outcomes, data

1

collection on the indicators, implementation of the outcome measurement system, analysis and reporting of findings, improvement
of the assessment system, and use of the findings. The United Way
program is based on the concept of management by objectives and
focuses on defining outcomes as measurable objectives that clients
hope to achieve through a specific service activity. The training
program offers guidance on the use of objective measures of behavior change, client self-reports, and informant ratings of behavior change. It provides a procedure to quantify the achievement
of individual client goals. The United Way training and manual
are good companion pieces to this book.

The focus of this book, however, differs from the United Way
training. The goals of this book are to acquaint managers with
more advanced concepts of program evaluation, emphasize the
manager's role in program evaluation, embed program evaluation
within current management practices, and relate evaluation to
managed care concepts, some of which are at odds with the goals
of human service organizations. The preparation of human service professions for managed care (Mordock 1996, 1997, 1998) and
current managed care practices in child welfare (Mordock, 1999a)
have been addressed elsewhere. These volumes, however, did not
consider the recent merging of managed care concepts with the
use of "scientific management" practices (as promulgated by
Fredrick Taylor in the early 1900s) that can have an adverse effect
on human service agencies. This issue is addressed in this book.

The Impact of the Managed Care Movement

Most human service agencies engage in program evaluation only
when required by outside forces, and usually only under special
circumstances. Often, evaluations are tied to funding for a specific
program or service, which carries with it the stipulation that the
agency provide the funding source with a report of the results that
have been achieved from time-limited services. For most agencies,
the major outside force driving program evaluation in human services is the managed care movement.

Managed care—and with it, the recent upsurge of interest in outcome research—is set within an environment in which efforts are being made to apply business practices, or "the corporate model," to the field of human services. In spite of the empowerment and "human relations" movements in modern business practices, scientific management is still alive and well in the business world. Taylor (1911) believed that productivity and efficiency would be increased if work were broken down into specific steps, or sequences of activities, that could be replicated by all workers. His concepts led to the use of assembly lines in the manufacturing industry. The application of these concepts is now being seen in the downsizing efforts of many corporations and the "reinvention" of human services.

As managed care concepts have arrived in the human services, nonprofit enterprises have been required to base policy decisions on profit and loss considerations. The emphasis is now on the cost-effectiveness of services. To achieve cost effectiveness, managed care organizations have demanded that human services identify specific processes that contribute to outcomes, eliminate ineffective processes, and "manualize" the resulting methods so that all workers can apply them in the same manner. As processes have become more important than people, human service workers, like factory workers, have come to be seen as interchangeable.

The effort to develop and uniformly apply specific intervention protocols is clearly a "scientific management" effort. Scientific management concepts, however, have never been successfully applied to more complex and conceptual work, including human service activities. It has never been possible to devise the "single most effective procedure" in various types of white collar work nor to determine how to enforce their use if they were developed. The difficulties in this regard are heightened by the fact that direct, detailed supervision does not take place in human service activities. Most human service providers operate relatively independently. Supervisors do not join them in intervention sessions, accompany them on home visits, nor join them in their work with groups of clients. More often, supervision takes the form of consultation, as workers present their difficult cases and seek supervisory advice and direction. Human service workers typically learn from one another, and peer supervision is a primary form of training and supervision. In fact, the freedom to self-manage attracts many people to the low-paying jobs in the human services.

Scientific management is now being applied, however, in human services. Many professionals oppose this development and object to efforts to develop specific intervention protocols. Fears center on concerns that their use will cause an erosion in professional relationships with clients, the employment of less educated workers to apply these protocols, and the loss of the essential ingredients of helping relationships. Some of these fears already have been realized. In the mental health field, managed care organizations, applying market-based fee-setting procedures, refer more clients to social workers than to psychiatrists and psychologists and employ utilization reviewers to approve and then to closely monitor treatment delivery. Clients now experience brief encounters with providers rather than meaningful relationships with them, receiving "fast food" instead of "home-cooked meals." At the same time, "downsizing" is occurring as professionals are pressured to see more clients and are removed from managed care providers' lists when they cannot comply with such requirements because they are located in low-use areas.

Managed care organizations currently look primarily at costs as outcomes. They focus on the costs of serving a client, as opposed to the costs of achieving client outcomes. When they do examine client outcomes, there is little interest in how the outcomes are achieved and far greater interest in high client satisfaction ratings (the criterion often used to retain providers as part of the managed care network). The focus should be, instead, on which interventions assist clients to reach their objectives. With this goal in mind, managers must be able to work with staff to develop specific intervention protocols, ensure their correct implementation, perform outcome assessments, and identify the specific features of interventions that make them effective. When managers work with staff, program evaluation efforts can lead to employee empowerment rather than to the dehumanization that accompanies scientific management.

Research Consultants and Research Departments

Human service agencies often face program evaluation pressures from private and governmental entities that fund specific programs or services. As an example, a substance abuse treatment center recently applied for and received funds from a foundation to develop a new parent training program for their patients who are parents of young children. In another case, a foundation awarded a child welfare agency the funds to provide a 10-week parenting course to parents of children in foster care. Both agencies were able to implement their programs only with external support. In both cases, the funding sources asked the agencies to demonstrate the effectiveness of their parent training programs. Neither agency had existing evaluation programs, and undoubtedly, neither would have evaluated the proposed services had the funding sources not required it. The staff in both agencies lacked experience in program evaluation, and as a result, each agency hired an academically based researcher as a consultant to help the agency to evaluate the effects of the funded programs.

Quite frequently, research consultants assume full responsibility for program evaluation. Typically, they (and their graduate assistants) perform the entire evaluation from its inception—designing, analyzing, interpreting the data, and writing the report. Their relationship with the agency ends after the evaluation is completed, and agency staff are no better equipped to perform evaluations in the future. When the need again arises to evaluate a program, the agency most likely will contract with the academic researcher who performed the last program evaluation.

Some large nonprofit agencies have their own research departments, but rarely do these departments help program staff to evaluate ongoing agency programs. Typically, the research departments are semiautonomous units that rely primarily on extramural funds (government or foundation monies) to maintain themselves. The research performed by staff usually is tangential to the existing services the agency delivers, with funding obtained for research or demonstration projects that interest the funding sources themselves. Research directors in nonprofit agencies continually are on alert for requests for proposals from government agencies and private foundations that will fund projects that have some bearing on the agency mission and in which agency clients can serve as research subjects.

An example of the realities associated with agency research departments can be drawn from the author's experience as coordinator of research at the Devereux Foundation in Devon, Pennsylvania. The agency received funds for a number of research projects that enhanced agency services during the grant period, but which were not part of the ongoing service delivery system prior to the research project. The agency, for example, received funds from the Rehabilitation Services Administration to evaluate the effects of a training program on the coordination skills of children suffering from minimal cerebral dysfunction. Because the agency had more than 300 children in care who suffered from this condition, it was one of the few centers in the United States that could undertake such an evaluation project. Nevertheless, the exercises developed for the evaluation were not used throughout the agency prior to the research project, nor were they widely used after the project's completion. The physical therapist responsible for the development of the exercises, the "Program Champion" (a term used to designate a strong supporter of a program or service) and a consultant to the agency, died a short time after the project concluded and there was little interest in continuing the training exercises.

Similarly, the director of research at The Devereux Foundation who preceded the author received federal funds to develop a behavior rating scale for children. Using public school children and agency clients for the standardization sample, he developed the Devereux Child Behavior Rating Scales. Although the scales were sold to others and widely used throughout the nation (primarily by researchers), they were infrequently used at the Devereux Foundation itself, largely because advocacy for the scale's use in assessment procedures came from research staff. In fact, at the time the director of research was developing an adolescent scale, he took a research position at a different agency, completed that instrument, and named it after his new agency (the Hannimen Adolescent Behavior Rating Scales). It is likely that this scale is not used extensively at that agency.

Shortly after the author left, Devereux disbanded its research department. Twenty years later, the agency reestablished the department, and one of the first projects was to revise, sell, and distribute the Devereux Child Behavior Rating Scales. A second project was to examine program outcomes using the scales to differentiate among client groups. Within five years, the research department, once again, was disbanded.

As these examples well illustrate, human service agencies should not rely on research consultants or research departments within the agencies to conduct evaluations of its services. Instead, evaluation should be viewed as a management task. Evaluations should be performed by agency staff on an ongoing basis and not by outside consultants or by members of an agency research department.

Program Evaluation as a Management Task

Federal and foundation-funded research, although of value to an agency, should not be the only research in which an agency engages. To the contrary, an evaluation component should be built into all agency programs, particularly in the current managed care environment. Ongoing program evaluation is important because managed care contracts often require that agencies evaluate both the efficiency and the effectiveness of their services. Evaluation should not be an activity that the agency performs every now and then to please a funding source. It should be an integral part of the agency's service delivery system. Although it has its complications, program evaluation is not "rocket science," and any reasonably intelligent person can conduct evaluations and, in fact, enjoy the process.

Every manager in a nonprofit agency should perform program evaluations so that all programs and program components

(services) are regularly assessed. Program evaluation has important benefits. Involving staff in program evaluation efforts adds a
positive dimension to their work. Most human service workers are
curious about why services do or do not work; many, because they
were trained in one of the social sciences, identify themselves with
disciplined inquiry. Program evaluation also can increase consumer involvement in agency programs and enhance an agency's
standing in the larger community. When an agency is viewed as
one that "evaluates what it does," it typically attracts more qualified personnel, particularly those willing to trade a "positive organizational culture" for less pay.

Importantly, program evaluation is necessary to maintain the
integrity of programs. Good management and program
evaluation go hand in hand. In the absence of program evaluation,
staff will continue the activities that they have utilized in the past,
even if other activities are more relevant. They may fail to see that
what they do best may be done better. Staff trained in a proven
intervention may drift away from the approach or even reinvent
the activity. Such changes in programs are more likely to occur
when staff is not held accountable by an organizational culture
that demands the continuation of effective programs until
another program is proven more effective.

The role of management is to challenge untested assumptions
and methods; evaluate the efficiency and effectiveness of existing services; and continue the effective programs while discontinuing the ineffective. Management also is charged with identifying, refining, and ultimately disseminating the specific
processes of interventions that work well, discontinuing interventions that lead to disappointing results, and substituting alternative processes for interventions that are not working.

Program Efficiency and Effectiveness

Agency executives often view program evaluation in less than
positive terms. They invest little energy in the periodic evaluations their agency performs, and they breathe a sigh of relief when

each evaluation is completed and the funding source is provided with the results. Some agency executives see program evaluation as an unnecessary academic exercise designed to demonstrate quantitatively what they already know qualitatively: the agency's services are effective. Although they may believe that services could be delivered more efficiently, they are of the opinion that, having stood the test of time, their services have been "proven" effective. After all, why would the agency provide services if they were not effective? In many cases, such assessments of service effectiveness may be correct. The important issue is whether the services that are delivered are the best services to achieve the desired result. Thirty sessions of family therapy may achieve a desired mental health result, for example, but so might 10 sessions of group parent training. Six months of a group home placement with outpatient treatment might achieve the same results as six months of residential treatment.

A number of questions must be answered about each service an agency offers. How much client gain does the service produce? Does the service produce greater client gains than can be produced by other services? What is the cost of producing the client gains attributed to the service? Does the cost justify the use of the treatment? As one example, a family may achieve a relatively higher degree of success after 30 sessions of family therapy than after 10 group parent training sessions, but the family may prefer the less successful parent training because it saves them time and money. As another example, staff in a mental health treatment center may deliver 15 sessions of group self-esteem training and outcome data may support the program's effectiveness. Further analysis of the actual gains made by the treatment group, however, may suggest that staff time could have been put to more cost-effective use.

When large human service agencies offer the same service in a variety of settings, other questions should be asked. Is the service equally effective across settings? If not, what factors contribute to effective delivery in one setting and ineffective delivery in another setting? This last question is particularly important to maintaining service integrity. When the factors that contribute to successful implementation of an effective service are known, it is much easier to replicate the service.

Some human service agencies deliver inefficient and ineffective services; and staff judgments about the efficiency and effectiveness of programs or components of programs can be, and often are, wrong. Quality assurance studies in agencies that undertake such evaluations demonstrate that many program components are inefficient. Outcome studies demonstrate that some programs not only are ineffective, but are actually harmful. Some programs directly harm consumers, and others are indirectly harmful because they raise false hopes that services will produce a positive change, if not a cure. Even in the face of ineffectiveness, when an agency is the sole provider of a service in the community, consumers may continue to utilize the service because they cannot choose another provider. Eventually, however, a rival service provider will appear; the agency will suffer a gradual loss of clients; and, without major corrective action, it may have to close.

Inefficient and Ineffective Programs

There are many examples of programs and services that prove to be inefficient and ineffective. Some programs subsequently are determined to be entirely inappropriate for the clients they are designed to serve; others offer "new" approaches that nonetheless yield little benefit; others offer false hopes. And still others prove to be inefficient and ineffective despite staff judgments to the contrary.

Examples of Inappropriate Interventions

There are a number of examples of interventions that initially were supported but later proved to be inappropriate. Early pioneers in the field of mental retardation, for example, believed that they could cure the disorder by admitting children who were mentally retarded to centers that specialized in intensive habilitation. Eventually these centers became extremely large, as society turned over more and more individuals to the experts for care and habilitation. Even individuals with moderate levels of mental retardation were seen as needing institutional care. The early pioneers who were the "Program Champions" of this approach eventually learned that mental retardation could not be cured, and disillusioned by their failures, went elsewhere. The large institutions regressed into human warehouses where clients deteriorated. Their deterioration was considered a feature of their retardation and not the result of the impoverished institutional conditions in which they were living. It is now clear that home care is preferable to group care for all but the profoundly retarded, and even those individuals receive better care in small group homes than in large institutions.

Similarly, after the passage of Public Law 94-142 (a federal law that stipulated that all children regardless of their physical or mental condition were entitled to a public education), children with disabilities were thought to be better educated in small, highly structured classes and taught by teachers trained and certified in special education. For many years, children were taught in self-contained classrooms. Some children were sent to specialized day and residential schools. The majority of students with serious emotional disturbance (SED) (98%) were placed in segregated special class settings. In some states, they represented more than 50% of students with disabling conditions in residential placement.

Nevertheless, outcome studies suggested that most of the children placed in special classrooms were making little progress. By contrast, handicapped children who remained in regular classrooms were doing no worse than children in special classes. Some handicapped children in regular classrooms were doing even better than children in special classes. Studies further suggested that the children who had profited least from special education programs were children with SED. Many children with SED continued to display the behavioral problems that resulted in their removal from mainstream classrooms, and a large number failed to make any academic progress and dropped out of school or were referred to day treatment, residential programs, or correctional facilities (Wagner, 1995; Wagner & Blackorby, 1996). Eber and Nelson (1977, p. 389) remarked that "services [became] part of the

student's program because they [were] part of the self-contained
EBD [emotional and behavioral disabilities] classroom, not because they [were] interventions likely to produce targeted outcomes for that pupil." Special education turned out to be "not so
special." It did not produce the results that were anticipated and
had some unanticipated harmful effects on children because they
were isolated from normal social interactions. Many educators,
believing that children with disabilities should be taught in regular classrooms, supported the general education initiative or in-
clusion movement.

Other examples of inappropriate interventions can be found
in the mental health field and in youth corrections. Initially, mental health embraced long-term therapy. But research demonstrated that many patients could make substantial progress in relatively few psychotherapy sessions and that some clients in
long-term therapy became emotionally dependent upon their
therapists. Some programs that provided emotionally disabled
children with group academic instruction and treatment (such as
in day treatment programs) found that children's conditions worsened instead of improved. Studies also found that a number of
programs for delinquent youth made them more, rather than less,
delinquent. A study in Canada reported that youth who received
mental health services in addition to probation department services had a higher recidivism rate than youth receiving only probation services.

Examples of New Approaches Yielding Little Benefit

For many years, psychoanalytic theory dominated the field of
mental health. Many mental health professionals (particularly
academic clinical psychologists who were heavily invested in developing treatment methods unique to psychology), however, were
disenchanted with what they viewed as the "mystical" medical
treatment methods of those who utilized a psychoanalytic framework. Based on principles of learning theory, psychologists developed what came to be known as the "behavior therapies." Because
they were new, they were considered better. The seemingly suc-

cessful recovery of a few individuals with severe disorders, such as anorexia nervosa, resulted in exaggerated claims regarding the superiority of the "new" behavior therapies over the traditional therapies. Research supported such claims as single-subject research designs replaced traditional research methodologies. When behavior therapies were subjected to scrutiny by more objective researchers, however, they often were found to be no more efficient and no more effective than traditional treatments. For example, patients whose anorexia was considered cured by behavioral methods experienced relapses. Autistic children whose behavior improved when treated with behavior modification returned to their former states when the therapy was discontinued. Even when they were shown to be effective, research indicated that the new methods were not necessarily more efficient. Studies showed that programs that taught parents of youth with conduct disorders to reinforce and extinguish their children's disruptive behaviors often required up to 50 treatment sessions, more sessions than were provided by staff schooled in other procedures. Although the early behavior therapies have evolved into "cognitive-behavioral therapies," which have been empirically verified as effective techniques, many regard the initial wholesale adoption of the crude early behavioral procedures as a step backward in the mental health field.

On a smaller scale is the experience of the John Tracy Oral Preschools for the Deaf, which was stimulated by the movie "The Miracle Worker " and spearheaded by the wife of actor Spencer Tracy. The preschools received substantial funds to provide oral language instruction for deaf children, which the founders of the program considered superior to traditional sign language instruction that characterized the education of the deaf at the time. There was a long waiting list, and the few children who gained admission were considered fortunate. Very few children, however, acquired recognizable speech in the program. As adults, students of the preschools fared more poorly than did individuals who as children attended the less well-funded state schools for the deaf that taught children to communicate in sign language.

Examples of Programs Leading to False Hopes

In the 1940s, both the *Reader's Digest* and *Women's Home Companion* ran articles stating that at long last, a scientist had developed an educational procedure that would increase the IQ of children with mental retardation to the normal range. These articles referred to a study that appeared to demonstrate that children classified as retarded (mean IQ of 52) increased nearly 20 IQ points in intelligence following three years of special educational training. After five years of post-school experience, their IQs had increased nearly 40 points and approached average. In reality, many of the subjects in this study were not retarded but rather were from disadvantaged backgrounds. Closer inspection of the children's records also suggested that many children actually had IQs in the 70s rather than in the 50s, and as a result, could have achieved improved intellectual functioning solely from special schooling. Children who were clearly retarded and not simply socially disadvantaged typically had retest scores within 10 points of their original IQ score.

Similarly, many promises of positive results have been made by the program, D.A.R.E. (Drug Abuse Resistance Education), which is widely used throughout the United States and in 20 countries abroad to prevent substance abuse among youth. Nonetheless, research has found that the program has no long-term positive effects. Studies that demonstrated positive effects after completion of the program also reported that the effects faded over time. Several studies, in fact, reported greater use of marijuana and hallucinatory agents after completion of the D.A.R.E. program.

Evaluations of several youth employment programs for disadvantaged youth have revealed poorer outcomes for program participants than for nonparticipants. One explanation for these findings is that program participation stigmatized youth. In one study of a youth employment program, the researchers studied wages at follow-up of youth who had participated in the California Conservation Corps (CCC), a state-funded youth employment program that provided youth with full-time jobs and training opportunities for up to one year (Grossman & Tierney, 1993). The researchers found that the wages of CCC youth were lower than those of the nonparticipants. However, they attributed the unexpected findings to their inability to create a similar comparison group in spite of their sophisticated efforts to do so.

There are many examples of other programs that have raised false hopes. The Doman-Delacato Patterning Program for children who have been brain damaged, for example, promised high levels of success for these children. The parents of many children, however, found that their children had been adversely affected by the demanding routine of the patterning program because it limited their contact with children of their own age at school or at play. Other examples of programs that have raised false hopes include the use of megavitamin, foods high in glutamic acid, and sugar-free diets for children who are retarded, autistic, or hyperactive.

Even treatments that have solid research support may be of benefit to only a portion of the group for which they were originally intended. As one example, in phenylketonuria (PKU), diet treatment originally was predicted to cure the disorder (in which mental retardation is believed to result from an inborn error in metabolism). The treatment, however, has been found to be effective for only a portion of those afflicted. Less dramatic examples can be found in services or programs that are less effective than others or that are equally effective but more costly (that is, less efficient). Self-help groups, for example, can be as effective as psychotherapy for some mentally ill patients. Some early childhood intervention programs have demonstrated substantial long-term results for some patients but have been found to be relatively ineffective for others. Some therapeutic interventions are more efficient or more effective with certain emotional disorders than are other interventions.

An Example of an Ineffective Program Despite Staff Judgment to the Contrary

Programs may be found to be ineffective despite staff beliefs to the contrary. In the 1960s, the Irving Swartz Institute for Children and Youth in Philadelphia provided a day treatment program for young children. The children were taught in highly structured classrooms; individualized instruction occurred in carrels rather than classroom settings; and children had minimal academic interaction with one another. The children usually remained in the program for two years. After the program had been in operation for approximately three years, it was decided that children would fare better following discharge to public schools if they were taught in a public school classroom structure prior to their discharge. Consequently, during the children's last six months in the program, the staff abandoned individualized instruction in carrels, taught children in desks that were arranged in rows, and provided group instruction. A follow-up evaluation revealed, that contrary to staff opinion, the children who had been instructed in the individual carrels before the change in program design were doing better in public school than those taught in the "transitional classroom." The key variable turned out to be academic rather than social proficiency as those children closest to grade level upon discharge did the best in public schools. More children taught in the structured classrooms throughout their stay in the program achieved closer to grade level at discharge than those instructed for six months in the transitional classroom.

Program Attributes Associated with Effectiveness and Efficiency

Because of the emphasis of managed care on developing best practices and assessing outcomes, a number of human service agencies, in preparation for managed care contracts, have attempted to assess outcomes for clients they have served in the past. Although these efforts are a beginning, the results will be of little value unless they are tied to best practices, a concept discussed later in this chapter.

What often is lacking in agency efforts is a clear definition of the attributes associated with effectiveness and efficiency. As an example, an agency might feature a bar graph in its newsletter that shows that 85% of the clients discharged from one of its programs are doing well on postdischarge measures of functioning. This "success rate," however, could be the result of the clients receiving an array of community support services after they were discharged rather than the result of the agency's intervention. Even if success were attributable to an intervention, would an agency with an 85% success rate at follow-up be "better" than an agency with a 75% success rate? The answer would be "yes" only if the clients served were drawn from the same population of clients, received different services, and were discharged to similar communities. If the agency with the 85% success rate cannot concisely describe the services the clients received while in the program (allowing program replication by others), the "success rate" is meaningless.

An agency might claim that its success rate is the result of unique milieu ingredients that cannot be measured or even clearly described. It may, for example, point to staff enthusiasm, staff morale, staff camaraderie, staff commitment to clients, family-friendly staff attitudes, professional-paraprofessional communications, participatory decisionmaking, and meaningful treatment team planning. If such factors are the unique ingredients of the agency's success (their "best practices"), how can the agency assure their continuation? If they cannot be described or measured, they are not likely to continue. In addition, such success-based factors may even be myths. A visit to a "less successful" agency, for example, may reveal that it also attributes its success rate to the same factors. If it were possible to measure these attributes, the less successful program might actually possess more of them. And if so, what then?

There are many other examples of assumptions about success-related program attributes. The success of inpatient treatment, for example, often is attributed to the frequency and quality of staff-patient interactions. Hospitals stress their small staff-to-client ratio in their milieu environments as the key to successful inpatient treatment. Yet, in a study of 30 adult inpatient programs, staff-client interactions ranged from a low of 43 exchanges to a high of 459 exchanges per hour and the total attention received by the

average patient varied by more than 1300% across institutions
(Paul, 1986). Similar variations occur in staff-client ratios and interactions in child care and other child services programs (Fulcher,
1991; Moos, 1974).

As these examples make clear, managers should clearly define
the attributes that are likely to be associated with efficiency and
effectiveness, and evaluate whether such relationships exist. Little
is achieved through assumptions about success based on abstract
factors that cannot be measured.

Maintaining Program Integrity

Once it is established that a program or a specific service is efficient and effective, managers must direct their efforts at maintaining the program as originally conceptualized. Maintaining the
integrity of a program means that it remains the same and does
not deviate from specific standards for any reason, including staff
turnover. Agency programs can suffer from "institutional drift" or
the whims of newly hired or promoted staff (sometimes referred
to as "reinventing") unless there are ongoing program evaluation
efforts supported by executive and professional staff and the
agency's board of directors. Drift typically occurs with the passage
of time and turnover of staff, particularly when staff who strongly
advocated for a program or a program component ("Program
Champions") leave and are replaced by others who wish to implement their own, often untested ideas. Although managers should
encourage innovation, they should remember that innovations in
proven interventions should proceed with caution. On the other
hand, efforts to revise the interventions that have not been proven
effective should be most welcome.

Three Examples of Failures to Maintain Effective Programs

There are dramatic examples of failures to maintain program
integrity that result in programs that enjoyed notable reputations
for efficiency and effectiveness eventually becoming mediocre or

disappearing all together. The first example is that of a well-known day treatment center for emotionally disturbed children, which for many years delivered services under a specific theoretical model with demonstrated effectiveness. An early director of the program implemented the model; when he was promoted to a higher position, he hired program directors experienced in the model's use. As the theoretical model evolved, programmatic changes rapidly became "institutionalized" because they were in keeping with the model and the organizational culture that grew around it. The institutionalization process was facilitated by four factors: the first director of the program held a theoretically-based assumption about conditions that produced positive changes in emotionally disturbed children, supported by research findings; specific program components that followed from these assumptions were implemented; new staff were taught solutions that worked consistently for the program; and staff eventually took the assumptions for granted, sharing a common philosophy that dictated actions and brought staff together as a community.

Although the program drifted from the model over the years, the drift was not significant until the first director (the "Program Champion") left the agency, followed by the departures of the last program director to operate the model and many clinicians and classroom teachers. The new program director, with no significant experience in milieu treatment but with many ideas, implemented changes that were not based on empirical findings. For example, he allowed newly hired teachers to discover for themselves techniques to manage children (sometimes referred to in the management literature as "country-club management"). The new teachers implemented a variety of procedures because there was no culture that encouraged them to employ historically successful practices; organizational "amnesia" occurred; and the program rapidly went into a state of "disequilibrium."

A second example is drawn from a school-wide reading program that was established many years ago in a nationally known treatment center. The agency's director of education was responsible for educational programs throughout the agency (a matrix model of management). The director observed that children in both the residential school and the day school were not making substantial improvement in reading (which he believed was the key to the children's ultimate success in life), even in small classes of eight or nine children. He also was concerned about the children's behavior early in the day, believing that maximal success and motivation depended on experiences at the start of the school day.

The director initiated a new approach, having children taught reading in small groups of no more than four children that met the first period of each day (a "school-wide model"). All available rooms in both schools were used, and all educational staff (teaching assistants, teachers, and special subject teachers) was assigned to teach the children in these small groups. A reading specialist tested the children, assigned them to homogenous groups, selected the grade level material for use in each group, circulated among the groups as instruction took place, and met with each reading group instructor when guidance was needed. The program enabled children to receive reading instruction at their comfort level rather than at their frustration level. The children experienced success that seemed to motivate them for other academic work when they returned to their regular classrooms.

After the program had been in place for several years, the director examined the reading achievement scores of children who had received instruction under the school-wide model and compared them with the scores of children who had received reading instruction in their classrooms prior to implementation of the new model. The gain scores of children receiving reading instruction in the school-wide reading program were significantly better than those receiving instruction in regular classrooms. Achievement test scores obtained on a yearly basis showed a one-year gain in reading for each year in the program, approximately a three-month improvement over gains made prior to program implementation. Before enrollment in the school-wide model, most children had gained less than half-a-year in reading grade level for each year they were in school. Following the implementation of the school wide model, both the state and federal governments recognized the residential school as an exemplary school.

Following the departure of the director of education (and no replacement for that position) and two other supporters of the school-wide reading model (the administrator in charge of community mental health programs and the program director of the day treatment center), the program was abandoned at the day treatment location. The new director of the center informed staff via a memo that reading instruction was to take place in the classrooms and that only licensed teachers would provide reading instruction. His immediate superior, also new to the agency, had given him blanket approval to make any program changes he desired. With the stroke of a pen, the new director arbitrarily disbanded a significant component of a nationally recognized program.

A third example is that of a residential treatment program for children located some distance from the community where the majority of its clients resided. After a number of years of operation, the agency redeployed its social work staff to a community-based center where many of the parents of the enrolled children could conveniently receive family therapy, either at the center or in their homes. A consultant was hired to train and supervise the social work staff in family therapy techniques so that the staff would be skilled in delivering this treatment modality. Previously, social workers traveled great distances to provide supportive services to mothers in their homes, mostly during the day when their other children were in school and their partners were at work. In some cases, parents and caregivers talked with social workers before visiting with their children at the center.

The results of consumer satisfaction surveys (one measure of perceived program effectiveness) suggested that the parents who lived near the community center and received family therapy placed more value on social work services than did those who received only traditional supportive counseling. In addition, their children were discharged sooner than were the children who received only supportive social work services. The children's average length of stay was also shorter than the institution's past average. Both the efficiency and the effectiveness of family therapy were established. Unfortunately, the community center was closed when the agency was forced to admit children from a number of counties throughout the state instead of only from the county where the center was located. Within several years, the agency had returned to providing traditional supportive casework services to the mothers of the enrolled children.

Some readers might maintain that such changes could not happen at their agencies because they or their executive directors would never permit such a development. Unfortunately, most readers would be wrong. Few executive directors are involved in the day-to-day operations of programs under their administration, and if they were, their boards of directors would question their delegation skills. Fewer still are grounded in theories of behavior change and, as a result, they leave such matters to their clinical and professional staff. As a result, program changes like those in the three examples are more likely to be the rule rather than the exception.

Avoiding "Drift" and "Reinvention"

Most agencies have a clearly stated mission statement that recognizes both efficiency and effectiveness as organizational goals. In spite of such statements, however, programs and services experience both "drift" and "reinvention." To prevent these two phenomena, an agency must put in place a process by which efficient and effective programs are maintained until they are replaced by more efficient and effective programs. This process must not depend upon a particular staff member or a specific staff position. In order to free efficient and effective programs from the influence of particular personalities or particular positions, programs must be described in writing in the agency's policy and procedures manual.

In the three examples, the program or program component had demonstrated effectiveness. Staff judgments of client progress and follow-up studies demonstrated the effectiveness of the day treatment model. Reading achievement test scores proved the effectiveness of the school-wide reading model. Client-satisfaction surveys and length-of-stay data proved the efficiency and effectiveness of family therapy with families of children in residential treatment. Nevertheless, none of the agencies had in place a mechanism to prevent changes from being made in the programs.

Drawing from the last example, program drift occurred to some extent as a result of unavoidable changes in admission practices. However, if the agency executive staff had been committed to maintaining program integrity, they would have found ways to deliver family therapy to the new group of clients. Why did they revert to less efficient and less effective practices rather than find a way to sustain the new effective approach? The answers likely lie in the changes that had occurred in agency leadership and the board of directors and the fact that the agency had no process in place to ensure the maintenance of efficient and effective programs during or following these leadership changes. Because the maintenance of program integrity requires certain management practices, management and program evaluation must go hand in hand.

This example provides insight into the role of leadership advocacy in effective programming. Some years after the center-based family therapy was abandoned, the clinical staff became concerned about the drift away from family therapy and reinstituted a program of family therapy for those families who regularly visited the center. The new administrator, however, admonished the social work staff because they were failing to meet the state social service regulations that stipulated a specific number of home visits for children in care. Social work staff had not been regularly visiting the homes of families who came to the center for family therapy and had, instead, seen families at the center, usually more often than was required under the state home visiting regulation. Although it goes without saying that agencies must meet state regulations, an agency administrator committed to the delivery of effective services would have traveled to the state capital and discussed the situation with state officials. In many states, regulation waivers are granted to agencies desiring to demonstrate more effective service options or best practices. The role of management is to remove obstacles to the delivery of efficient and effective services, not to create them.

It is likely that members of the boards of directors in the three examples were unaware that the programs at issue had demonstrated their efficiency or effectiveness. It also is likely that board members did not hold the philosophy that programs that have demonstrated their efficiency and effectiveness should be continued as designed until alternative programs have demonstrated their superiority.

Procedures to Assess Proposed Changes

Autocratic leadership is no longer popular in the present era of employee empowerment. There is one area of leadership, however, where autocratic policies should be practiced. No one should be allowed to change an efficient and effective practice without subjecting the proposed change to evaluation. Simply because one staff member or one group of professionals believes that a change in service delivery is needed does not mean change is indicated. There is nothing inherently wrong with staff resisting proposed programmatic changes with the statement, "But we have always done it this way," when "this way" has been proven efficient and effective. "Change for change's sake" should never be practiced.

To avoid change for change's sake in efficient or effective programs or services, agencies should institute a number of practices. First, an agency should have a clearly stated written policy that efficient and effective programs and services should not be changed without first evaluating the results of the proposed alternative service and comparing with the results produced by the established and proven service. Each agency should have a professional staff organization (PSO) that oversees these efforts. The PSO should provide the agency's board of directors with a list of programs or program services that have been proven efficient and effective and data that support these conclusions. The board of directors should hold the agency executive director accountable to maintain these programs until proposed alternative programs have proven to be more efficient and effective.

Second, any staff member wishing to change an efficient or effective practice should be required to take his or her case to the executive committee of the agency's PSO for approval. Alternative programs or services should not be introduced simply on the whim of a single staff member. Third, approval should be granted only when the elected head of the agency PSO, in keeping with the recommendations of the executive committee, is satisfied that: (a) The proposed alternative is in keeping with client needs; and (b) an appropriate evaluation procedure will be put in place to evaluate the proposed change against the traditional program or service. Fourth, before wholesale adoption of an alternative program or service, the executive committee of the PSO should be convinced that the data indicates that the new program has produced results superior to those produced by the established program.

If the executive committee of the PSO in the agency that implemented the effective school-wide reading program had followed these procedures, it would not have permitted wholesale abandonment of the program. The program director who wanted to replace the school-wide reading program with reading instruction in the classrooms would have been required to make the case that instruction in the classroom would be superior to the school-wide model and establish an evaluation procedure to prove his case. Because the new program director's suggested change was simply a return to a former and inferior practice, this proposal would have been denied at that point making evaluation unnecessary.

These procedures should not be applied to services that have never been evaluated because they would severely dampen innovation. Changes might be suggested, for example, in a group therapy program for sexually abused girls provided at a mental health clinic. If the clinic has never evaluated the service, any proposed changes in the group format should follow normal agency procedures for implementing suggested changes. If, however, a formal evaluation has proven the group format to be effective, any proposed changes should be subjected to the above procedures.

When staff replicate a format found effective with similar clients at another agency, the format is considered to be an efficient and/or effective format and is often referred to as a "best practice." An agency does not have to independently evaluate effective (or "best") practices that it replicates, but it is good practice to do so. Staff should use the evaluation procedures when they believe that their clients differ in important ways from clients in the original study.

These principles can be illustrated with an example. Several public schools in the United States have introduced an educational practice called the Strategies Intervention Model (SIM). SIM involves cognitive strategy instruction, peer tutoring, and cooperative learning. The effective implementation of this model requires lengthy (often multiyear) teacher training, teacher planning, administrative support, and additional instructional staff in some cases. Evaluation suggests that SIM results in modest improvement in academic outcomes for students with mild disabilities.

A principal in a day treatment center for seriously emotionally disturbed children wants to try the model in the center's educational program and asks the program director for approval to do so. There is some empirical support for the model's use with special education students, but the students in these evaluations were mildly impaired children in public school classrooms and not seriously emotionally disturbed children who had been removed from the public schools and placed in an off-site day treatment center. The current day treatment educational program has been producing favorable outcomes for the majority of the children enrolled.

Applying the above principles and procedures, the agency should require the program director to confer with members of the executive committee of the PSO and weigh the evidence. One possible result would be that the PSO would grant approval to introduce the model on a small scale and then evaluate the results. The program director, given this approval, could authorize the implementation of the model in, for example, two of the eight classrooms operated by the center. As the next step, the program director and principal together would develop a plan to evaluate the effects of the model, present the evaluation plan to the executive committee of the PSO, and with the PSO's approval, build the plan into the model's implementation.

Best Practices

The term "best practices" refers to services that have been proven to be efficient and effective with specific groups of clients. Evolving from the emphasis of managed care organizations on cost-effective services, best practices have come to mean a performance standard. A best practice is a state-of-the-art practice, intervention, or service that will optimize client outcomes at the least cost. Through evaluation procedures, agencies can identify the services that they provide that would be considered best practices. There are six steps in defining a best practice (each of which will be discussed in detail in Chapters 2 and 3):

1. Specify who is eligible for the service.

2. Identify the content of each service component in a program.

3. Identify the number of staff or staffing ratios required to deliver the service.

4. Specify the credentials of staff who deliver the service.

5. Identify the expected frequency of service sessions or the length of stay in the service.

6. Describe how service components fit together to form a program.

When several best practices are involved in providing a service to a client, they are called intervention paths. Specifically, an intervention path is a coordinated treatment plan for a specific condition utilized throughout the course of an intervention. The purpose of an intervention path is to standardize best practices and guide all staff involved in the management of the client's treatment or care. As an example, if a mental health clinic offers a 10-session group therapy program for children who were sexually abused by strangers, the outcome of the intervention should be determined. A protocol should be developed for the program in the form of a therapist's guide to each of the 10 sessions (a cookbook of sorts). Based on the determination of outcomes, the protocol may need to be revised to produce more favorable outcomes for the participating children. As Freeman (1995, p. 40) notes, agencies must develop "validated practice guidelines that are improved by outcome measurements." This approach is particularly important in a managed care environment. Dubin (1995, p. 35) states that "capitation can be adequately controlled to protect patients by the emergence of specific professional performance standards and treatment protocols along with regulation, accreditation, and monitoring of quality measures."

Very few human service agencies currently provide practices that would qualify as a best practice or an intervention path. Educational services for children served by child welfare agencies provide an example. Many child welfare institutions operate schools (which typically have a special education component) on the grounds of their facilities. Other child welfare agencies enroll children in special education classes in local public schools. In either environment, children may be served in resource rooms or in self-contained classrooms ranging in size from 6 children taught by 1 teacher and 1 teacher aide to 15 children taught by 1 teacher.

Services along the special education continuum typically are poorly described, and the types of children best served in each service option along the continuum are not clearly delineated. It is generally recognized, for example, that children with more significant impairments need a smaller staff-to-student ratio. However, very few special education programs have written eligibility criteria for placement in different special education options; even fewer programs have written descriptions of the services unique to each educational option; almost none delineate the child's expected length of stay in each option. And none can give the expected outcome of each service.

Similarly, although some residential treatment centers for emotionally disturbed children have demonstrated that children fare well after discharge, their findings cannot be applied to other centers because each center offers greatly varying services. In the absence of clearly delineated intervention paths, institutions that similarly describe themselves as residential treatment centers will not produce the same outcomes. More than 35 years ago, Franz

Alexander (1956), who coined the term "corrective-emotional experience" to denote the chief goal of any treatment, noted:

> The effectiveness of any form of psychotherapy can be evaluated only by a record which not only shows the initial state of the patient and his condition after termination of treatment, but also gives the precise account step by step of the psychological processes which have taken place in the patient in response to the therapist's interventions. (p. 13)

Managed Care and Performance Standards

Managed care organizations (MCOs) typically expect that agencies will deliver empirically validated best practices. MCOs customarily rely on published research data to determine the most cost-effective interventions for the treatment of particular diagnostic conditions or problems. They then expect agencies to utilize those cost-effective service interventions as empirically validated. An MCO may learn from the research, for example, that although 75% of mental health clients with an anxiety disorder may profit from 30 or more sessions of outpatient psychotherapy, an equal number profit from 10 one-hour sessions of training in self-monitoring, self-relaxation, and appropriate self-assertion. The MCO would expect implementation of the second procedure. If the published research suggests that children with a certain mental health disorder can be treated effectively with a telephone-based, supportive/self-directive parent training program, a MCO will have many questions if a clinic treats such children instead with fifteen 60-minute sessions of family therapy. The clinic will be required to demonstrate the superiority of family therapy over the other intervention in order to remain a provider for the MCO.

In addition, MCOs typically maintain "Behavioral Health Report Cards" on the agencies with which they contract. They assess the agency's functioning in four areas: (a) service access, (b) quality, (c) client satisfaction, and (e) outcomes. Agencies are required to provide ongoing data in each of the areas and will need evaluation procedures to meet this requirement. Both the gathering and provision of data are evaluation tasks.

Service Access

Agencies must track and report their service response times and their utilization rates. The American Managed Behavioral Healthcare Association and the National Association of State Mental Health Agencies (1995) have suggested access standards for mental health services, standards that could be applied to any human service agency. These standards provide the following:

- An average speed of answering the telephone of 10 to 30 seconds, with a rate of abandoned calls of less than 3%.

- Telephone access to critical staff within five minutes for emergencies and three business days for nonemergencies.

- Availability of on-call professional staff 24 hours a day, 7 days a week.

- Initial, routine appointments made within four to seven business days.

- Face-to-face initial evaluation within 6 hours for emergencies, 48 hours for urgent (or emergent) cases, and 10 business days for routine care.

- Resolution and response to written complaints within 15 business days.

- Resolution of appeals within 30 business days.

It appears that well managed mental health centers can meet the rapid access standards for their adult patients, but can generally only meet these standards for child patients in their outpatient programs. Difficulties meeting these standards primarily occur when children need an array of services that are under the control of another agency or funding source.

Quality

Agencies must routinely collect certain data to demonstrate that services are of high quality. Minimally, human service agencies should track the:

- percentage of clients reporting improvement in the presenting problem,

- percentage of clients reporting satisfaction with the intervention specialist,

- percentage of clients prematurely withdrawing from services,

- percentage of clients who do not appear for initial appointments,

- percentage of hospital admissions from each service or program in one year, by diagnosis or other meaningful category,

- percentage of inpatients with at least one outpatient visit within 30 days of discharge (which demonstrates a minimal standard for adequate aftercare planning).

Client Satisfaction

An agency should regularly gather formal feedback from clients about access, administrative efficiency, clinical quality, and satisfaction with frequency and length of treatment. Three factors that clients report as promoting their sense of well-being are: (a) they feel that staff listen to them, (b) they feel validated and respected, (c) and they are given information. Satisfaction surveys (discussed in Chapter 7) should include questions about these three factors. Client satisfaction should be analyzed by functional status, race, sex, and primary language. Agency approaches to gathering and using client feedback vary. Some agencies hire consultants; some use consumer advisory boards to help them analyze the degree to which they are family-friendly and to guide them in making their services more accessible to clients. Others develop consumer satisfaction surveys that are used agency-wide.

Outcomes

Osborne and Graebler (1993), in their insightful book, *Reinventing Government*, state that "what gets measured gets done." Nevertheless, they describe three problems in measuring the performance of public institutions: there is a vast difference between measuring process and measuring results; there is a vast difference between measuring efficiency and measuring effectiveness; and there is an important difference between program outcomes and broader "policy outcomes." Some of these problems are discussed in Chapter 8.

Despite these problems, human service agencies are expected to assess and report on the outcomes of the services they offer and relate their findings to effectiveness and efficiency. Effectiveness is a ratio of units of outcomes to some standard unit (which can represent maximum improvement or some set standard of improvement). Efficiency is a ratio of units of outcomes to units of program output or resource input. Agencies can anticipate that it will take considerable time and effort to relate their findings to both effectiveness and efficiency.

There are three types of outcome measures: (a) client satisfaction (the client's subjective measure of the helpfulness of the intervention and/or current status); (b) case status or proximal outcomes (such as whether the client still displays admission symptoms after exceeding the average length of stay or the exhaustion of benefits, whether a child has been adopted, the amount of time that a child remains behind academically after one year in a self-contained classroom, or the client having met seven of eight objectives); and (c) client status or distal outcomes (i.e., the client has not been readmitted for services, the child missed five days of school in the year following discharge from care, the client rates himself as improved, or an informant rates the client as improved or symptom-free). Each of these outcome measures will be discussed in greater detail in Chapter 7.

Summary

Program evaluation is a management practice. Every administrator in a human service agency should be able to implement program evaluation procedures as part of the ongoing quality assurance procedures of the agency. Evaluation can be as simple as assuring that intervention plans are being implemented for each client (for example, the client receives the recommended dose of each treatment rather than a smaller dose, or the child receives the recommended 20 minutes of remedial reading as opposed to 15 minutes). Alternatively, evaluation can be as complex as demonstrating that a group treatment format results in a decrease in symptoms associated with the trauma of rape or sexual abuse or that youth in a group home participating in an afternoon tutorial program do better in school than those in a group home without the tutorial program.

Once a program or a program component has been proven efficient and effective, the agency should have procedures in place to ensure program continuation and prevent unnecessary tampering with the program or program component. Proposed changes in effective programs should be granted only by the executive committee of the agency's professional staff organization. When employees receive such approval, they should be required to formally demonstrate the superiority of the proposed change over the existing format before any change is officially adopted. At first glance, such approval procedures may appear to damp creativity, but it is important to emphasize that the procedures should be applied only to proposed changes in interventions that have been proven effective. Because it will be difficult to prove the effectiveness of many services, innovations will continue in organizations that encourage them. In organizations that value innovation, effective interventions will eventually be replaced by even more effective ones.

Chapter 2:
Defining the Characteristics of the Clients Served

Chapter 1 described a study in which an intervention claimed to turn children who were mentally retarded into normally functioning children. It is an early example of the failure to follow one of the basic principles of program evaluation: The population served must be clearly described. Had the evaluator gathered information other than IQ scores about the children, including their emotional and social maturity, it would have become apparent that many of the children were not mentally retarded.

Many program evaluators continue to violate the basic evaluation principle of an adequate description of the population served. Although a plethora of outcome information exists in the human services, much of it is not useful because the characteristics of the individuals served have not been clearly described nor have the services received been clearly delineated. Studies of the same service, consequently, may report very different findings. Some studies, for example, show that domestic violence programs reduce abuse among participants; some show no reduction in abuse; and yet others show similar remission rates for populations of abusers who received no services. Some studies show that veterans benefit from substance abuse treatment programs; and other studies suggest otherwise.

Without an adequate description of the populations served, little is learned than can be applied to intervention planning. As an example, the man who is violent with his wife, abuses his children, uses alcohol excessively, and is 10 years his wife's senior may need different services than the man who is violent with his wife and does not possess any of these other characteristics. Similarly, an older veteran with civilian job skills and social skills may be able to stop his or her substance abuse more easily than the younger veteran lacking in such skills. Collecting specific data on each client and his or her family members is the first step in efforts to relate client characteristics to intervention outcomes.

In child welfare, children admitted into therapeutic foster care should differ from those admitted into group home care, who in turn should differ from those placed in institutional care or in residential treatment centers. Although this principle suggests that children with more severe problems are placed further along on the service continuum, an examination of the admission criteria for child welfare programs in many communities does not support this assumption. The criteria are relatively vague and quite similar across settings, suggesting that similar children receive different services. In many communities and even in many comprehensive agencies, the criteria for admission to different child welfare services are identical and movement along the continuum of services traditionally advances by failure. Children initially are placed in foster family care, moved to group home care following poor adjustment to foster care, and then moved to institutional care following poor adjustment to group home care.

The failure to clarify the distinct populations of children needing different levels of services has important implications. If children served in these settings prove to be the same, it could be argued that all children should be placed in the least expensive service, family foster care. Similarly, if it becomes evident that children admitted to high-cost residential centers and those admitted to low-cost community-based care have similar outcomes on follow-up, communities could be justified in closing their residential centers and developing more community-based facilities. One recent study, in fact, demonstrated that adolescent delinquents served in foster family homes did better than those served in group homes, suggesting that group homes also might be closed.

The Need to Define the Clients Served

The need to clearly define the population of clients who benefit from different services and from varying levels of services can best be illustrated with examples. Project Re-Ed, a brief residential program model that was introduced some years ago, provides an example of the need for definitions. This model was lauded as a more efficient and effective option for children than traditional residential treatment offered by child welfare agencies. But, Project Re-Ed never provided a clear description of the clients that the program served, and the follow-up period was only six months. Consequently, not only was their claim of superiority over other programs unwarranted, but the type of child they effectively served was unclear.

More recently, a study that gained wide publicity claimed to demonstrate that children residing in a community with a full continuum of mental health services (the experimental group) did no better than children residing in two communities that had only outpatient and inpatient services (the comparison group). The investigators concluded that "more is not always better" (Bickman, 1996). Unfortunately, children's psychopathology and assessment of change were defined primarily by their scores on measuring instruments rather than by external factors. The researchers did not provide clear descriptions of the admission criteria to the different services in the published writings about the project. Data were presented in an appendix to the report (such as the number of special education placements, juvenile court appearances, and arrests), and the data suggested that the children in the study were a mildly disturbed group. These data indicated that the children who benefited from the more limited services were unrepresentative of children who usually make use of intermediary services along the mental health continuum. The authors recognized that they had failed to define admission criteria for the various mental health services, but they attempted to minimize this oversight through a second study where they found that clinicians differ significantly on the criteria they use to make placement decisions.

The development of best practices rests on an adequate description of the clients served in each intervention. Such descriptions should reflect an understanding of clients' pre-morbid (pre-service) factors, particularly risk factors; state what types of clients are effectively served by what types of programs; and outline the specific criteria for placement in different service options. It is only when the characteristics of clients are clear that agencies can begin to delineate and describe the specific services clients receive and relate them to observed outcomes.

A number of studies have indicated strongly that preinterventio characteristics relate to outcomes. Studies, for example, show that more severely depressed clients respond less favorably to cognitive-behavioral interventions; that family support is crucial in psychoeducational interventions for schizophrenic adults; and that preadmission variables relate more to outcomes for children in residential care than do intervention variables. Studies also show that, among children served in mental health clinics, children whose parents are neglectful, who reside in high crime neighborhoods, and who have hostile-destructive relationships with their mothers have the poorest outcomes.

Findings may be wrongly attributed to interventions when client or family characteristics are not considered. Shorter lengths of stay for children placed in residential centers, for example, have been attributed to the family's involvement in family counseling. The involvement of the family in the child's life prior to and during placement, however, may be the significant factor in a child's early discharge and not the family's involvement in counseling. It would be important to assess the impact of family involvement as opposed to the impact of family participation in therapy on a child's early discharge from care. To make such an assessment, it would be necessary to study two groups of equally involved families, one group whose members participated in family treatment and one whose members participated in another form of treatment.

The Development and Use of Admission Criteria

To intervene in a cost-effective manner, agencies must identify in writing the specific characteristics of clients (and, when relevant, their families) whom they serve across their continuum of care. These characteristics are called admission criteria. Some human service agencies use very limited admission criteria. For example, the only admission criteria in programs providing shelter or food for the homeless may be that the consumer has no home. Similarly, a well-baby clinic may have the sole criterion for admission that the woman is pregnant or the mother of an infant. Nevertheless, if these agencies wish to provide different services or assist clients with problems that they may face in the future, they may decide to develop more rigorous admission criteria. One well-baby clinic, for example, observed that when pregnant adolescents were served by the same team of professionals (doctor, nurses, and social service staff) at each prenatal and postnatal clinic visit, they attended well-baby sessions more frequently and avoided future pregnancies more often than did adolescents served by the professionals who happened to be available on the adolescents' scheduled days of service. Based on this observation, the clinic might more rigorously define the characteristics of adolescents who seemed to be responding favorably to the team approach and the characteristics of adolescents who seemed satisfied with the traditional approach. The clinic could create criteria for admission to both approaches based on the different characteristics of each group. This process may not be necessary if the team approach proved to be economically and pragmatically feasible with all clients.

As another example, the staff of the well-baby clinic may discover that a number of their young clients had engaged in physical abuse of their infants. Clearly, the best interests of children and of prospective mothers would be served by identifying the characteristics of young pregnant women who are at greatest risk of abusing their infants in the future (and a number of researchers have attempted to make such identifications). Having identified the characteristics of these high-risk pregnant women, the agency could provide specific services to targeted individuals to prevent future abuse. Further, the agency might identify the traits of women who respond positively to the prevention program and develop an alternative service for women who do not respond well. Eventually, a variety of prevention programs could be offered. Instead of a process in which women fail in one prevention program and then are placed in another, clients could be matched at the outset with the program most suitable to their specific needs. It can be anticipated that having an array of prevention programs based on client characteristics would impact dropout rates from service (rates that tend to be quite high in abuse prevention programs for pregnant adolescents). Delivering the most suitable prevention service from the outset is efficient and effective and maximizes client participation.

One example of the use of admission criteria is with hospital diversion services (in which an on-call clinician is always available to families). These programs have been found to be effective in preventing psychiatric hospitalization. Hospitals with successful diversion services have studied outcomes for patients who failed in diversion programs and required hospitalization. This work has led to clear definition of criteria for hospitalization, including a requirement that the client (or parent) failed to create an initial treatment contract with the diversion worker.

An example of a program in which admission criteria cannot be developed appropriately is D.A.R.E, the drug prevention program delivered in many public schools throughout the United States and described in Chapter 1. Studies demonstrate that the program, administered to all students at a specific grade level, has no measurable impact on the future drug use of children. D.A.R.E. participants and nonparticipants lay the same use rates of drug use. D.A.R.E. proponents suggest that the program would be effective and more efficient if it were provided only to youth identified as at high risk for substance abuse. This outcome is doubtful. If D.A.R.E. participants had shown a reduction in drug use (no matter how small), further refinement of the program for high-risk youth might produce larger effects. If there had been a difference between D.A.R.E. participants and nonparticipants but the difference failed to reach conventional levels of statistical significance (that is, there was a large probability that the difference could have occurred by chance), children considered high risk for substance use could be culled from the participant and nonparticipant groups and their use patterns compared. But the trends are in the opposite direction. Some critics even suggested that the D.A.R.E. program may stimulate some youth to experiment with drugs. Because the program has produced no measurable effects or even trends, it would not be appropriate to attempt to define more specific admission criteria.

When an agency attempts to develop admission criteria though precise definitions of the type of clients it best serves in each of its programs, it should make clear to staff that they do not have to rigidly adhere to these criteria for each admission. In the real world of nonprofit management, it is common that when a program has a vacancy, a client will be admitted even if the client does not exactly fit the admission criteria. Empty program slots translate into an underfunded program, and the result is likely to be over-enrollment towards year-end or an unacceptable year-end fiscal deficit. At the same time, an agency may not wish to reject a client who is clearly in need of services. In some cases, a child who does not meet a program's admission criteria, for example, may be accepted while an alternative placement is being sought or efforts are being made to refer the child to a more appropriate setting.

No matter how well a program has related client characteristics to services delivered and outcomes obtained, there always will be situations in which the relationship between admission criteria and benefit does not hold. Children will be admitted for treatment who meet the criteria for admission and who do not make progress, a situation known as a "false positive." There also will be some children who do not meet the admission criteria but who make progress, a situation known as a "false negative." There has never been an instance where 100% of clients with delineated characteristics for program admission have responded favorably to treatment or where 100% of individuals without the delineated characteristics responded poorly to treatment. In fact, in the early stages of program evaluation, an agency can be satisfied with the process if 60% of the clients who meet admission criteria respond well to the treatment. More will be said about this topic in Chapter 6.

Development and Use of a Database

In order to adequately describe the clients served by each service, a core database should be established. Certain elements should be a part of any human service database, and additional elements should be included depending on the field of service. The data should be expanded to include information on the individual client's situation.

Elements of a Core Database

There are multiple elements of a database that must be in place to support an adequate description of clients. First, there should be data related to pre-morbid factors. These data relate to a client's interpersonal and family history and should include:

- age of all family members in and out of the home;

- socioeconomic status;

- precipitant for the current episode of care;

- history of the current problems;

- history of previous services, including outcomes;

- family history of any previous high risk incidents, such as self injurious acts, injury inflicted on others, or hospitalization;

- family history of physical and mental illness, substance abuse, and diagnosis (when applicable);

Table 2.1 Common Data Elements	
Client Demographic Information	Record Number Social Security Number Zip Code Date of Birth Gender Race
Program Information	Admission Date Referral Source Presenting Problems Date of Discharge Placement at Discharge Living Environment at Discharge
Living Situation and History	Living Environment at Intake Out-of-Home Placements
Family Information	Number in Family Number of Siblings Siblings Placed Out-of-Home
Educational Information	Grade Level Completed Special Education Vocational Education
Medical Information	Health Status Alcohol and Substance Use Mental Health Treatment Medications (Past and Present) Date Medications Prescribed Primary Physician
Intervention History	Interventions Prior to Admission Services Requested Services Delivered Services Delivered to Others Services Planned at Discharge
Untoward Incidents	Incident Dates Incident Types
Outcomes	Client Satisfaction Staff Ratings Informant Ratings Objective Instruments Living Environment Social/Work History Follow-Up Services Provided

- family history of school and vocational functioning (seeking such information as enrollment in special educational services and the number of times that the client or adult family members have been unemployed);

- history of placements of family members outside of the home as children;

- family member involvement with the social service, justice, or juvenile justice systems; and

- family variables (including such factors as domestic violence, parental neglect, stepparents or paramours who are punitive or authoritarian, parental support of children and their interests, religious commitment, involvement of extended family in positive and negative ways, and family involvement in the community).

Certain principles apply when such information is obtained from clients. Careful attention should be paid to the subtleties and nuances of clients' lives when questions are constructed and asked. Professionals should show respect for the client and an understanding of how the information affects the client.

Second, there are core data elements related to the services provided. These elements should include:

- the recommended intervention plan, including types of services, modalities of treatment, and recommended length of stay;

- problems, situations, symptoms, or developmental difficulties that are or were the primary focus of services;

- an operationalized estimate of the severity of the targeted problems (through the use of family functioning scales), symptoms (through symptom rating scales) and, when appropriate, developmental problems (through such measures as global assessment ratings and developmental attainment schedules).

The two sets of elements comprising the common database should be entered on a common data sheet. The common data elements are presented in Table 2.1.

Each agency should add items that are unique to the services that it provides. Mental health agencies, for example, also should collect aggregate data, such as the following:

- the readmission rate (number of clients readmitted in a benefit year for treatment of the same or similar condition);

- average number of service visits (analyzed by provider, diagnosis, and treatment protocol);

- percentage of clients served with brief intervention protocols (less than 10 service sessions) and percentage of clients served with long-term interventions (more than 20 service sessions); and

- percentage of clients who are served with group intervention protocols.

Appendix A outlines a database for child welfare programs.

Additional Client Data

Client descriptions should not read like an academic research study. Although admission criteria tend to be limited to general descriptions and differ among programs, a client's record should contain easily retrievable information. To avoid duplication of effort, common intake forms should be used to meet the needs of all professionals who will work with the client. At the same time, each record should contain different information about the client and the client's family, depending upon the earlier information that was gathered. For example, if parents admit to domestic violence, information should be gathered about the nature of the violence, the suspected causes, and the parents' perceptions of the effect of the violence upon their children.

Data gathering should use decision trees. In decision tree formats, one answer brings forth a group of related questions and another answer does not. As an example, if an agency used the data set described above or the child welfare data set in Appendix A, a question would be asked about parental alcohol or other substance use. If parents answer "yes" to this question, additional questions related to substance abuse should be asked, including questions about the frequency of substance abuse, history of outpatient and inpatient treatment, and past and present involvement in services such as Alcoholics Anonymous (AA). Under the heading "parental problems associated with drinking," for example, the following data could be collected:

- need for daily use,

- absences from work,

- convictions for driving under the influence of alcohol,

- dishonesty/evasiveness,

- violence while intoxicated,

- sexual activity while intoxicated,

- child abuse when intoxicated,

- general acting-up while intoxicated,

- withdrawal symptoms,

- amnesic period,

- binge episodes,

- blackouts,

- arguments and other difficulties with family,

- compromised values,

- delirium,

- tremors,

- problem denial, and

- related health problems.

Although professional staff can gather most of the data on client characteristics, clients themselves can contribute considerable information, particularly about living arrangements, past usage of community resources, prior services, health status, and child-rearing practices. Clients can complete such instruments as the Health Status Questionnaire (also called the SF-36), the Beck Depression Inventory, and the Child Behavior Checklist (described more fully in Chapter 7). These instruments can be completed on a computer or over a phone line where touch-tone responses are made to computerize recordings.

Detailed Descriptions of the Clients Served

Many researchers fail to adequately describe the population served by their interventions. In fact, the typical published outcome study usually gives only relatively general descriptions. The following descriptions are typical:

> The subjects were 60 patients who were diagnosed as suffering from major depression. The mean age was 42.7 years (SD 13.4 years) with a range from 18 to 71 years. Patients were recruited from the Brisbane community through media releases seeking individuals suffering from depression who were willing to participate in a research project involving cognitive therapy.

> The patients were 110 clients seeking treatment for panic disorder. Clients with a diagnosis of panic disorder with or without accompanying agoraphobia were admitted for treatment. Excluded were those with active symptoms of substance abuse, psychosis, or mental disorder caused by a medical condition. Forty-seven percent met the criteria of moderate or severe phobia.

> The subjects were 50 parents of 66 children who had been referred to a university-based psychological clinic

for treatment of noncompliant behavior. The parents ranged in age from 27 to 42, and the children ranged in age from 8 to 13.

In each of the three studies, the treatment had a positive effect on the clients served. In the first study, depressed patients in cognitive therapy made more progress than did clients placed on a waiting list (wait-list controls). In the second study, patients who received a 15-session Cognitive Behavior Therapy Protocol (treatment manual approach) did better than did clients receiving other therapies (concurrent treatment controls). In the third study, children whose parents received a 10-session parent training program on managing defiant behavior were less defiant upon treatment completion than children who received traditional clinic treatments (such as assignment to a clinician for treatment). The overall findings were positive in all three studies, and the researchers demonstrated what they wanted to demonstrate: the approach they preferred was effective. Consequently, no further description of the population was deemed necessary.

The good service provider cannot be content with general descriptions of clients served. If a clinic director, for example, is considering more parent training groups for parents of defiant children, the director should consider a number of factors. The director knows from the research that a number of the children became less defiant after their parents completed the group-training program, and fewer children had reduced defiant behaviors after completion of the traditional approach to treatment. The director should be more interested, however, in how many children improved (that is, reached the targeted behavioral objective) in each treatment approach than in the statistical significance of the overall findings. The director also should be interested in the characteristics of parents and children who profited and who failed to profit from the different treatment methodologies offered; the factors that contributed to the failure to reach the target objectives; and the specific components of the parent training program that produced the desired effect. The director cannot have a full understanding of these factors unless the characteristics of the children and families served are fully delineated.

Summary

When the exact characteristics of the population served by an intervention are known and the nature of the services provided is clear, it is possible to determine what is helpful for whom. The intervention has been proven effective for a certain client group. A best practice has been established as the current, most cost-effective intervention. However, without a clear description of clients served, best practices cannot be determined. For example, there is often an inadequate description of the clients served through briefer forms of treatment for disorders that traditionally have required more lengthy treatment to produce change. Evaluation may reveal that the clients served in the brief intervention were quite different than the clients served through traditional modalities. They may have been less impaired than those served in traditional treatments; the goals for the client may have less comprehensive; or the outcome measures may have been questionable. If, however, the population of clients served in the brief intervention is found to be identical to the traditionally treated group, the briefer intervention becomes a "best practice." Agencies can adequately describe the clients they serve by establishing a core database and using decision-trees to gather additional data.

Once evaluation has established the effectiveness of an intervention for a certain client group, further evaluation may be undertaken. For example, evaluation may reveal that the intervention also can assist clients with characteristics that differ from the clients originally served. Alternatively, it may indicate that another approach that is easier to deliver or a briefer intervention is as effective as the first approach. A second intervention may prove to be more cost-effective for the provider and for the consumer as well.

Chapter 3:
• • • • • • •• •
Describing the Services Provided

Ensuring that staff deliver efficient and effective services requires a description of the clients served, as discussed in Chapter 2, and a description of the services that are delivered. An agency must be able to describe precisely the actual services provided to each client. It is not sufficient, for example, to state that a patient receives mental health services, a family receives social services, or a client receives peer support or homemaker services.

Defining the Content of Each Service

When an agency defines the content of a service, it should describe the services in as much detail as possible. An agency that provides a parent education program, for example, should develop a written description of the program, including a parent education protocol and a parent education manual to guide staff in providing the service. The agency can be assured that all staff are appropriately providing parent training and assessing parenting deficits only when the agency monitors and supervises staff performance based on implementation of the parent education manual. Without ongoing training and supervision, professionals may give child-rearing advice based on their own parenting experiences. "My child didn't eat any vegetables. Don't worry about it, it's not worth the arguments." Similarly, when clinical staff in child care institutions provide structured group treatments for children with specific problems (such as their

51

parents' substance abuse or sexual victimization) or offer groups to help children with transitions (such as discharge preparation groups), the agency should develop group intervention protocols. The effectiveness of the protocols can be assessed, and others can replicate the groups.

One chief task of management is to require staff to define the nature of their services. In order to determine what works for whom, one first has to define the "what." Bickman (1997) states:

> Better means of describing non-manualized treatments and services are clearly needed. Until such means are developed, the best one can do is locate where the services occurred (e.g., hospital, office) and the number of time units (e.g., days, hours) but little else. (p. 563)

In many human service agencies, however, professionals operate as if they were independent providers, offering services in a nonspecific manner and making it difficult to determine exactly what it is that they do. Clinicians in a mental health clinic, for example, may be allowed to treat clients in whatever fashion the clinicians think best. The "clinic," in such a case, is merely a group of professionals working independently under the same roof. Staff ratings of client progress or client ratings of improvement may reveal that 70% of the clients demonstrated perceived improvement. Under such circumstances, however, clients may have improved without clinic treatment (an issue discussed in greater detail in Chapter 6). Client improvement may have been even more pronounced if clients received specific symptom-targeted treatments rather than a general treatment provided in a loosely organized practice.

Similarly, a child welfare agency may offer group psychoeducation for parents who have abused their children and allow each group leader to operate the group as each leader sees fit. In such a case, there would be no specific intervention procedure to evaluate. Client satisfaction surveys or independent assessments of client progress may reveal that the group therapy was perceived to be effective. The results, however, could be attributable to certain group leaders rather than the group format itself, and the findings could not be replicated by others. If positive outcomes were the result of the group format, the next step would be to determine the factors that produced the reported changes and were common to successful groups. The beginning stage in treatment protocol development involves the isolation of such factors and the requirement that all group therapists implement these factors in the groups they lead.

Some clinicians may disagree with the need to standardize service delivery, believing that the group process itself (a process that produces critical feedback in the presence of peer support and an opportunity to "try out" new behaviors in a protected environment) are the key factors that create client changes. It is true that group leadership skill and the group leader's behavior are prerequisites for the development of a positive group climate. Such skills are described in books on group therapy, and clinical staff can draw on these sources to create group treatment protocols for unstructured groups. Nevertheless, many unstructured and open-ended treatment groups have not been effective. In fact, some unstructured treatment groups for children have been found to be not only ineffective but "disasters" because therapists spend entire group sessions disciplining unruly children. Other evidence of the ineffectiveness of unstructured services can be found in adult services in community mental health centers where adults assigned to open-ended treatment groups have the highest dropout rates.

The alternative to unstructured programming is a structured approach that uses a treatment protocol written down in a treatment manual. A treatment manual gives the specific procedures staff members are to follow (the protocol) to ensure uniform delivery of a service. Such uniformity is evident, for example, in surgical procedures where agreed-upon protocols are followed. The same approach can be used in human services. If, for example, the treatment is a 12-session parent training program for abusive parents, a manual may present the group activities that are to take place in each of the 12 sessions. Use of the manual assures that each professional delivers the service in an identical fashion. Similarly, if two children are treated by two different student thera-

pists in a university clinic that utilizes a specific treatment protocol for treatment of depression (such as the Beck's treatment protocol), the two adolescents will receive almost identical services.
This result contrasts with the very different treatments the two
depressed adolescents are likely to receive if they are seen by two
different professionals in the typical mental health clinic.

In mental health, the American Psychiatric Association
and the American Association of Child and Adolescent Psychiatrists developed general practice guidelines for many of
the adult and child disorders they classify. These guidelines
identify the types of services to be provided to clients displaying each disorder and serve only as guides to treatment. Although they are not very useful to clients or to clinicians, they
provide a starting point in the effort to standardize intervention procedures. More specific procedures, known as intervention or service protocols, or "manualized" procedures, represent the next step in protocol development.

The Development of Service Protocols

In the field of mental health, there are manualized treatment procedures for specific childhood disorders: oppositional defiant disorders, enuresis and encopresis, bulimia, attention-deficit disorders, and traumatic stress disorders. There also are manualized
treatment protocols for assisting parents in dealing with their
children's mental health problems, including services to parents
whose own anger is a factor in their child's conduct or oppositional
disorder; who are experiencing child-rearing difficulties; whose
children have oppositional and attention/deficit and hyperactivity disorders; and whose children have anger management problems. Some manuals offer different intervention options at each
step in the treatment process. Some are so detailed that they can
be given to children and parents as workbooks to be used as self-
help resources when treatment is concluded. Manualized procedures have been developed for most adult mental health disorders, but the procedures with the most empirical support are those
for patients with depression, panic disorder, pathological grief,
posttraumatic stress disorder, and the delusions and hallucina-

tions associated with psychosis. Manualized procedures generally do not address the comorbid personality disorders that are found in many patients referred to mental health centers, and work is needed to expand protocols to cover a variety of conditions.

Group treatment protocols for children and for adults have been described in professional publications (see Mordock, 1999b). In many cases, however, general treatment protocols for various conditions have been developed but have not been published or empirically validated. One example of treatment protocols that have been empirically validated is the work of Miller and colleagues (1992) at the Department of Child Psychiatry at Columbia University. They developed a 142-page treatment manual to guide clinicians when they provide six-session cognitive-behavioral family therapy for adolescents who have attempted suicide and their families. In the 35-page introductory section, they describe the treatment philosophy, a model for understanding the interactions between the adolescent and the family, general methods and special techniques, assessment of imminent danger, a triage plan, difficult treatment situations, and use of the manual. The 107 remaining pages list the goals and objectives for each of the six treatment sessions, the rationale for the goals and objectives, and the procedures to follow. The manual also lists all the needed materials. It further provides the therapist with a word-for-word script for each session as a concrete example of how to do the exercises that constitute the therapy. The expectation is that after the therapist reviews a session and is able to explain the process to the client, the therapist will begin to use his or her own words.

Other examples of detailed protocols are Beck's treatment manual for adult depression; Barley's *Defiant Children: A Clinician's Manual for Parent Training* (which outlines the step-by-step delivery of 10 group sessions for parents of children with oppositional defiant disorders); the manual by Boswell and Bloomquist for treating children with Attention-Deficit Hyperactivity Disorders; and the Horowitz manual, *Stress Response Syndromes,* for treating stress related disorders in adults.

Outside the mental health arena, descriptions of interventions tend to be very general. Perhaps the most replicable intervention in child welfare is that associated with crisis intervention services designed to prevent the foster care placement of a child. The *Homebuilders Model* has been replicated by many child care agencies across the country and by mental health professionals to prevent the immediate hospitalization of clients. The 11-step plan (presented in Table 3.1) is the initial service offered to all families who contract for the service. It provides an example of a written intervention protocol in the field of child welfare. After implementing these steps, the intervention worker typically helps the family to take immediate concrete actions to resolve the identified problems. When counseling services are provided, the intervention worker uses cognitive-behavioral procedures with children and solution-focused interventions with parents.

A second replicable program in the field of child welfare is the Professional Parenting Program in Boy's Town in Nebraska (Phillips et al., 1974). Couples hired as cottage parents are trained in very   specific behavioral techniques that characterize the milieu environment of each Boy's Town cottage. Each couple receives a training manual, and the boys receive a student handbook that outlines the positive and negative consequences of their behaviors. Visitors to the different cottages note the similarity of the milieu environments in each cottage. Although the warmth and commitment of cottage parents are prerequisites for their employment, it is the program model (as opposed to the traits of cottage parents) that is the key factor in producing positive changes in the children. The Professional Parenting Program model has been replicated at a number of child care institutions.

A third replicable child welfare intervention is the Home Rebuilders Model, a program designed to expedite the discharge of children in foster care (Mordock, 1999a). The program is composed of a number of service components: social work services; reduced caseloads; services from a substance abuse counselor and from former clients who serve as parent advocates; assistance with housing needs; and classes in child care, spiritual life, and avoidance of domestic violence. Unlike traditional service models, the Home Rebuilders program is not limited to 90 days. Parents may request a change in social worker with no questions asked, and

Figure 3.1 Homebuilder Model: Intervention Protocol

- Actively listen to the concerns of each family member.

- Communicate hope and optimism to the family that the crisis can be resolved without the child's placement out of the home.

- Provide factual information about the intervention program and how it functions.

- Formulate the present problem situation with the family.

- Predict the future consequences of various courses of action.

- Develop a specific contract with the family regarding the child at risk (with a focus on the course of action the family is to take when there is a risk that they may harm the child).

- Develop a specific agreement with the family regarding compliance with the contract (with a focus on the course of action the family is to take when there is a risk that the family will fail to comply with the agreement).

- Identify with the family the changes that will contribute to resolution of the child's immediate problems.

- Identify the goals related to changes that the child and parents would like to make.

- Obtain the family's commitment to take certain actions immediately after the worker leaves their home and they are left alone with the child.

- Emphasize the 24-hour availability of the worker to help the family meet concrete goals.

parents may dictate the time and place of services. Unfortunately, replication of the program is limited by the fact that a specific intervention manual has not been developed to guide social workers in the provision of each service component.

A fourth replicable model is Therapeutic Foster Care (TFC), a program that focuses on treating emotionally disturbed children in the community instead of in institutions. Foster parents have a high level of responsibility and are a meaningful part of each child's treatment team. They receive higher monetary remuneration than traditional foster parents. TFC parents are trained in behavioral management and treatment techniques. Outcome studies have indicated that children in TFC show significant improvement in the level of restrictive placement they need (at discharge and at the one-year follow-up) relative to a comparison group in alternative community placements. In one study, a group of adjudicated delinquents was randomly assigned to a TFC or to a group home program. Compared to the group home youth, TFC youth were less likely to run away and more likely to complete the program. TFC youth had fewer criminal referrals and self-reports of criminal activity at the one-year follow-up. One study also showed positive outcomes for the foster parents themselves. The study compared a group of TFC parents with a conventional group of foster parents and found that TFC parents provided foster care for longer periods of time and reported feeling more valued and appreciated in their roles.

A number of service components in group care facilities (whether operated by mental health, child welfare, juvenile justice, developmental disabilities, or substance abuse treatment agencies) require more precise descriptions if their effectiveness is to be evaluated. These components include educational and vocational services (even if children attend local public schools or vocational training programs), the living group component, nursing services, recreation, family services, and clinical services. Within each of these service components, a number of specific service activities typically must be identified. These service activities are important because some practices may not be effective standing alone but may be powerfully effective when combined with other practices. As an example, an agency may provide a broad range of services that individually and collectively produce positive outcomes. An agency's school may utilize a curriculum, providing subject matter in a specific order and at specific time periods. Basic academic instruction may be supplemented with reading, language therapy, social-skills training, and prevocational opportunities. Clinically, the agency may offer individual play therapy for certain children and special group interventions, such as discharge preparation groups or groups for children who have been sexually abused. Family therapy may be provided with clinical and child care staff serving as cotherapists with the social work staff. A detailed description of each service component would be necessary to determine the effectiveness of each activity and the program as a whole.

The initial treatment protocol for a service component should list the variety of services that are provided. The protocols should be written so that a new staff member can easily understand the protocol and the training needed to implement it. Management should utilize a quality assurance program to ensure that staff who deliver a treatment protocol or treatment modality, including newly hired clinicians, receive the training and supervision necessary to deliver it effectively.

Ongoing Treatment Protocol Development

After a large number of individuals or families have been treated with the initial protocol, the agency should analyze clients' clinical records. This review will reveal the most frequently delivered services. These services should be highlighted in the treatment protocol or manual and further refined. For example, an analysis of 60 children treated in a crisis intervention service may reveal that in 60% of the cases, the worker consulted with public school staff and attended meetings of the Committee on Special Education. This finding would suggest that workers could profit from training in special education regulations and procedures, and in effective school consultation practices so that they could make more sophisticated recommendations to public school staff. The consultation procedures, once developed, should be included in the written treatment protocol. The review also may indicate that anger management training is needed in many cases. Once the clinical staff determines the type of anger management training to be provided, a description of that service should be added to the treatment protocol.

Opposition to Protocol Use

Not all clinicians are interested in using specific treatment protocols to deliver services, viewing the process as restrictive of their clinical freedom and not in their clients' best interests. Trained in universities where academic freedom is prized, they (like their university professors) view efforts to apply a specific treatment protocol to a group of clients as an infringement upon their freedom. Some clinicians have been influenced by the efforts of university professors and their graduate students to resist the introduction of managed care concepts into universities. From their perspective, managed care is an effort to increase the "efficiency" and "productivity" of the university at the expense of its faculty and students.

The opposition of some clinicians is based on a view of protocols as another example of the routinization of behavioral health care that leads to a "cookbook" approach to treatment and that stifles innovative practice. Protocol use is seen as leading to a "one size fits all" approach. From this perspective, protocols are seen as the major drawback of managed care, supporting its emphasis on short-term interventions for all clients, regardless of problem severity or clinical diagnosis. Clinicians may stress that clients need treatment tailored to their individual clinical needs, which they believe that protocols cannot provide.

Analogously, some physicians have been reluctant to apply medical treatment protocols to the care of their patients. As these protocols have proven to be effective in clinical trails and consumers have become knowledgeable about their proven effectiveness, however, almost all physicians have employed them in their daily practice. Similarly, specific human service practices ultimately will be proven effective; resistance to their use will wane; and protocols will become more widespread.

Managers, however, should keep mind that the effort to develop specific treatment protocols is a management practice with roots in the past. Even though management has now moved well beyond the early principles of Taylor, his ideas continue to influence present thinking. Based on the tenet that "every single act of every workman can be reduced to a science," he believed that any piece of work could be broken down into a series of prescribed tasks that could be predicted and controlled. The assembly line developed by Henry Ford and others, with its efficient but dehumanizing aspects, deconstructed work performed into its simplest components, ensuring maximum control with minimal product variability. The appeal of work routinization or standardization and the application of scientific management principles rests on promises of efficiency, predictability, and control. Their overuse, however, can create erosion of professional autonomy as staff begins to question their authenticity and their use of self in the therapeutic situation.

The manager who is clear that "practice wisdom" can be as important as protocol delivery should be able to prevent these problems. In implementing the development and use of protocols, an effective manager will delegate responsibility to the agency's professional staff rather than imposing protocols from outside the organization. Without the support of the agency's professional staff, specific intervention protocols either will not be developed or, if developed elsewhere, will not be widely used. Management needs to gently push clinical staff to form committees to develop protocols and ensure that a number of trained individuals are always available to deliver each protocol. Management also should enlist the support of the medical or clinical director. Most comprehensive agencies create professional staff committees whose members oversee the development and use of intervention protocols, specify the types of clients suitable for each protocol, and monitor the results of their continued use. Program supervisors typically are involved in ensuring that the protocols are in keeping with agency policies and are applied as described, particularly as the staff who developed the protocols leaves the agency.

Elements of a Service Description

There are five elements in each service description: the staffing ratios to deliver the service, client eligibility, the expected frequency and length of services, the relationship of service components, and the exact dates of programmatic changes.

Staffing Ratios

There is great variation in staffing ratios of human services. For example, a federal report recently examined the staffing patterns in 440 child caring institutions that called themselves residential treatment centers. Some institutions with as many as 100 children had only 2 mental health professionals on staff, and other centers with as few as 60 children had 10 mental health professionals.

A clear delineation of staffing ratios is the first step in developing a service description. Agency administrators should answer a number of questions about staffing ratios. What is the caseload of each intervention worker in each service provided by the agency? What should the caseloads be? How many psychiatric aides are needed in each psychiatric unit at various periods during the day? How many teachers in the educational service or how many child care workers in the child care program are needed to effectively deliver those services? What is the justification for the current caseloads? What efforts are being made to establish empirical evidence to support these levels? For example, why do the agency's psychologist and psychiatrist have different caseloads than the social workers in the mental health outpatient clinics? Why are two staff members required to deliver a parent education group?

There generally is little empirical evidence to support staffing patterns at the beginning of program evaluation efforts (and, in some situations, there may never be). Nevertheless, attention must be given to the arbitrarily set staff ratios that characterize human services. Some child care institutions, for example, have 15 children in a living unit supervised by 2 child care workers during programming hours, and others have 10 children in a unit supervised by 1 worker. Special education classrooms vary in size from one teacher for 15 children to one teacher and 2 teaching assistants for 6 children. In the educational arena, the desirable ratio of teacher to students in terms of classroom size is not well understood. Although studies reveal that children in regular education do better in smaller classes, there has been no research on classroom size in special education and little attention to the tremendous variability in college classroom sizes. Opinion as to staff ratios varies greatly, although most line workers and some administrators believe that "more staff is always better."

In spite of the need to define and justify staff ratios, agencies may encounter challenges when they change staffing ratios and patterns. The following example illustrates the dilemmas. When the author first joined the staff of Astor Home for Children in Rhinebeck, New York, the agency's institutional school was funded and operated by the New York City Public Schools. Staffing consisted of 8 classroom teachers for 64 children, a shop teacher, a head teacher with no classroom responsibilities, and a part-time physical education teacher. The agency additionally supplied an art and cooking teacher as well as a remedial reading specialist who taught a classroom of children with reading disabilities. As part of the evaluation process, children with reading problems were matched and each member of a matched pair randomly assigned to the classroom of the remedial reading specialist or to a regular classroom. Year-end achievement test data suggested that children placed in the reading specialist's class made greater academic progress than the matched controls. Although the positive results could have been attributed to the reading specialist's personality or motivation rather than the remedial reading techniques used, there was a very low likelihood that the teacher was better or more motivated than each of the eight classroom teachers who taught the matched controls. After four years, the reading specialist's classroom was converted into a resource room so that more children with reading disabilities could be served.

During this period, the teaching staff was on a New York City pay scale and lived in upstate New York. They felt supported by the agency, and, consequently, turnover was very low. But, as the

agency increasingly accepted children from upstate counties into
the school, the New York City School system could no longer le-
gally operate the program. The school became an approved institutional school and its tuition rate was fixed by the New York State
Department of Education. The size of the educational staff more
than doubled with the addition of a teaching assistant to each
classroom, two floating assistants, a crisis counselor, a speech
teacher, a physical education teacher, an art teacher, two school
psychologists, a head teacher, and a building principal. It was determined that the art, cooking, and remedial reading specialists
were no longer needed.

Changes also were made in the agency's scheduling of child
care workers. Initially, the agency made a small cadre of child care
workers available during the day to assist sick children, help the
head teacher with crises, and attend treatment team meetings.
Often a child care worker would accompany a child in crisis to the
living group and remain with the child until he was sufficiently
calm to return to school. With the change to an approved institutional school, child care workers no longer were scheduled during the day. The changes in staffing allowed funds to be freed to
enrich the child care department and develop a recreational department. Initially, almost everyone was pleased by the change.

Was the second staffing pattern more effective in providing
the educational program? Did the children perform better under
the new and enriched staffing pattern? As time passed, not all staff
assessed the changes as positive. Some staff felt that the friction
between teachers and teaching assistants caused management
problems in many of the classrooms. Because many special education jobs were available in the surrounding school districts (most
of which served less disturbed children and offered better pay or
better benefits), teacher turnover was high. In contrast, the turnover of teaching assistants (who had relatively few other opportunities and who were better paid than teacher aids in the public
schools) was low. Newly hired teachers had difficulty acquiring the
skills necessary to manage the children because the more experienced teaching assistants quickly and more efficiently handled
discipline problems. Some teachers came to rely on teaching as-

sistants for classroom control. Conflicts between teachers and teaching assistants escalated, and the building principal spent considerable time on staff interaction problems, frequently transferring teaching assistants from one classroom to another.

Some staff expressed concerns regarding the impact of the new staffing pattern on the children. Some clinicians, for example, felt that the children felt safer in the presence of both a teacher and teaching assistant and acted out more often because they knew their fights could more easily be interrupted by two adults. Children seemed more willing to escalate interpersonal conflicts because they knew they would be able to save face through adult intervention. Some staff believed that the staffing pattern increased children's opportunities for meaningful adult relationships, but others believed the opposite, viewing the large number of staff as diluting children's relationships with adults. Some staff felt that the child care workers (who knew the children and their families more intimately than the school crisis counselor) had not only been able to turn each crisis situation into a learning experience for the child but had assisted the child in developing meaningful relationships. For these staff, a meaningful relationship leading to a corrective-emotional experience was the key to positive change. Their views were bolstered by the fact that after discharge, many children corresponded with or inquired about their New York City teacher and only a few such communications occurred under the new staffing pattern.

As this example illustrates, it is important to objectively compare the effectiveness of different staffing patterns. If in the Astor Home for Children situation, the children admitted under the two staffing patterns had been found to display similar characteristics, the two patterns could have been compared (using such measures, for example, as the number of behavioral incidents, achievement test scores, the number of children who viewed their teacher as a model, length of stay, and postdischarge academic adjustment). No concerted effort to compare the two staffing patterns, however, was made. A preliminary analysis revealed that achievement test scores and intellectual gains were similar for the two groups, and there was a period when the number of restraints under the new staffing pattern far exceeded the number of time-out room placements under the old pattern. Critics, however, noted that the more recently admitted children were more disturbed than children admitted under the older staffing pattern and that incident recording was spotty under the old staffing pattern. Because in all likelihood these observations were correct, further study would have served no practical purpose.

In any event, it would be a rare administrator who would recommend a study of alternative staffing patterns given the possible implications. When a service has enjoyed an enriched staffing pattern, as was the case with this agency, staff is unlikely to accept reductions in staff size. In other cases, including many child welfare and mental health agencies, salary levels are fixed by state funding mechanisms. As a result, monies saved through staff reductions could not be used to increase the salaries of remaining employees.

Client Eligibility

As discussed in detail in Chapter 2, program evaluation efforts must include written client eligibility criteria for each program and for each service within each program that the agency provides. Client eligibility should be an integral part of each service description.

As an example of client eligibility criteria, a group home program may admit only children with IQs within a certain range or may exclude children who display certain behaviors, such as sexual abuse of peers or fire setting. A therapeutic foster care program may expressly exclude children with serious relationship problems, whereas a residential treatment center may specialize in treating children with such characteristics. A juvenile justice program may have different admission criteria for each of its programs, using criteria related to the seriousness or chronicity of the juvenile's offense. A psychiatric hospital will likely have clearly stated admission policies for emergency admissions (criteria on which about 60% of psychiatrists agree). On a smaller scale, family therapy may be offered only to families who display certain characteristics, and speech therapy may be offered only to children with certain language disorders.

Expected Frequency and Length of Services

The third element of a service description is a delineation of expected frequency and length of services. In the human services, there is great variability in the extent to which service frequency and length is defined. For example, in the mental health arena a specific number of treatment sessions may be specified, or alternatively, a range of sessions or a maximum number of sessions may be recommended (such as 8 to 10 sessions or up to 20 sessions). In practice, it is not uncommon to find in some clinics that clients with a wide variety of problems are assigned to a brief treatment service; in other clinics, brief treatment based on manualized treatment procedures is limited to clients who display specific disorders; and in yet other clinics, brief treatment is provided across multiple client disorders in keeping with particular models of brief therapy, such as solution-focused therapy or brief psychoanalytic therapy. An example of service frequency and length in the child welfare arena can be seen in the Home Builders Model where clients are seen as often as necessary but only for a total time of up to six weeks.

In many human service programs, neither the expected frequency of a service nor the expected length of stay in each service is stated, and both parameters remain open-ended. When children are admitted to special education programs, for example, they tend to remain in these programs throughout their schooling. Children in public school are given speech therapy or individual counseling with no stated end dates. There is, in fact, almost no data that informs a parent or a provider about the number of speech therapy, physical therapy, or occupational therapy sessions that are needed to ameliorate a specific problem.

At the same time, there is little evidence to support service delivery method in relation to frequency or length of service. Empirical validation is needed to determine the most efficient and effective methods of providing services and delineate the type and length of treatment required for maximal gains. As an example, in some states, speech therapists in public schools carry a caseload of 60 children and see most children in groups. There is, however, no evidence that supports group speech therapy as the most effective method for addressing either the wide variety of speech problems that children in public school tend to have or for achieving outcomes within a specific period of time. Although the group method may appear more efficient (more children can be served at a given time), efficiency must be related to effectiveness. In the case of speech therapy, a therapist will be efficient if she meets with the children assigned to her on time and for the recommended time period, but she will be effective only if she is able to improve each client's communication skills using the most efficient methods. If it takes children twice as long to make progress in group treatment as opposed to individual treatment, it will not be efficient or effective.

If empirical study were to prove that individual speech therapy was more efficient and effective, a therapist could continue to see the same number of children, but instead see them in waves. During a 40-week school year, for example, a therapist could deliver 5 hours of direct service each school day, or 25 hours of therapy per week. Fifty half-hour therapy sessions could be delivered to 15 children, approximately four sessions per week for each child for up to 10 weeks. This wave of children could be followed by treatment of another wave of 15 children for a second 10-week period, with subsequent waves of children treated throughout the school year.

In addition to determining the most efficient and effective methods of providing services and the type and length of treatment required to maximize outcomes, professionals also must determine a cutoff point after which further treatment results in minimal gain. When such information is available, an agency can utilize frequency and length of service data to construct appropriate caseload size, as discussed above.

Relationships Among Service Components

Although most clients receive a variety of services, most agency policy, procedures, and service manuals do not state how the different service components work, or fit, together. The manuals may state that interdisciplinary team meetings are held to determine the client's goals and objectives, and that a team coordinator ensures that each service component is implemented in keeping with team goals and objectives. How the components work together, however, is not described in sufficient detail to replicate. The typical descriptions (such as regular meetings of department heads and periodic meetings of program-wide staff) do not permit replication of the component-fit aspects of a program despite the fact that these "fits" may be the keys to the program's effectiveness. As one example, Moos (1974) demonstrated that team functioning relates to client outcomes. It was only after his study of outcomes and his comparison of the traits of ineffective and effective interdisciplinary teams, however, that effective team functioning could be described and the skills of effective team leaders identified.

As another example, in some residential centers, the psychotherapists' offices are housed in children's cottages, and in others, the children go to a clinical center for psychotherapy. When housed in a children's cottage, the therapist becomes easily and intimately involved in the child's milieu life. When housed in a clinical center, the therapist may be involved only minimally in the child's milieu life. It may be the case that the center-based clinician spends each afternoon in the cottage, facilitating discussion groups with children and remaining after the group to interact informally with them. The therapist may be equally, if not more, involved in the child's milieu. An office in a cottage, consequently, would not necessarily guarantee meaningful involvement with children.

Irrespective of the location of the therapists' offices, the program manual should specifically describe the services that the clinician is expected to deliver in the milieu and the milieu activities in which the clinician will participate. If, for example, the clinician is expected to accompany children on field trips and help child care staff with child management, the agency should include this expectation in the manual, monitor its actual occurrence, and solicit opinions about the clinician's child-management skills from child care staff. This description will provide clear information on how the clinical and the child care program components fit together.

The author once visited several children at a state mental hospital (considered a model treatment center) and was invited to visit the children during occupational therapy. "Occupational therapy" was, in reality, a period during the school day when children played pool or Ping-Pong with other children in a room that was staffed by an occupational therapist. The therapist explained that each child in the hospital received the service and that the occupational therapy goals for each child were the same: "to learn to play together cooperatively with other children and to master the perceptual-motor skills inherent in the games of Ping-Pong and pool." The occupational therapist knew very little about the children outside of his own observations while they were in the room. Treatment team meetings were held in another campus building, and the therapist's schedule did not allow him to attend. He viewed his attendance at such meetings as meaningless, however, because each child received occupational therapy and the pros and cons of the service for each child were not subject to discussion. The therapist, however, wrote monthly progress reports on each child, which were available for the monthly team reviews. Interestingly, during the author's visit, four different children played pool or Ping-Pong together, all very cooperatively and all very well.

In marked contrast, the occupational therapist at Astor Home for Children assessed each child's self-help, fine and gross motor, and recreational skills. Only children who displayed developmental deficits received occupational therapy. The therapist worked directly with recreational and child care staff, assisting them in offering appropriate therapeutic activities for children within the milieu environment. Approximately 70% of the therapist's direct service time was spent in working with other staff. Despite the clear integration of occupational therapy and child care at Astor Home, the interdisciplinary functioning of the occupational therapist could become "institutionalized" only if written in agency policy. Otherwise, the component-fit would be an unknown influence on program outcomes. Outcomes could be favorable, but if the networking services of the therapist were not written down, they could not be replicated by others. Newly hired staff could easily decide to function quite differently (and, in fact, often do). The effective program could rapidly become ineffective.

As another example, in a relatively well known residential treatment center, children received individual psychotherapy only during academic-subject time periods. Therapists reported that children resisted therapy when asked to leave art, shop, cooking, or gym classes. Therapy sessions, consequently, were routinely scheduled during periods of academic instruction. This scheduling pattern created ill feelings among the teachers. Upon the appointment of a new clinical director, the treatment team was given the authority to decide when a child would receive therapy. For the most part, the team scheduled children for therapy sessions during art, cooking, shop, or gym unless the child had a pronounced need for one of these subjects. If, however, the child was disruptive in mathematics and mathematical skill was not considered a priority at the time, the team might decide that the child would be seen during the math period. The team also decided that many children should be seen after school or during the evening so that all of their learning needs could be addressed sufficiently during the school day. The clinical director mandated that each clinician work a flex-schedule that included evening time. Teachers and child care workers also received instruction in what to say to children when therapists arrived to take them for their therapy sessions. This structure provided consistent support throughout the milieu for children as they left their ongoing activities for their therapy sessions.

The research literature and the agency's own follow-up studies indicated that, following these changes, children closest to grade level at discharge had favorable academic outcomes regardless of their reported gains in psychotherapy. Feedback from staff six months after the new system was implemented was favorable, including feedback from clinicians who reported that the flex-schedule created opportunities to interact with the children in more meaningful ways. This program-component fit, however, was never written nor did it become official agency policy. Shortly after changes in the executive director, the clinical director, and the school principal, flex hours vanished; clinicians returned to working a 9-to-5 day, and children attended therapy sessions only during art, cooking, shop, and gym classes. When the author recently visited the agency, the school principal described the teacher-clinician friction around therapy times and stated her belief that it had always existed. Organizational amnesia had set in.

As this experience well illustrates, the saying, "If it's not written down, it doesn't exist," (repeated ad nauseam by compliance monitors from licensing and accreditation agencies) is not bureaucratic nonsense.

Exact Dates of Programmatic Changes

Typically, it is not possible to determine the actual date when an agency implemented a change. Without such dates, it is not clear which clients received what services and for how long. Rarely are changes made in programs to coincide with a new group of admissions. As a result, after a change is made, some clients will have received both the old and the new service prior to their discharge from the program. Although the data sometimes can be retrieved from usual agency sources, typically far more work is required. As an example, an agency at one point offered group therapy to children who had been victims of sexual abuse. The therapists who developed the groups left the agency, leaving no written group therapy protocols. With their departure, groups for sexually abused children were discontinued. The remaining clinical staff addressed the issue of sexual abuse in individual psychotherapy, but several clinicians thought that groups should be reintroduced. They were unsure about the structure of the previous groups and did not know whether they had been effective. No one knew when the groups had been held, although they believed that it had been approximately five years previously. Fortunately, several staff remembered the clinicians who had provided group therapy, and the personnel office provided information on those clinicians' employment dates. It was then possible to identify the children who had been in the program at the time the clinicians were with the agency. Based on a reading of therapists' progress notes in more than 250 of these children's clinical records, the staff was able to identify 80 children who had received the group treatment. The notes indicated that four to six children had been in each group, and the groups lasted for 20 sessions. Usually four groups were held each year over a four-year period.

This process was hardly an efficient way to determine the start and end dates for a service or to learn more about it. Information about the activity and identification of the clients served would have been easily obtained if the agency had required written service protocols and retained them; recorded the beginning and ending dates for all services; and maintained a client database that included the services each client received.

Standardized Data Collection

Once a service is clearly described, it is possible to assess the outcomes for clients who received that service. Appendix B provides an example of a form that may be used to abstract data from children's clinical records. This form has been used to abstract data about children and families who received intensive home-based mental health treatment, but could be used for other services as well. It provides for a standardized collection of information about each child and family that the program served and the exact nature of the services provided to them. Such information can be related to outcome data for each client, enabling staff to determine relationships among child and family variables, treatment variables, and outcomes.

Summary

Efforts to evaluate a service will be relatively meaningless if the specific nature of the service provided to a specific group of clients is not clear. Clarity requires that this information be in written form in program manuals and specific service protocols. Although a number of programs have reported positive outcomes, the descriptions of their programs often lack sufficient detail for replication. These descriptions often fail to identify how the services were delivered or how the service components fit together. Program manuals should describe the content of each service; contain service protocols; state the staffing ratios required to deliver each service; specify consumer eligibility; and state the expected frequency of service sessions for each service. The manual should also specify how the different service components fit together. Finally, when changes are made in a program, a program component, or a specific service, the agency should document the dates of those changes.

Chapter 4:

. . . .

Monitoring the Integrity of Service Delivery

After a written service protocol is developed and implemented and efforts are underway to assess its effectiveness, management must ensure that the protocol continues to be used and that its use remains unaltered. The fact that a treatment methodology has been implemented or its effectiveness has been proven will not guarantee use of the protocol as described or its continued use in the future. Monitoring the integrity of service delivery involves two key efforts: the development of quality assurance processes and the development of staff evaluation processes that focus on performance competencies. Both processes are described in this chapter.

Quality Assurance

Management practices are required to ensure the correct use and the continued correct use of a specific service protocol or a best practice. For some time, educators have known that attention must be given to the ongoing and correct use of protocols. Although research may demonstrate the overall positive effects of a new curriculum in a school system, further analysis typically reveals that the curriculum is not equally effective in all classrooms. In some classrooms, children demonstrate greater gains when the new curriculum is used than the average gain made by the total school system (that is, the curriculum has high implementation success). In other classrooms, students perform better when the traditional curriculum is used (that is, the new curriculum has low implementation success). Qualitative research typically reveals that teachers with whom the new curriculum enjoys high implementation success follow the curriculum guidelines more closely, understand the strengths of the new curriculum, and profit more from the training provided prior to the adoption of the curriculum. Similarly, in a national study of Head Start Centers, some centers were found to be more effective than others, even though their staffs utilized the same educational materials and delivered family support services. Qualitative research studies revealed that staff in the more effective centers more closely followed the curriculum guidelines and provided more meaningful outreach services to families than did staff in the less effective centers.

In any outcome study, there are proximal and distal outcomes. Proximal outcomes are short-term or intermediate outcomes that are expected to contribute to distal outcomes. Distal outcomes are long range goals that a client is expected to achieve following the successful implementation of an intervention. The following are examples of proximal and distal outcomes.

> In studies of curriculum effectiveness, proximal outcomes are changes in teaching behavior and distal outcomes are changes in student achievement test scores.

> In studies of psychotherapy protocols, proximal outcomes are changes in the psychotherapist's activities (such as the correct application of a treatment protocol) and distal outcomes are changes in client functioning.

> In studies of the effectiveness of residential treatment, proximal outcomes are changes associated with the correct implementation of treatment components. Proximal outcomes may be staff-related outcomes, such as the correct delivery of an implementation procedure, more interpersonal contact with children, the arrangement of more visits for children, more social service contacts with parents, more social work visits to the child's home school prior and subsequent to discharge, and the provision of more remedial reading. Distal outcomes for children may

be improvements in academic achievement, behavior control, and language use, as well as developmental advancements in self care, social skill, and gross and fine motor skills. Another distal outcome for children may be adequate community functioning six months after discharge.

In a study of a community mobilization effort to decrease the adverse effects of alcohol use in a community, proximal outcomes might include changes in the alcohol serving practices of restaurants and bars following employee training programs, implementation of an alcohol prevention curriculum in health education classes in the public schools, level of mass media coverage and programming on alcohol issues, and the number of roadside checks performed by the police. Distal outcomes might include decreases in the number of DWI tickets issued, the amount of alcohol refuse found at schools, or the number of individuals who report frequent driving after drinking in community surveys. Positive distal outcomes also might be decreases in alcohol related traffic incidents and the total number of alcohol involved injuries.

In any of these studies, there are distinctions between intervention components that relate to the implementation process itself and intervention components that relate to the impact of the intervention. Before the effects of a curriculum can be evaluated, teachers must correctly implement the curriculum. Before a treatment protocol can be evaluated, clinicians must correctly implement the protocol. In the community-based alcohol-use reduction program, the effects of efforts by restaurant staff and police can be evaluated only if, after training, restaurant staff and bartenders engage in different alcohol-serving behavior and the police correctly use breath analyzers and increase the number of roadside checks. When neither proximal nor distal outcome measures show change after program implementation, the efforts may be considered ineffective. Before reaching this conclusion, however, it is important to use qualitative research procedures that provide detailed descriptions of intervention settings and intervention delivery. The failure to achieve a desired result may be the result of incorrect implementation of the intervention procedures rather than the intervention itself.

The Importance of Process Variables

Unfortunately, in the typical human service agency, management practices have been divorced from formal evaluation practices. Ensuring program continuation and maintaining program integrity requires ongoing evaluation of staff performance variables related to service protocols. These variables often are referred to as "process variables." Process variables are critical because even when a service activity has been proven effective, staff may discontinue its use for variety of reasons. Chapter 1 provided three examples of agencies that failed to maintain effective services. Similarly, a clinic that demonstrated success from a 15-session cognitive-behavior therapy protocol in the treatment of patients who suffered from panic disorder subsequently found that clinicians discontinued its use. Clinicians reverted to their preferred but less effective and often less efficient method of treating the disorder. They simply concluded that the intervention protocol did not meet the needs of individual clients.

A manager would do well to remember that unless staff is continually supported in their use of specific intervention procedures, they often find it easier to use methods other than the specific treatment protocols. For example, it may be easier to simply follow a child's lead in play therapy than to structure the play so that core conflicts are aroused or ego-support is enhanced. A therapist may find it preferable to treat disturbed children individually than to see them in a structured treatment group that takes considerably more time to plan and infinitely more patience and endurance. Similarly, in child welfare, staff may find it easier to see parents of children in foster care in individual counseling sessions than to coordinate structured group counseling sessions on child management problems. Substance abuse treatment professionals may prefer to discuss parenting problems with patients in individual counseling than to arrange for multiple-family group parent education for children and their caregivers. Probation officers may find it easier to talk with youth in their offices than to make home visits and deliver a psychoeducational- lrogram to parents on effective discipline.

In any human service field, maintaining staff adherence to standardized intervention protocols requires continued staff training, support, and encouragement. It does not require that management continually supervises or monitors staff or that management applies scientific management concepts to professional practice. Staff cannot be forced to apply effective interventions; they must want to do so. Managers must allow time for staff to learn the use of a specific intervention and to prepare for its delivery. For example, in group therapy for children, staff may need planning time for group treatment and assistance in seeing that once a specific group treatment protocol is developed, its future delivery is easier. At the same time, management should anticipate uneven implementation of service protocols. For example, management may find in a 12-step alcohol clinic treatment program that some staff are less actively engaged in teaching clients the 12-step rehabilitation approach; some staff fail to link clients with existing Alcohol Anonymous (AA) and Narcotic Anonymous (NA) meetings in the community; and other staff fail to ensure that AA and NA sponsors are recruited and prepared in adequate numbers. If any or all of these problems exist, it is unfair to compare the outcomes of clients in 12-step alcohol clinic programs with clients receiving alternative clinic services because the 12-step approach would have been incorrectly implemented.

The Role of Quality Assurance

Program integrity is maintained through monitoring process variables that are part of the service protocol. These process variables, often called "performance indicators," are monitored through quality assurance (QA) efforts. QA is designed to assess the quality of program implementation and involves efforts to determine how closely actual program delivery is to intended program delivery. The chief task of QA is to ensure that best practices regularly occur because these practices are most likely to influence outcomes. Formal QA activities should be in place in all agency programs to supplement ongoing staff training and supervision and to minimize the effects on program integrity of supervisory differences in skills, interests, and theoretical orientations.

QA efforts involve three components: (1) assessment of adherence to intervention guidelines (including best practices); (2) assessment of the amount of intervention exposure (how much intervention was delivered to the target group); and (3) assessment of reinvention (the extent to which the implementation deviates from the program standard being evaluated). This third component is critical because, as Rogers [1983] demonstrates in *The Diffusion of Innovation,* program designers often experience spontaneous implementation of an intervention outside of the program design.

QA programs regularly monitor process variables. The QA process typically involves the identification of the process variables that staff believe are related to outcomes or that empirical evidence has related to outcomes, the identification of a procedure that allows the ongoing assessment of the presence of these variables, and the implementation of the assessment procedure. How assessment is conducted will vary, depending upon a number of factors, including the size of the agency. Staff may conduct the assessment in turns, or they may designate one or more staff members to perform the assessment. When the variable being assessed is adherence to an intervention, peer review procedures can be used. The agency may choose to use role-play instead of observing a staff member's work with clients. If the staff member cannot display the specific techniques in role-play, it is unlikely that he or she can display those techniques in interactions with clients. Such procedures can highlight staff support and training issues.

Another approach to assessment is a second-party review of clinical records for the presence or absence of process variables. For example, the author conducted a review of clinical records of staff who were treating children who had been sexually abused. Ten staff had been trained in the use of structured play techniques to help children elicit feelings about past sexual abuse. The review, however, revealed that two of the staff showed no evidence of using the techniques in treatment at all. In addition, the children treated by these two clinicians never revealed or discussed their abuse with the therapists, although most of the children did so with the other eight therapists. The author discussed this finding with the supervisor of the two staff members. The supervisor remarked that the first therapist was extremely client-centered and did not believe in structured approaches to play therapy. The second therapist was described as being uncomfortable with the topic of sexual abuse. The supervisor stated, however, that both therapists were effective in helping the children deal with a host of other problems. After determining that the remaining eight therapists believed in the value of the techniques and were providing effective services, the supervisor no longer assigned sexually abused children to the two staff members.

The Evolution of Quality Assurance Activities

Only recently have QA activities been conceptualized as an integral part of program evaluation. When QA activities were first introduced into nonprofit management, there was considerable confusion about their purpose. At that point in time, few agencies had written service protocols, and many had no clearly established service models that staff were expected to follow.

The Role of Accrediting Bodies in the Evolution of QA

Accrediting bodies contributed to the initial confusion around QA because they required agencies to implement ongoing monitoring activities before agencies had demonstrated that any of the services they delivered were effective. The Joint Commission on Accreditation of Health Care Organizations (JCAHO), for example, directed agencies as to what to monitor; determined which practices contributed to quality client care; and required agencies to utilize JCAHO standards for monitoring. Among the initial standards that JCAHO imposed were that client assessments and discharge summaries cover a number of specified areas of client functioning; that agencies complete assessment, treatment planning activities, and discharge summaries within specific time frames; and that safety and infection control procedures be put in place. As JCAHO representatives visited agencies and learned how they operated, they added standards and within a short period of time, the number of standards had increased 100-fold. Agency QA departments sprang up almost overnight and agencies were forced to hire staff for the sole purpose of ensuring compliance with JCAHO standards. Some agency directors determined that complying with JCAHO standards took an estimated 10% of staff time. In some facilities, efforts to maintain JCAHO standards interfered with performing meaningful program evaluation. Staff was busy monitoring compliance with JCAHO standards and had no time to monitor the integrity of their ongoing services (Mordock, in press). Service protocols remained unwritten; other protocols were not followed; organizational amnesia set in; and programs "drifted away" from their original models. Accrediting agencies brought scientific management practices into agencies; innovation and creativity were stifled.

As these developments indicate, many agencies developed an elaborate superstructure of JCAHO activities despite the fact that the foundation upon which this structure was based had never been adequately evaluated. At the same time, agencies that varied widely in their service delivery approach received JCAHO accreditation. JCAHO staff assumed that compliance with their standards (which they viewed as indices of quality) automatically translated into delivery of quality treatment services. Many in the field, however, knew that some of the accredited agencies provided inferior care and treatment (even those accredited "with accommodation," meaning they met almost all of the JCAHO standards). These critics pointed out that success at dotting the "i's" and crossing the "t's" did not mean quality care.

To date, there have been few studies of the relationship between perceived quality and actual outcome. Although there may some agreement on the essential ingredients of a quality service (at least among professionals who share a common theoretical perspective), it continues to be necessary to establish empirically that a "quality service" is both efficient and effective. To this end, meaningful QA activities are needed to demonstrate that a service produces favorable outcomes in a cost-effective manner. At minimum, QA efforts can ensure that services are delivered as conceptualized in a program manual or service protocol and that staff follow specific treatment protocols or delineated intervention paths (that is, the specific performance standards, or "quality indicators," associated with the service protocol).

QA has evolved through four generations, although few agencies currently engage in fourth generation activities.

First Generation QA Activities

Current QA procedures evolved from earlier, or first generation, efforts to monitor treatment delivery in keeping with standards set by accrediting bodies. First generation quality assurance activities in mental health and child welfare tended to monitor activities that were related to but were not core treatment activities. These activities included staff credentialing, safety, incident management, and infection control procedures to ensure that the client was treated by qualified professionals in a safe environment. They did not include efforts to measure staff-related proximal outcomes.

In the first generation of QA, independent evaluators regularly reviewed clinical records for compliance with written standards. Compliance was monitored with such accreditation standards as measurable client objectives, treatment reviews every three months, and written discharge summaries completed within 15 days of the client's discharge. Agencies established committees to review aggregate compliance data and make recommendations for improvement. Although some might equate compliance with the achievement of proximal outcomes, staff generally did not see that meeting such standards indicated that clients had made progress.

Second Generation QA Activities

Second generation QA activities went one step further. Quality indicators were established, and staff activities were monitored for evidence of the indicators. Clinical record reviews expanded from monitoring to determine compliance with accreditation standards to assessments of the presence of predetermined quality indicators. Some indicators were established from surveys of professional staff, others from surveys of present and past clients, and yet others from standards of accrediting bodies. No quality indicators were related to outcome findings.

As an example of second generation QA, a residential treatment center may have determined that a child's successful discharge to a foster home depended on the child's acceptance of the foster care placement. It would be expected that the child's record would reflect the child's agreement with this plan. There would be regular reviews of the records of children referred for foster home care to assess the progress each child was making in relation to the transition. Reviewers would expect to find that therapists' notes for older children would describe efforts to help the child verbalize feelings about previous out-of-home placements and to help the child understand the reasons that his parents could not care for him. Reviewers would expect therapists' notes of their treatment of younger children to reflect similar efforts in psychodramatic play therapy.

Third Generation QA Activities

In the third generation, QA activities moved from monitoring indices of quality to attempts to improve quality at all levels in the organization. This process is called total or continuous quality improvement. Participatory management practices were at the heart of such efforts, and staff members themselves identified and solved problems. The goal became continuous efforts to improve rather than efforts to simply meet current standards. Quality was defined based on the consensus of staff opinion, but such consensus was largely lacking. As a result, total quality improvement efforts often led to agency-wide micro-management. Professional staff made suggestions to improve agency forms, secretaries suggested better use of their time, and recreational staff in day and residential programs suggested hiring temporary help for seasonal responsibilities. Numerous improvements in internal operations were suggested, but no one examined whether the services were effective. In essence, better ways were found to "clean up the operating room," but no one was sure what the actual operation entailed or could prove that the "operation" was a success.

Fourth Generation QA Activities

In the fourth generation, the stage being addressed in this book, quality is evaluated through examining outcomes. It recognizes that the only true measure of program quality is perceived client progress. The fourth generation of QA focuses on assessing the effects of service activities and specific treatment protocols on outcomes; modifying activities and protocols to improve outcomes; and continuing programs that make a positive impact on clients' lives. In this generation of QA, refinement in treatment procedures is followed by further refinement. Few agencies have reached this stage of QA practice.

The Current Status of QA Activities

Currently, many human service agencies deliver services without formal ongoing quality assurance activities. Although both the juvenile justice and special education systems have mechanisms in place to preauthorize services and perform ongoing utilization review of all cases, other first-stage quality assurance activities have yet to be introduced. In most school systems, educational staff members are unfamiliar with the procedures associated with quality assurance. Although some larger educational organizations have implemented "quality teams" comprising selected staff members who meet regularly to discuss needed educational changes, many of these teams have been short-lived, and their influence on the system as a whole has been relatively negligible. In the field of child welfare, only larger nonprofit organizations have formal ongoing quality assurance activities and generally only to satisfy accreditation requirements. Few county departments of social service use formal quality assurance activities to monitor and improve their service delivery systems. Rehabilitation agencies, particularly those accredited by the Council on Accreditation of Rehabilitation Facilities (CARF), have implemented second generation QA activities, but these efforts fall far short of outcome assessment. Leaders in child welfare, juvenile justice, special education, rehabilitation, and other human service agencies face considerable challenges in implementing the fourth generation QA practices described in this book.

Monitoring of Service Plan Implementation

Maintaining program integrity requires ongoing monitoring of service plan implementation. Monitoring should take place at the level of individual clients and at the agency-wide level.

Quality Assurance at the Client Level

Quality assurance efforts begin at the level of individual clients. In most human service agencies, clients have a written plan for services. In outpatient mental health settings, the plan may include a number of distinct services, and in a residential treatment center or a psychiatric center for children, the plan may involve many service components that are related to one another. A child's treatment plan in a residential treatment center, for example, may include a combination of therapeutic and educational services and ongoing milieu activities. As an example, a child's initial intervention plan might list the following:

1. Two 50-minute periods of play therapy a week, with a focus on the child's prior history of sexual abuse;

2. Meals low in calorie content to help the child lose weight;

3. Individual speech therapy, twice a week for 30-minute periods to remedy the child's articulation disorder;

4. Participation in family therapy twice a month, with a focus on sibling rivalry;

5. Reinforcement of the child's defenses of projection and blame throughout the milieu;

6. Recreational therapy focusing on the development of the child's interest in nature and animals; and

7. Weekly trips to town to purchase fish for the child's fish tank.

A study conducted some years ago at a nationally recognized residential treatment center suggested that children's treatment recommendations, as contained in the child's plan, were not necessarily carried out. The study indicated that when the agency's services format was weekly clinical rounds by the team psychiatrist, only 70% of each child's recommendations were implemented. The rate improved to 90% when the format was changed to a treatment team approach and team meetings were held quarterly and chaired by the team psychiatrist. After the agency developed a new role of team clinical coordinator, 95% of the recommendations were carried out. If formal QA activities had been in place at the time of these developments, it may have been possible to achieve implementation of 100% of the recommendations.

A reader employed at a residential treatment center may believe that these findings indicate that something must have been wrong at this residential treatment center. A reader may believe that 100% of the recommendations for children's treatment would be carried out at his or her agency and that there would be no need for any "fancy QA program" to determine the agency's quality.

It is highly likely that in 9 out of 10 cases, the reader would be wrong. In reality, numerous untoward events disrupt treatment plan implementation, and in fact, it is the exceptional case when a plan is fully implemented. In the example of the treatment plan of seven services described earlier, a child may resist play or speech therapy, and the therapists, as a result, may be able to engage the child in sessions that last fewer minutes than stipulated in the plan. The play therapist might not be skilled in implementing structured approaches with sexually abused children and may not be able to address the child's real conflicts. Family therapy may be unable to address sibling rivalry issues because the child's sibling refuses to participate. Staff absences, crises, and weather may prevent the child care staff from taking the child on the recommended weekly trips to town. Newly hired recreational staff may neglect to actively encourage the child in nature activities and, instead, may include the child in the gross motor activities they typically deliver to the child's living group. The supervisor may fail to assign a specific recreational worker the responsibility for encouraging the child's interest in animals. An outdoor nature activity that has been planned for the child may be cancelled because it rains, and no backup activity may be planned. Child care workers and teachers may not support the child's use of projection and blame when the child is anxious and, instead, may confront the child when immature but needed defenses are employed, "forgetting" that the child will now employ even more primitive defenses such as fight or flight. Crises in the child's family may prevent the weekly family therapy sessions from occurring as often as recommended, and instead of 20 times in a 20-week period, family therapy may take place only eight times. To quote a maxim, "The best laid plans of mice and men often go astray," and to quote Murphy's Law, "If something can go wrong, it will."

The reader might ask why formal QA systems are needed to correct such problems. It might seem that staff would recognize failures to implement aspects of a treatment plan. In some cases, staff do, but in other cases they do not. A recent personal experience of the author, whose 91-year-old mother was in the hospital, illustrates this point. Above the bed was a printed sign stating, "Cut the food into small pieces and hand-feed the patient." The staff in this teaching hospital repeatedly brought whole solid foods, placed the tray of food in front of my mother, and left her to feed herself.

Many milieu treatment programs for both adults and children have found it necessary to assign one staff member (often called the team coordinator) the responsibility of carefully monitoring each client's intervention plan and ensuring that each plan is carried out by the treatment team. One individual, however, cannot do it all. To ensure routine 100% compliance with treatment plans, a staff member who is not a member of the team must periodically review each client's plan. This reviewer should read the client's record and the intervention plan and examine subsequent information to determine if the plan is being implemented. In most cases, the reviewer will discover that some aspect of the client's intervention plan has been neglected. For a child in a residential treatment center, for example, monitoring may reveal any one of the following situations: a recommended neurological evaluation was never completed; recommended biweekly family therapy sessions were not scheduled; the play therapist failed to provide the recommended structured play designed to elicit feelings about sexual abuse. The reviewer (who functions as an internal compliance monitor) should send case review findings to the team coordinator, who may take a number of actions. In some cases, a client's plan may be altered to reflect current realities (for example, new information indicates that the neurological evaluation is not needed, individual parent counseling is working better than the recommended family therapy, or the child is not ready to deal with the trauma of sexual abuse). In other cases, the team coordinator may remind supervisory staff that the plan has not been implemented and that staff must take corrective actions.

When a plan is modified in keeping with current realities, there is an accurate record of the interventions provided to a client. Services to clients cannot be evaluated unless the services they receive are clearly identified. In the above example, if the intervention plan remained as originally developed, the child (for whom, for example, structured play therapy for sexual abuse was recommended but not provided) might have been included in a study of the effectiveness of a service he never received.

Quality Assurance at the Agency Level

An agency-wide quality assurance process involves a number of components. A staff member who acts as the agency's compliance monitor (usually a member of a program or of an agency-wide QA committee) records aggregate findings about treatment team functioning; the agency records the aggregate findings, distributes them to staff, and ensures that they are discussed in staff meetings; and the agency makes efforts to correct deficiencies through corrective action plans. The agency's compliance monitor might find that one or more of the intervention teams consistently fails to implement all the components of their clients' intervention plans or that one department consistently fails to implement a portion of the recommendations within their area of responsibility. The recreational staff, for example, might be implementing only 80% of the recreational plans. With a total quality improvement goal of 100% (the management literature refers to this percentage as "zero defect tolerance"), the recreational department would be required to develop and implement a corrective action plan. After a period of time has elapsed, the agency would assess the effectiveness of the corrective action plan by reexamining clients' intervention plans with a specific focus on recreational services.

Department directors and staff should not feel threatened by the quality assurance process. They must believe in and actively support the concepts of total quality improvement, value self-inspection and self-improvement, and strive for greater success. Just as professional athletes recognize that reviewing videotapes of their performances is uncomfortable but necessary to produce winning teams, staff must be willing to engage in self-examination. If staff feel threatened by the process, they may develop fewer intervention plans or limit the variety of plans they develop so that they can be found in compliance in future evaluations. Compliance rather than perfection may become the goal.

Once treatment team functioning has been assessed and corrective action plans are in place, formal QA activities can include the assessment of other aspects of staff functioning. The staff assigned to perform QA functions can examine intervention protocol implementation and component functioning within and across agency settings. As an example, staff might determine whether suicidal precautions are being implemented correctly in all units of an inpatient psychiatric hospital; the number of children in a residential treatment center who meet the intake criteria and the reasons for the exceptions; the number of clinicians in an outpatient mental health clinic who utilize the agreed-upon processes variables in their clinical interactions with clients; or the extent to which the recreational department in a group child care setting employs developmentally appropriate recreational activities. As the sophistication of QA activities increases, many findings can be related to other variables. For example, the delivery of developmentally appropriate recreational activities in a child care institution can be related to months of the year, days of the week, time of day, weather conditions, or staff attendance. Once these influences are understood, the agency can develop action plans to minimize negative influences and maximize positive influences on service delivery.

Staff Competencies and Evaluation

Although formal QA activities are key to maintaining program integrity, staff performance is most affected by ongoing staff supervision, evaluation, and peer review. Like QA, these processes are key to monitoring and maintaining program integrity, but generally, they are not well implemented. Surveys reveal that supervisors and peers rarely observe human service providers as they deliver services to clients. Agency year-end (or summative) evaluations, which accreditation and licensing bodies require of human service agencies, rarely lead to improvement in employees' intervention practices or client outcomes.

In the teaching profession, for example, public school teachers report that their supervising principal observes them either not at all or only for one or two brief periods during the school year. They also report that when they are observed, the observation periods are not long enough to arrive at a justifiable opinion about their performance. The few teachers who report that the observation periods were appropriate also indicate that they were more likely to implement the principal's recommendations for instructional improvement.

Scientific management successfully streamlined production, but it also reinforced the belief that labor efficiency requires a reduction in the freedom of workers. Taylor believed that organizational efficiency demanded that a worker "not produce any longer by his own initiative," but "execute punctiliously" the orders given by management, "down to their minutest details." Taylor made it clear that the engineering of labor required not self-management (which was associated with waste), but close supervision. The history of scientific management practices in industry is a story of managers' attempts to reduce worker autonomy and workers' attempts to increase it. This history should not be duplicated in the human service professions.

Evidence suggests that when management stresses labor discipline, the organization is weakened in the long run. Tightening supervision neither saves money nor improves operations. At the same time, squeezing labor costs hurts rather than helps innovation and does not, as proponents may assert, increase revenues or improve services (Dougherty & Bowman, 1995). Human-relations theorists, in contrast to scientific management theorists, trace productivity to quality relationships, collaboration, and creativity rather than to sheer efficiency and economy.

Although beginning human service workers may actively seek supervision, experienced staff value self-directed activities. Experienced staff may seek case consultation from peers or supervisors, but they resist active monitoring of their work. The manager's job is to orchestrate staff efforts to supervise themselves, enabling them to achieve goals that they have set, and to implement interventions that staff value because they have participated in efforts that prove the effectiveness of those services. Improvements in practice will take place only when service providers see the need to make improvements.

The staff evaluation process should encourage each professional to engage in self-evaluation about his or her performance. Most human service providers enter the profession to help people, and if they believe that supervision and evaluations can help them better serve their clients, most will participate in the process. Evaluation should help professionals set their own goals and objectives. The staff member and supervisor should jointly agree on the staff member's goals for improved performance and the performance objectives to help him or her reach those goals.

Staff are likely to feel less threatened by evaluations at year-end if they have received frequent progress evaluations throughout the year. The evaluation process should parallel the process by which professionals evaluate client performance. Typically, a professional helps the client set goals for improvement; involves the client in a self-appraisal to assess the current status; helps the client set long range goals and short range objectives; prescribes, in concert with the client, what he or she must do to reach each objective; measures progress toward objectives; provides regular feedback for ongoing revision of objectives and intervention procedures; and measures goal attainment. Ongoing staff supervision and the year-end evaluation should follow the same process.

Staff Competencies, Indicators, and Descriptors

As the first step in developing a staff evaluation process, an agency should ask staff to develop a list of the intervention skills and personal and professional characteristics they deem essential for effective and efficient performance. Staff may draw on outcome literature in developing the list of specific intervention skills or "competencies." As one example, they may focus on research that shows that clients make greater improvement, regardless of the intervention protocol that is used, when they feel that the professional understands and empathizes with them. Such client perceptions contribute to a "therapeutic alliance" or "helping alliance," as described by Lester Luborsky, a highly respected outcome researcher. Drawing on this work, staff may identify communication of understanding and empathy as a competency. By involving staff in this process, the agency sets the foundation for expectations that all staff ultimately will have a firm understanding of intervention procedures and their efficient and effective delivery.

Once staff identify competencies that are key to effective performance, they should be asked to list for each competency the type of information that would reflect the effective and efficient performance of that competency. These "indicators" and "descriptors" should be listed for each competency. As an example, a competency in the provision of family therapy might be "accurate empathy" and the indicator and descriptors of that competency might be as follows:

Family Therapy Competency

Makes each family member feel understood, respected, and appreciated.

Indicator: Uses procedures that actively involve family members in initial sessions.

Descriptors:

a)   Actively listens to the concerns of each member and links concerns to future therapeutic activities;

b) Helps each family member recall past experiences or knowledge related to the presenting problem;

c) Simulates discussion by asking each family member thought-provoking but non- threatening questions; and

d) Helps each family member appreciate the degree to which they are affected by the current problem.

Because assessment is a critical area in family therapy, multiple competencies may be identified in this area. The following illustrates three competencies in assessment by family therapists, along with an indicator and descriptors for each:

Assessment Competency 1

Makes each family member feel involved in assessing the presenting problem.

Indicator: Employs techniques that actively involve family members in the assessment process.

Descriptors:

a) Family members verbalize the purpose of the assessment;

b) Family members verbalize an understanding of what the assessment will include;

c) Family members verbalize an understanding of the importance of their participation in the process;

d) Family members verbalize an understanding of how the assessment will be used to explain the presenting problem; and

e) Family members verbalize an understanding of how the assessment will help them to set goals to ameliorate the problem.

Assessment Competency 2

Helps family to clearly identify the presenting problem.

Indicator: Employs techniques to obtain detailed information about the problem.

Descriptors:

a) Family members verbalize who is involved in the problem;

b) Family members verbalize how each member is involved in the problem;

c) Family members verbalize how others outside the family are involved in the problem;

d) Family members identify the intensity of the presenting problem: the degree to which each family member is upset by the problem, the crisis nature of the problem, and the vulnerability of each family member to harm;

e) Family members identify the longevity of the problem;

f   Family members reveal history pertinent to the problem; and

g) Family members state their motivation and commitment to engage in work to alter the problem.

Assessment Competency 3

Helps family members to understand the interventions planned.

Indicator: Employs techniques that enable each family member to understand the treatment process.

Descriptors:

a) Family members verbalize how the therapy method specifically can help them;

b) Family members verbalize the mutually agreed upon defi-
    nition of issues that need to be addressed in treatment;

c) Family members verbalize the expected outcomes of their
    work; and

d) Family members verbalize how the work of each family
    member will proceed.

The identification of competencies as well as the personal and
professional characteristics essential for effective and efficient
performance should be tied to job descriptions. Job descriptions
should be written to reflect the performance competencies that
staff identifies (or which may be identified in the research). Although professionals may differ on the personal characteristics
they believe are related to performance competency, they typically agree on such characteristics as organization, good judgment
and reasoning, and the capacity to relate to others. These characteristics, at minimum, should be included in job descriptions.

Once staff have participated in developing competencies, and
indicators and descriptors of each competency, the agency should
involve staff in developing instruments to assess the extent to
which staff demonstrate the identified competencies. An agency
may develop two separate tools: a "Self-Appraisal Instrument" and
an "Intervention Observation Instrument." Both tools should be
objective, descriptive, and diagnostic; and their final form should
be approved by staff and administration. In addition, the agency
may involve staff in designing tools that clients may use to evaluate provider performance. The use of these tools is described in
greater detail in the next section.

The Staff Evaluation Process

Once the content of staff evaluations (competencies, indicators,
and descriptors) has been developed, the agency can develop an
evaluation process to assess staff performance, provide feedback,
and ensure that staff receive the support they need to perform
most effectively. The three components of the process are pre-assessment, formative evaluation, and summative evaluation.

Preassessment

The first step in a staff evaluation process is the staff member's assessment of his or her strengths and weaknesses in providing the range of interventions that he or she is expected to deliver. Each staff member should use the "Self-Appraisal Instrument" to assess his or her skills in each competency area and his or her personal and professional traits. With his or her supervisor's assistance, the staff member should use the results to generate specific goals and objectives to improve her intervention skills in the areas determined to be weak. The supervisor also should assist the staff member in identifying ways to use his or her strengths in achieving objectives. A performance plan (which includes goals and objectives) should be developed to guide the ongoing evaluation process and the worker's efforts at self-improvement. The effort to develop a performance plan, in and of itself, can have positive results, as the research on planning with families in clinical settings suggests. In one study, it was found that working with a family to develop a plan of mental health services for their child produced positive changes for the child even when the family withdrew from services before the therapy was provided. Another study demonstrated that when a family was asked to count or chart a child's misbehavior, the child's targeted behaviors decreased. These findings suggest that drawing attention to performance issues can have positive effects, irrespective of the subsequent steps that are taken.

A second component of the preassessment is a staff development plan that outlines the training that the staff member will obtain to further strengthen his or her intervention skills. Many professionals recognize that they need additional training, either on the job or through enrollment in special institutes or other programs. Unfortunately, some providers believe that their academic degrees or life experiences are all that is needed to function adequately. These staff, for example, may say, "I was a single parent so I know what single parent's need;" "I'm a problem solver so I can help others to problem solve;" or "Treatment is just the application of good common sense." The preassessment process should be used to assist staff to overcome attitudes such as "my view is the world's view" and define their needs for further training.

Formative Evaluations

Formative evaluations focus specifically on helping staff to improve their delivery of the intervention strategies identified in the written performance plan. Formative evaluations are conducted by a staff member who serves as observer. This individual should not be responsible for the summative evaluation (discussed next). Formative evaluations also may take place through staff mentoring, where experienced professionals mentor new staff and peer supervision is provided to experienced staff. When formative evaluations are performed by mentors, the process should include arrangements for the staff member to observe the mentor's or another professional's use of the intervention procedures in the performance plan.

In the formative evaluation, the evaluator (whether designated staff member or mentor) observes the professional's delivery of services over a designated time period, with a focus on the intervention behaviors related to the goals and objectives developed in the pre-assessment phase. The staff member and the evaluator should agree on observation frequency. During the employee's probationary employment period, however, there should be no fewer than four observation periods for each identified intervention. After the probationary period, there should be no fewer than four observations of each intervention each year. Because objective-related behavior is the focus, observations should be scheduled in advance and at times agreeable to the staff member. Each observation period should be for at least 30 minutes.

During each observation, the evaluator should complete an Intervention Observation Instrument and rate the staff member on each competency as "satisfactory," "unsatisfactory," (or, alternatively as "present" or "absent") or "needs improvement." Following the observation, the evaluator should confer with the staff member to discuss the observation and the evaluator's ratings and allow the staff member to share her own observations about the intervention. This aspect of formative evaluations is particularly important because it provides staff with corrective feedback through written results of each observation and directly observable data. The meeting should result in suggestions for improvement, the revision of objectives, and/or the development of new courses of action when needed. A specific performance plan should be developed when the evaluator rates any competency as "needs improvement." The evaluator and staff member also may refine the staff development plan made during the preassessment phase. If they revise this plan, a new agreement should document the training objectives and action steps.

Summative Evaluation

The summative evaluation is conducted at year-end, and like the results of formative evaluations, it should stimulate service delivery improvement. Unlike the formative evaluation, the summative evaluation includes assessment of the staff member's personal characteristics and professional attributes in addition to his or her process skills. The summative evaluation also should include client evaluations of the staff member and information regarding outcomes for the staff member's clients. The summative evaluation bears a relationship to the Self Appraisal Form that the staff member completes and gives to his or her supervisor during preassessment and to the Intervention Observation Instrument that evaluators complete and provide to the staff member after each observation. The summative evaluation form should rate the staff member on his or her intervention skills using the same ratings system utilized in the observation form, It should also contain sections for comments so that the staff member's notable contributions can be listed and provide an opportunity for the staff member to list notable contributions and strengths (if the administrator concurs). Like the formative evaluation, the summative evaluation should reflect a generous sampling of the staff member's professional behavior over time.

The summative conference typically occurs at the end of each year of employment and includes a professional improvement plan for the coming year. This plan outlines the means that will be used to assist the employee to overcome deficiencies and make improvements; describes how an evaluation of improvement will take place; and sets time lines for improvement. The summative evaluation should be made part of the employee's permanent personnel file.

As a final point regarding summative evaluations, staff members typically view year-end evaluations as administrative in nature (such as promotion, salary increases, transfer, and dismissal) and see the chief purpose as the elimination of incompetent staff. Summative evaluations should not be used to inform staff for the first time at year's end about the deficiencies in their performance. The results of the summative evaluation should come as no surprise. From the perspective of progressive discipline, a staff member can be expected to make improvements in his performance only after he or she has been informed in writing of his or her deficiencies and has signed a corrective action plan. Staff must be afforded ample time for corrective action, a process that will only be delayed if the agency waits until year-end to identify performance deficiencies.

Evaluation of the Staff Evaluation Plan

The effectiveness of a staff evaluation process can be assessed in several ways. Data can be gathered from several sources before and after the implementation of the staff evaluation program. Data may include pre- and post-plan measures of client improvement, client satisfaction information (or satisfaction surveys of parents, teachers, or employers), and information on untoward incidents. For example, in a children's residential treatment program, the staff evaluation process may be based on behavioral incident reports, time-out room placements, parent complaints, injuries, student illness, and staff absences before and after the process was implemented. If the staff evaluation process involves teachers, for example, it might be expected that the evaluation process would result in improvements in student performance (as reflected in higher achievement test scores or improved physical fitness); higher levels of student, parent, and staff satisfaction; and fewer untoward incidents in school following the implementation of the teacher evaluation program.

Summary

In order to effectively implement any intervention, staff who employ the intervention must value its use. Research has established that although some treatment protocols may achieve better results than others, the most effective service providers are professionals who convey empathy and genuine concern for clients. Staff would find it difficult to convey such attitudes if they are forced to apply a protocol. Agencies must create a culture in which training is provided; innovation is encouraged; there is support for evaluation of interventions; and peer supervision is valued. Evaluations of staff performance must be consistent with this culture. Evaluations may include observation of the professional's provision of services, examination of clients' intervention plans, client evaluations of provider performance, and objective outcome data that reflects the provider's performance. Ratings of professionals' performance should include relevant, descriptive, and verifiable data that are collected on instruments developed by the agency's professional and administrative staff. The final evaluation system should reflect the general consensus of all relevant staff and be endorsed by the agency's administration.

Managers must view implementation failures as the result of system problems and not staff problems. Managers must continually ask two questions: "What are the obstacles that prevent staff from delivering this intervention?" and "What can be done to remove these obstacles?" Supervision and evaluation within this context will be supported by staff, and clients will prosper.

Chapter 5:

Assessing Client Participation in Services

Although most academic researchers are concerned with distal outcomes, program evaluators must be concerned with proximal outcomes. Distal outcomes, which will be discussed in Chapter 6, are long-range goals that a client is expected to achieve following the successful implementation of an intervention. By contrast, proximal outcomes are short-term or intermediate outcomes that are expected to contribute to distal outcomes. If proximal outcomes are not achieved because the participant has not received the service, the intervention is unlikely to produce favorable distal outcomes. As an example, the protocol for a group for adolescent sexual offenders may require offenders to write apology letters to their victims and identify the feelings that led them to abuse others. These two behaviors, both of which are proximal outcomes, are expected to occur before an adolescent will give up his or her abusive behavior (which might be defined as the distal outcome of "no incidents of sexual abuse up to two years after treatment completion").

When assessing client participation, an agency should focus on three issues: determining whether clients are fully participating in the intervention protocol, as opposed to participating in only certain services within the protocol or none at all; determining the client's level of exposure to an intervention, both in terms of optimal dose and actual attendance at intervention sessions; and determining the client's level of engagement in the service as an active or inactive participant. These factors are key to assessing the achievement of proximal outcomes.

103

Participation in the Intervention Protocol

An evaluation of an intervention will be possible only when the clients, whose outcomes are studied, fully participate in the intervention protocol. For example, when examining the effect of a specific medication on an illness or condition, there must be assurance that clients took the medication as recommended, cooperated with treatment, and followed the entire treatment protocol. If a doctor prescribes a treatment for an illness and patients follow only half of the protocol, the effectiveness of the medication cannot be assessed. In such cases, implementation failures flow from clients' failure to participate fully in the protocol, as opposed to staff failure to implement the intervention.

The same situation may occur in human services. In rational-emotive psychotherapy, for example, completing homework assignments is considered a key component of the therapeutic model. In behavior therapy, practicing progressive muscle relaxation procedures at home is an important treatment element. If a number of clients do not complete key components of the protocols (their homework assignments or relaxation procedures at home), evaluative results will be contaminated by implementation failure because clients have not fully participated in the interventions. In neither case could negative outcomes be attributed to the interventions themselves. Interventions can be considered ineffective only when fully participating clients make no progress.

In many instances when clients fail to fully participate in intervention protocols, researchers will remove uncooperative or nonparticipating subjects from the samples. However, in some cases so many subjects are nonparticipants that it is clear that the intervention design must be modified. For example, in the study of medication effects, so many patients may fail to follow the protocol that it becomes necessary to substitute nurse-administered medication for self-administered medication or add home visits to supervise home medication administration.

It is important to determine why clients fail to participate in protocols. In human service terminology, it is common to describe clients who fail to cooperate with specific intervention procedures as "unmotivated." In reality, it may be that a different intervention would change the motivation level of the client. Years ago, Wilhelm Reich studied individuals who had failed in classical psychoanalysis. He identified the characteristics of clients who had not succeeded in psychoanalysis and offered a different form of therapy to individuals who displayed those characteristics. He found these clients to be more amenable to face-to-face therapeutic communications, an approach that was the forerunner of modern psychotherapy and counseling. He discovered that the clients were not unmotivated with regard to psychoanalysis but that psychoanalysis was inappropriate for them. His work established an alternative intervention that benefited certain clients. As this example suggests, the failure of clients to fully participate in a protocol should be an indication that alternative interventions may be needed for those experiencing problems in participating in the intervention.

A more recent study of the characteristics of participants and nonparticipants was conducted by St. Francis Homes, a treatment center for boys with conduct disorders. The study compared the outcomes of boys who completed treatment with nine different subgroups of noncompleters. The best outcomes were achieved by boys whose parents withdrew them from the program (one of the noncompleter groups). The next best outcomes were achieved by boys who completed treatment. Successively poorer outcomes were achieved by groups of noncompleters in the following order: boys who were negative leaders, had chronic problems, deserted the program, engaged in acute misbehavior, were incarcerated, were expelled from school, were withdrawn from the program by others, and engaged in drastic and acute misbehavior. This study provided important information on client characteristics that could be used to assess alternative interventions.

Individuals may be nonparticipants in a study for a variety of reasons, including life circumstances that make it difficult for them to participate fully in the treatment protocol. A mother living with an abusive husband may be unable to provide the recommended discipline to her child because her husband interferes. Alternatively, her proper use of the recommended procedure may be preceded and followed by her husband's inappropriate discipline. In this case, the mother would be a participant in the study, but the father's nonparticipation might exert more powerful influences on the child.

In summary, an evaluation of an intervention can take place only when clients fully participate in the intervention under study. Participation is directly observable, unlike "motivation" (which is a postulated, mediating variable) or "compliance" (a more recent term but equally value-laden). A client, for example, either does or does not complete homework assignments. If tracking the number of clients who fail to do homework or who produce incomplete homework assignments results in a large number of clients, the agency should identify the characteristics of those clients. At that point, the agency should either modify the intervention or provide a completely different intervention.

Level of Exposure to the Intervention

Determining exposure to an intervention is more than simply recording the client's presence or absence, although this factor is important. Equally relevant is the concept of optimal dose.

Optimal dose refers to the level of treatment that is necessary to produce changes. For example, a mental health agency may hypothesize that six months is the optimal dose for a treatment program that addresses adolescent behavior. The agency may determine optimal dose empirically by correlating attendance with outcome and establishing critical cutoff points. Findings may reveal that a client must attend day treatment at least 80 days (of the total 120 days) in a six month period to achieve any gains and must attend 100 days or more to achieve the greatest gains. Studies with moderately disturbed children reveal that little progress is made in mental health clinic treatment, regardless of the protocol employed, in less than six sessions and that optimal gains are made after 14 or 15 sessions. Other studies have suggested that some treatment approaches are as effective after a certain number of sessions as they are with additional sessions, reflecting a point of diminishing returns. A client's level of exposure should be compared to the determined optimal dose for the specific intervention.

Second, exposure relates to the extent to which the client is physically present at each intervention session, that is, the client's attendance. A child enrolled in a day treatment program, for example, may spend a major portion of the intervention day in time-out rooms or the school principal's office, be subject to in-school suspension, or be sent home on numerous occasions halfway through the treatment day. Although the child may attend the day treatment program for 100 days, his disruptive behavior may cause him to be isolated from full program participation for as much as 20% of program time. This attendance pattern should be recorded in the child's clinical record and related to outcome scores.

The complexity of recording intervention attendance varies, depending on the type of program. In community-based intervention settings, recording is a simple task. The therapist in an outpatient mental health clinic makes dated progress notes after each treatment session, including comments about the specific intervention method employed and the client's responses. In other settings, attendance records are more complex to keep. A child in a residential treatment center, for example, receives a variety of services and tracking the child's attendance at each service may be quite involved.

In the early days of residential treatment before specific treatment objectives and timetables for objective attainment were included in clinical records, psychotherapists wrote monthly progress reports that included dates of therapy attendance. They recorded whether the child attended for the full session. For the most part, psychotherapists' notes contained information that could be used to determine the child's engagement in therapy (discussed in the next section). In "the old days," child care workers, teachers, speech therapists, art therapists, and other professionals also submitted monthly progress reports. Although these staff members typically did not record the amount of time a child spent in a particular milieu activity, they recorded information that could be used to assess level of exposure and the nature of the child's relationships with caregivers. A child care worker's notes might indicate that a child spent considerable time alone and observed, rather than participated, in activities.

Current recordkeeping practices are not as focused on attendance, and consequently, greater attention should be given to maintaining attendance records for all services. For example, in a day treatment center where the author worked, the agency added a therapy attendance section to the weekly progress summary form that the state required all therapists to complete on each client. Program evaluators should ensure that records include each client's attendance at each service and that the QA process monitors case records for such information. A child in a residential treatment center, for example, may work with a community volunteer, in which case the number of meetings with the volunteer and the amount of time the child and volunteer spend together should be recorded. This information will assist the agency in assessing the effects of the volunteer program. A study of the volunteer service would be meaningless if, for example, an evaluator were to create an instrument to assess child, parent, staff, and/or volunteer satisfaction with the experience, only to discover later that many children referred for volunteer services spent almost no time with a volunteer. A number of developments may contribute to this situation and also should be recorded: volunteers may have been lost to the program; the child or the volunteer may have been ill or otherwise absent when meetings were scheduled; or the child may have refused to spend time with his volunteer.

Similarly, in a residential treatment center, staff should record all parent contacts with their child in the child's record. This information should include the number of family therapy sessions that are conducted (with attendance records for each family member kept separately) and the attendance of parents at training sessions. If, for example, parents are provided a 15-session group parent training program and many parents fail to attend a significant number of sessions, the effects of the treatment cannot be evaluated because of implementation failure. When attendance is recorded for clients, it then can be correlated with outcomes, and critical cutoff points (in terms of optimal dose) can be established.

Level of Client Engagement

A third issue related to client participation is the extent to which a client engages in the service that is provided. An outpatient group treatment protocol for adolescent sex offenders may require, for example, that each offender accomplish a specific number of tasks during treatment. Staff should record in each participant's clinical record the date that each major task was successfully completed (that is, the adolescent's work on the task met the written standard in the treatment protocol). For example, an adolescent may be required to write an apology letter to the victim that contains specific content for the task to be considered successfully completed. It is possible that an adolescent could attend each treatment session and never write a letter with the required content. In such a case, implementation (as opposed to intervention) failure has occurred.

Different levels of client engagement also can be seen in play therapy. One child, for example, may engage in expressive activities such as drawing, puppet play, sand play, or conversation with the therapist about problems. Another child may avoid dealing with problems by repeatedly playing table games, building models, or constantly pressuring the therapist to allow him to go outside to shoot baskets. In this situation, the first child receives play therapy, and the second child simply plays with an adult. It is not appropriate in a study of play therapy effectiveness to combine children who receive play therapy with children who simply play during the sessions (although almost every investigator has done so). Instead, the two groups of children should be separated and their gain scores on proximal and distal outcome measures compared.

Assessing and Recording Level of Client Engagement

Unfortunately, today's records often lack information that can lead to an assessment of client engagement in interventions. In earlier days of service provision, staff notes emphasized content and it was relatively easy to determine levels of client engagement in services. As an example, in child care settings, records revealed whether a child actively participated in certain milieu activities and avoided participating in others. This practice changed in the early 1980s when compliance monitors from accrediting and licensing organizations visited agencies and read monthly progress notes in client records. They initially suggested and then required significant changes in recording practices. Compliance monitors viewed notes regarding what clients did or said in therapy as unnecessary. Instead, they focused on measurable objectives with a timetable for completion and the recording of objective attainment. The assumption was that if a therapy was delivered, the client received the service (although communication specialists know that a message sent does not necessarily mean a message received). As a consequence of early accrediting and licensing requirements, clinical records now typically contain the specific objectives a client is expected to achieve in different areas of functioning and a record of whether the objectives were or were not met. When objectives are not achieved, staff often simply extend attainment dates and rarely include their observations about the reasons that objectives were not achieved. Because clinical recordkeeping is a tedious chore, staff typically provide only what is required.

Record keeping should include an assessment of the client's level of engagement even if such information necessarily rests on staff judgment and staff judgment can be unreliable. (The same staff member will make different judgments on different occasions within a short time period [intra-rater reliability] or different staff members will make different judgments at the same time period [inter-rater reliability]). Staff in a residential treatment center, for example, can be asked to rate each child as an "active participant," a "marginal participant," or a "nonparticipant" in selected activities. Staff training in using such a scale will be needed, as even skilled staff may resist rating any child as a nonparticipant absent a clear definition of that concept. Each scale point should be operationally defined, and written examples should be provided so that staff fully understand the meaning of each scale point. Ratings need not be made frequently but can be submitted as global judgments each month.

Staff should keep data on the client's engagement level in all services regardless of beliefs about the relative contribution of the service. If a child in a residential treatment center, for example, receives volunteer services, the child's level of engagement should be recorded. Staff may ask the child, his parents, and the volunteer to complete questionnaires that provide information about the child's involvement and relationship with the volunteer. With such information, it is then possible to distinguish the level of engagement of one child (who consistently goes to movies with the volunteer, silently eats ice cream afterward, and then returns to the center) from that of another child (who goes bowling with his volunteer and freely interacts with the volunteer's family and friends). It can be expected that the first child learned little and the second child learned much more in the relationship. A well-constructed questionnaire can shed light on the reasons that a child does not actively engage in a service.

Level of Engagement and Outcomes

When evaluating a program or service, the key information is the number of clients who were fully engaged (actively participated) and the number of clients who were not fully engaged (passively participated). Evaluators can create groups of "Very Active Participants," "Active Participants," and "Passive Participants" and correlate gain scores with levels of engagement, comparing scores on various proximal and distal measures of performance (such as number of time-outs, developmental attainments, length of stay, academic achievement, status at discharge, and long-term outcome). Evaluators also can compare findings for clients with a comparison group of clients who were referred to the program but did not receive the service. Such information can give program planners information about service effectiveness.

It also is possible that an evaluation will reveal that members of each of the three engagement-level groups (very active, active, and passive participation) vary identically on a previously un-

known measure or on a known measure. For example, an evaluation may reveal identical variation among children in a residential treatment center on milieu activity participation. In such a
case, the agency must decide whether a service, such as a volunteer program, contributes incrementally to proximal and distal
outcomes or is an unneeded service. The services of a statistician
can assist in making this decision.

Participation and Proximal Outcomes

Proximal outcomes are client behaviors that are directly related
to intervention protocol efforts. They differ from client participation in that they are the short-term results of the intervention.
Levels of participation include general domains of client behavior, such as "the client discussed her feelings" or " the child played
out conflicts with dollhouse toys." Proximal outcomes relate more
specifically to the goals of the intervention, such as "the client discussed feelings about foster care" or "the child played out sexual
abuse scenes." Because it is assumed that a client must achieve
proximal outcomes before he or she achieves success on a distal
outcome, the achievement of proximal outcomes should be recorded in the client's record.

One might ask why levels of participation should be recorded
when it is of greater importance to record the attainment of proximal outcomes. Levels of participation are important because the
proximal outcomes that will lead to the achievement of distal outcomes are not always known. The selection of behavioral objectives requires the identification of behaviors from a class of representative behaviors, any of which could be used to measure
change. As an example, in the treatment of a noncompliant child,
only a few noncompliant behaviors will be selected to measure the
child's response to treatment. It may happen, however, that the
child will make changes in behaviors that were not selected for
study. For example, going to bed on time may have been the selected measure, but instead, the child stops teasing his sister. When
these changes in terms of the child's participation in treatment are

recorded, it is possible to examine behaviors other than those selected for study.

The relationships among participation, proximal outcomes, and distal outcomes can be seen in examples from child welfare and mental health. In the area of mental health services for children in foster care, psychotherapists may define certain tasks (proximal outcomes) that a child must complete in order to successfully adjust to her placement in foster care (distal outcome). These tasks must be achieved in order to consider therapy a success. One treatment protocol is the creation of a personal history book that outlines chronologically the significant events in the child's life. Investigators who study the effects of this protocol must know with which children the protocol was fully implemented (that is, the active participants), with which children the protocol was not implemented (the nonparticipants), and which children achieved "success," that is, a successful adjustment to placement in foster care. If the study reveals that participants and nonparticipants achieved equal success, the personal history protocol would be determined to be ineffective. Although some children may have achieved the proximal outcome of completing the personal history book, the achievement would be unrelated to the achievement of the distal outcome of successful adjustment in their foster homes. As another example, the relationship between the child's biological and foster parents (a proximal outcome) may be viewed as key to the child's successful foster home placement (distal outcome). Intervention efforts usually are directed at creating and maintaining good relationships between the two parties, and one proximal outcome may be that "the foster parent will avoid making unfavorable comparisons between the foster and the biological home." As with the example of the personal history book, foster parents' levels of participation in this activity should be determined and recorded.

Appendix C presents a very brief form that clinicians in an outpatient mental health center may use to track a child's participation and achievement of proximal outcomes, and summarize the reasons for a child's failure to progress in treatment. The use of this form over time allows for an aggregate analysis of such factors; facilitates utilization review of closed cases; contributes to the interpretation of outcome findings; and assists agencies in determining the clients who should be asked to participate in follow-up studies.

Summary

Quality assurance activities include monitoring not only staff activities but client responses (both general and specific) to these activities. When one type of monitoring occurs without the other, the results are meaningless. The monitoring of client responses in the form of proximal outcomes has found support in the recent emphasis on setting specific objectives for clients and monitoring their attainment. Such information, however, generally is not used in outcome studies. Similarly, goal attainment scaling (an evaluation methodology developed in the early 1970s) can be used to examine the relationship between goal attainment and outcome. This procedure, likewise, is rarely used. One of the problems encountered in using proximal outcomes is that many of these outcomes, particularly those set for clients in mental health treatment centers, are changes in symptoms and not changes in levels of participation. Because the symptoms of troubled clients wax and wane, it is far more important to know whether a client became an active participant in an intervention (such as, for example, whether the individual formed a therapeutic alliance with staff).

When examining attainment of distal outcomes, it is important to control for intervention exposure, levels of participation, and attainment of proximal outcomes. How much exposure clients had to an intervention and how much they engaged in the intervention process itself are key. Clients who attended an intervention for only a few sessions or who failed to complete intervention-related assignments should not be considered as part of the treatment group. Their scores on distal outcome measures should not be included with the scores of individuals who attended all intervention sessions and completed all intervention assignments. Noncompleters, even when identical to treatment completers on known variables (such as age, marital status, or earnings), may differ from completers on unknown variables (such as motivational level).

When time and costs are factors, noncompleters may be eliminated from follow-up studies. If time and costs are not factors, noncompleters can be included in studies for comparison purposes (they can serve as a quasi-comparison group) or to help determine relationships among treatment dose, attainment of proximal outcomes, and attainment of distal outcomes.

Chapter 6:
• • • • • • • • •

Assessing Service Impact

How is success measured? What yardsticks can be used to determine improvement as a result of a specific intervention? How
much of a difference might be expected between outcomes for
clients who participate in an intervention and outcomes for clients
who do not?

The real impact of an intervention can be measured only
when one knows what would have happened to participants had
they not received the service. An unbiased estimation of real
program impact is obtained by comparing the outcome scores of
clients who received an intervention with an equivalent group of
individuals who did not receive it. The perceived impact of a
service is the change that participants and others report following
an intervention. Perceived impact differs from real impact in that
the changes reported by informants may be the result of other
factors, often unknown, and not the intervention.

This chapter focuses on the evaluation of real and perceived
impact. Many agencies can evaluate the real impact of some of
their services, but for reasons discussed later, they are not able to
measure the real impact of other services. However, agencies can
always evaluate perceived impact. In some cases, agencies will have
to be satisfied with the evaluation of perceived impact.

Design Considerations in Assessing Real Impact

To assess real impact, an agency must compare outcomes for individuals who completed an intervention with outcomes for an

117

equivalent group of individuals who did not complete the intervention. Reports of improvement by individuals who received an intervention does not mean that the intervention itself was responsible for the reported changes. Perceived changes may result from the increased attention that accompanied the intervention or from events that occurred with the passage of time. For example, studies show that subjects who receive no intervention (such as individuals who are placed on waiting lists) often report improvement as the result of help that they received from other sources, having solved their problems on their own, or a natural resolution of the crisis that contributed to their problems.

Evaluators use two types of designs to evaluate real impact of services: experimental designs and quasi-experimental designs. In experimental designs, subjects are randomly assigned to the intervention (experimental) and nonintervention (control) groups. In quasi-experimental designs, evaluators develop comparison groups through a variety of procedures other than random assignment.

Ideally, agencies would develop a research base for each intervention based on randomized control trials. However, most human service agencies lack the resources to create a research infrastructure or to conduct research studies in the initial implementation of an intervention. Moreover, agencies generally do not collaborate on research until there is some evidence of the effectiveness of an intervention. Empirical validation of human service effectiveness, as a result, often is a developmental process in which an intervention is implemented; its perceived effectiveness is evaluated; preliminary evidence about real impact is gathered using a comparison group; and after preliminary evidence suggests effectiveness, fully randomized trials are conducted.

Any evaluation of real impact must include an intervention and a nonintervention group. The two groups must be equivalent on all variables that might affect intervention outcomes. If they are not, a nonequivalent variable, often called a "nuisance" variable, can produce outcome differences. A host of variables can influence outcome differences, including easily measured variables (such as age, earnings, household composition, socioeconomic status, number of siblings, birth order, and parental status) and variables that are more difficult to measure (such as level of problem severity, motivation, personality traits, marital stress, and self-perceptions). Nuisance variables can be controlled either through experimental designs (using control groups) or quasi-experimental designs (using comparison groups).

Formulation of Evaluation Questions

Because they cannot deny services to clients, the question arises whether human service agencies can evaluate the true impact of their programs. In the case of an agency that provides food for the poor, concerns may arise regarding withholding food distribution services. Evaluation of impact in this type of program does not focus on the need for food (or the essential value of the service to clients) but rather the manner in which the food is distributed. Evaluation involves an assessment of the impact of alternative forms of service delivery. In the case of an agency that provides temporary homemaker services for individuals who are ill, evaluation seeks to assess whether certain service variations are more helpful than others. If the purpose of the homemaker program is to assist clients in becoming more independent, evaluation may focus on the effectiveness of different instructional methodologies.

Similarly, the question to be answered in the case of probation services is not whether the services are effective. Probation is an alternative to incarceration and will not be eliminated from the range of criminal justice alternatives. The question that evaluators must answer is how best to deliver probation services. To answer that question, alternative forms of probation must be provided and their effects evaluated. Likewise, some large-scale policy studies may suggest that certain basic services, such as child protective services, have not met the needs of those they were designed to serve. These studies may advocate the elimination of basic services. As with managers of probation services, however, managers in county child welfare departments are not charged with performing evaluations to support the elimination of basic government services.

Elementary Probability Theory

When using control or comparison groups to measure impact, the number of participants must be large enough to rule out any between-group differences that could occur by chance. If a coin were flipped only 10 times, it might come up "heads" 8 times. If the "flipper" concluded that the coin was "weighted" to come up heads more often, the chance of being wrong about the coin's features would be quite high. The individual would wrongly believe there is an effect when there is no effect—what researchers call a Type I error. If the coin were flipped additional times, it would become apparent that the coin was normal. It may be necessary, however, for the coin to be flipped as many as 100 times before the results came close to the 50-50 heads-tails expectation of flips of a normal coin.

Similarly, it also is possible that a coin that is weighted to come up heads 10 times on an uneven surface nevertheless comes up with 5 heads and 5 tails. The "flipper" in this case might conclude that the coin is normal. In this situation, the "flipper" would wrongly conclude that there is not an effect when there actually is one—what researchers call a Type II error. If the coin were flipped additional times, the effects of the uneven surface would fade and more tosses would come up heads.

As a final example, if 100 coins were tossed in the air, there probably would be small clusters of coins containing more heads than tails and other small clusters containing more tails than heads. If only the clusters were examined (the small samples), investigators could draw incorrect conclusions about the true (or real) distribution of heads and tails. If they examined the entire group of 100 coins, they would correctly conclude that the distribution of heads and tails was identical. As this example illustrates, when a small sample is employed in an outcome study, even random assignment may not result in two equivalent groups. If there are only 30 clients who are randomly assigned to two intervention conditions, for example, it is possible that one group of 15 clients would include a greater number of older clients, more motivated clients, or more disturbed clients. When, however, 100 clients are randomly assigned to each group, such group differences are likely to disappear.

Variability

How large a group should be to ensure that chance plays a minimal role in the results achieved depends upon a number of factors. One factor is the variability among individuals in each group on the dependent variable. The dependent variable is the element that is believed to rely on the intervention that is manipulated in the study (the independent variable). If, for example, it is believed that members of one racial group are shorter than members of another, that belief could be tested by measuring the height of representative members of both racial groups. Height would be the dependent variable, and racial identity the independent variable. The question to be answered would be whether an individual's height is dependent upon the racial group to which he or she belongs. If there is a real difference in height between the two racial groups and the overlap in height between the two groups is small, it would be possible to measure the height of a relatively small number of individuals in both racial groups and conclude, based on a reasonable degree of certainty, that a true difference in height exists. In other words, if the majority of men in one racial group were tall and the majority of men in the second racial group were short, a small sample of men from each group would reflect the difference in height between the two groups. If the average height of one group of men was 5' 7" (with members ranging in height from 5' 5" to 6') and the average height of the other group of men was 5' 10" (with member ranging in height from 5' 8" to 6' 5"), a sample size as small as 15 in each group might reveal a difference, providing the samples were representative. In contrast, if the overlap between the two groups is large (that is, the height of each group's members vary widely from the group average), a much larger sample of subjects would be required before the true 3-inch difference in height would be observed.

It would not be correct to conclude that if the true average, or "mean," difference in height is small (1 inch, for example), a larger sample would be needed to reflect the difference. It is the degree of overlap between the two groups that is critical and not the average difference between them. For example, all men in each group may be of the same height (that is, there is no variability in height in either group). In such a situation, a small sample (even as small as one individual from each group) will detect the real difference in height between the two groups, irrespective of whether the difference is 1 inch or 10 inches.

If the variability in the heights of members of the two groups was large but there was no overlap in height between the two groups, a sample of one from each group would reveal that members of one group were taller than members of the other group. This small sample, however, would not demonstrate the average height difference between the two groups. If, for example, several individuals at the tall end of the range in one group and at the short end of the range in the other were selected by chance, the average height difference between the two groups would be greatly overestimated. A representative sample of perhaps 25 individuals from each group would have to be gathered to make a valid estimate of the average height difference. An additional problem may occur if, by chance, several men from both groups of the same height were selected. In that case, it would be incorrectly concluded that there was no difference in average height between the two groups. As the different scenarios related to height and racial group membership demonstrate, a small sample under certain circumstances may reflect real differences (including differences that result from interventions) but may not reflect the true magnitude of the difference.

Sample Size

Small samples can result in unequal groups and create both Type I and Type II errors. Type I errors occur when there is a measured treatment difference, but the difference is actually due to chance or to nuisance variables rather than to the intervention itself. Replication of studies (which is the equivalent of adding more subjects to the sample) typically reveals a Type 1 error. Small samples can also result in an overestimation or an underestimation of differences that are real. This situation leads to a Type II error, one in which the evaluator finds no difference between the treated and untreated groups when there is a true difference but uncontrolled nuisance variables mask the treatment effect.

When the effect of an intervention is large (that is, the majority of individuals in the experimental group are affected by the intervention and the majority in the control group are not, regardless of the magnitude of the effect), a small sample will reveal a difference. If the effect of an intervention is small (that is, only a small number of individuals in the experimental group is affected by the intervention), a large sample will be needed to reveal the difference. In statistical terms, an intervention effect is large when it explains a major portion of the variability between individuals in the experimental and control groups. Similarly, when the overlap in outcome scores between members of treated and untreated groups is quite large, large samples are needed to reflect the intervention effect. Adding more subjects to a study (that is, flipping the coin additional times) helps to eliminate the effects of uncontrolled variables. In very large samples, these variables would be expected to be distributed equally. Many researchers state that at least 30 subjects are needed in each intervention condition. Others state that at least 100 subjects are needed (although these investigators are those primarily concerned with avoiding Type II errors).

Control of Nuisance Variables

When researchers use small samples, they may attempt to avoid nuisance variable problems by matching participants on as many of these variables as possible (such as age, initial problem level, socioeconomic status, and parental status) and then randomly assigning subjects to experimental and control groups. However researchers must know the nuisance variables that can influence findings in advance so that they can create equivalent groups. Alternatively, after random assignment, researchers may determine whether any readily observable differences exist and then randomly add more subjects until the differences disappear.

As an example of how a nuisance variable could affect an evaluation, a clinic has been delivering two different treatments to adolescents who are depressed. Clinician judgments and client satisfaction surveys suggest that the two treatments are equally effective. The clinic decides to evaluate the true impact of each treatment. The agency constructs a patient profile: adolescents between 14 and 16 years of age who have symptoms of moderate depression, who live with single mothers between 35 and 45 years of age, whose mothers are relatively free from major mental illness or substance abuse and adequately support their families. Clients who fit this profile are identified at admission and randomly assigned to one of the two treatment conditions. The sample is small and by chance, one treatment group contains a larger number of patients who are seen in the morning, and the other treatment group contains a larger number of patients seen in the afternoon or evening. Staff had not related time of day – a nuisance variable – to outcome. It is possible (as suggested by research findings that clients seen by therapists in the morning make greater gains than clients seen in the evening) that one randomly assigned group would show more improvement than the other group, not because of the intervention but because of the time of day the patients were seen. Treatment outcome may be more associated with the effect of therapist or client effort or fatigue. The evaluator, however, might wrongly conclude that the differences in improvement were due to the interventions themselves.

Comparison Groups

As opposed to control groups, which comprise clients who receive no intervention, comparison groups comprise clients who receive a different type or level of intervention.

Examples of Comparison Groups

Comparison groups may be created in a variety of ways. For example, two small mental health clinics operated by an agency may decide to study the effects of a specific treatment protocol on a specific client group. Staff in Clinic A have been using the protocol for about one year, and client satisfaction surveys and clinician judgments suggest that clients treated with the protocol make more improvement than those treated with traditional clinic methods. Staff from Clinic A and Clinic B identify clients that fit a particular profile. As clients who fit this profile are admitted to each clinic, Clinic A staff provide treatment based on the protocol (the intervention group) and Clinic B staff continue to employ traditional treatment methods (the comparison group). Staff in both clinics administer the same pretreatment, concurrent (during treatment, such as after six sessions), and posttreatment outcome measures. The outcome scores are compared after 30 clients in both settings have completed treatment. Staff also keep a record of attrition from treatment (recognizing that one method may contribute more to premature withdrawal from treatment) and determine whether clients who withdraw prematurely from treatment differ in any way from clients who complete treatment. They additionally examine the cost-effectiveness of both treatments.

The findings of this study would be invalid if clients who received services at Clinic A were significantly different in some way from clients who received services at Clinic B. For example, Clinic A may serve more economically disadvantaged clients or more single parent households, and these factors may contribute to poorer outcomes. Nevertheless, if the agency suspected that these variables might have an effect on treatment, they could construct client profiles to control for them.

Alternatively, the agency could match selected subjects on the nuisance variables, although matching might not always be possible. If Clinic A, for example, primarily served rural Caucasians and Clinic B primarily served inner city African Americans, the agency may not be able to match subjects on race and geographic location. Nevertheless, if the agency found a difference favoring the protocol, the study could be replicated by having the clinics switch treatments. True replication, however, would be unlikely because the clinic staff who used the effective protocol would likely favor its continued use and be unwilling to reemploy the traditional practice. As an alternative, both clinics could use the protocol and compare the results of the studies. For example, it might be found that rural Caucasians responded more favorably to the protocol even though both groups benefited from it. The true effects of the intervention, however, may not be determined even with a series of studies. In this research, race would be confounded with geographical location in both designs. It may be that rural Caucasians would respond differently than rural African Americans to the protocol.

A second example of the use of comparison groups may be drawn from studies of curriculum effectiveness. Fifth-grade children in 20 classrooms in several different school systems may be selected to receive a new curriculum. As a comparison group, children in another 20 classrooms may be selected to receive instruction in the traditional curriculum. The use of 20 classrooms (as opposed to a smaller number of classrooms) would help to rule out the effects of individual teachers, school buildings, and school systems, all of which could influence outcomes. Random assignment of children to curriculum conditions would not be possible because children already are assigned to classrooms. If several school systems are involved in the curriculum effectiveness study, however, it is possible to randomly assign classrooms to curriculum conditions.

Random assignment in this type of study would be necessary because other assignment methods could influence outcomes. For example, if volunteers teach the new curriculum, the interest, enthusiasm, and motivation of the teachers become uncontrolled. If teachers are assigned to the two conditions, principal bias in selection (for example, the assignment of better teachers to the new curriculum if the principal favors that curriculum) and teacher responses to their assignments become uncontrolled factors. If only one school system implements the curriculum, using a similar school system in which classrooms employ the traditional curriculum as a comparison group will present problems because the school system or school building effects cannot be controlled.

In some curriculum studies, the comparison group often is composed of children who attended the school in the past. For example, the achievement test scores of fifth grade children who received the traditional curriculum in past years are compared with the scores of students who received the new curriculum. In such studies, the children who were enrolled in the past must be equivalent to children enrolled in the present, and the achievement measures must be gathered in an identical fashion. Such a comparison would be invalid if a large homeless shelter had been built in the community in the intervening years, resulting in a large number of lower achieving children enrolling in the school and receiving the new curriculum. Even if it were possible to eliminate homeless children from the study in order to create a more comparable group of children, their enrollment may impact the school in other important ways. For example, they may divert teacher attention from the larger group.

Representativeness of Comparison Groups

Comparison groups must be representative of the clients who receive the intervention. The challenges of constructing a comparison group are illustrated by the following example. A county mental health association (MHA) operates a social rehabilitation program for mentally ill adults. The program is multifaceted, and each client participates in a variety of activities especially designed for his or her unique needs. Some clients go bowling, develop computer skills, and participate in prevocational groups. Others receive therapeutic horseback riding, attend health and exercise groups, and learn library skills. A third group attends poetry workshops, life skills training, and social communication groups. Some choose to go on planned trips (including movies, operas, plays, picnics, shopping, miniature golf, and tag sales), and others do not. Given the variety and scheduling of the activities that are provided, no single patient's activities are identical to the activities of another. Because the program turns no one away, all referred clients receive services, but some clients receive many more services than others. All individuals who are informed about the program are encouraged to attend, but attendance is voluntary. At intake, clients complete brief questionnaires about themselves and their needs and MHA staff suggest activities which clients are free to choose or decline.

The National Association of Social Clubs (an organization of agencies that serve the mentally ill) has developed outcome measures, which they report are reliable and adequate measures of social and vocational improvement in clients who participate in

club activities. These measures could be used by the MHA to measure the impact of their social rehabilitation program. To measure
the true, as opposed to the perceived, impact of participation, the
outcome for the clients who participate in the social rehabilitation
program would have to be compared with outcomes of nonparticipants. How would the MHA find such a group? It could seek comparison group participants from the population of individuals
who live in community residences and sheltered apartments for
the mentally ill, the primary referral sources for their services.
They would probably find, however, that social workers in these
settings had already referred all suitable clients and that some clients had not followed through with the referrals. These individuals would not be an acceptable comparison group because they
could differ significantly from participants on a number of variables. Patients whom the social workers had not referred also
would not be an appropriate comparison group. It is likely that
these individuals either already displayed the skills the program
teaches or were considered too disturbed or too intellectually limited to profit from the program.

One way to evaluate the MHA program would be to establish
a group of waiting list controls. Referred clients would be randomly assigned to the program and to a waiting list condition. It
would be necessary to provide some services to clients in the waiting list condition as the larger mental health community would
not tolerate the denial of essential services to a large group of
needy clients, particularly when funds for service delivery are
provided by governmental sources. As an example, the comparison group might meet for recreational activities only and
not receive the intake assessment or any ongoing group counseling services that are considered the most significant components of the program.

Limits on Agencies' Ability to Evaluate Real Impact

Many small agencies will be unable to perform research that will
reveal the real, as opposed to perceived, differences resulting from
an intervention. Because of their size, many human service agencies cannot group together clients with similar characteristics and

Figure 6.1 Information Form

The following information should be provided to parents regarding participation in an agency's evaluation of mental health services.

You learned in your intake interview that, during the past year, clinic staff have provided two different treatment methods to treat children with your child's condition. Both of these two treatment conditions were described to you and you were told that feedback from clients suggests that both methods are equally effective. You stated at the intake that you had no preference for either treatment and tentatively agreed to volunteer to help us determine whether one treatment is actually better than the other.

We discussed with you then that although child and parent feedback is helpful in determining treatment effectiveness, we would like to determine if other measures of change would reflect treatment differences. We would like to give clients some objective measures of problem status before, during, and after treatment and compare the scores of clients who receive the two different treatments. If clients in one treatment group show greater gains on these measures than clients in the other treatment group and clients are equally satisfied with both treatments, then we will know that one treatment is better than the other treatment. We would then use this treatment in the future when treating clients with your child's condition.

In order to ensure that clients in both treatment conditions are similar, we will randomly assign an equal number to each treatment condition. Consequently, we do not know at this time which treatment your child will receive, but when you come for your scheduled appointment next week, you will begin the treatment condition to which your child has been assigned. You also should know that you have the right to withdraw your child from participation in this research project at any time during your child's treatment and that this decision will, in no way, jeopardize your child's continuing treatment. All material gathered in connection

---

Figure 6.1 (Cont'd)

with this project will be kept confidential and scores will be coded so that no names appear on any of the evaluation tools that we give to clients. You will also be informed about the results of this research project when it is completed.

If you have any further questions before treatment begins, feel free to speak to your intake worker. We thank you again for you willingness to help us in this project.

---

then involve a large number of professionals in administering an intervention procedure. For example, a county-operated, all-purpose mental health clinic may only have one or two staff who specialize in children's treatment and, consequently, would not be able to study the effects of children's treatment through the use of multiple outcome measures and comparison group methodologies. Because of their client base, it would not be feasible to randomly assign clients to different treatment groups and to a comparison group.

Likewise, many large agencies (even agencies working in collaboration) may be unable to assess true intervention effects in particular programs. As discussed earlier, program evaluation generally progresses through stages, beginning with perceived impact and employing more rigorous experimental designs only after evidence is available to justify the costs connected with their use. Once a program has some support (from perceived effectiveness studies, for example), clients may be unlikely to give their permission to random assignment, as discussed in the next section.

Client Consent

Although appropriate comparison groups can be constructed, such designs often are not possible in human service settings because clients are not willing to forego full services. For example, in the MHA study individuals assigned to the recreational activity-only group may request to participate in group counseling and other services. They may be upset if they are told after the fact that they must wait for these services while others, who applied at the same time, are receiving them.

It is essential that all clients (or their guardians) give their consent to participate in any study regardless of the condition to which they are assigned. Clients must be told in advance that if they are assigned to the comparison group, they will be required to wait for certain services. Clients must also be informed of the evaluation results. An example of the type of information that should be conveyed to clients about their possible participation in evaluation is presented in Figure 6.1. This information and client consent are essential to the integrity of any study, but they also can present challenges. For example, if only clients who agree to wait are placed in the comparison group, the comparison group may not be valid because these individuals may differ significantly from clients who do not agree to wait. They may be individuals who are highly anxious about treatment and eager for the chance for delay. Alternatively, if only a few clients agree to wait for services, it may not be possible to undertake the study or assess true intervention impact. Clients may agree to assignment to alternative treatment conditions, but if they seek a specific type of intervention, they should not be assigned to alternative interventions. They should receive the requested intervention and be excluded from the randomized design.

Consent and Client Preferences

Participation in comparison groups may be difficult to achieve if clients perceive a new intervention as superior to traditional methods. Some program evaluators attempt to skirt this issue by presenting participation in research as an opportunity to receive a new intervention. For example, a researcher may say to a parent, "There is a chance your child will get the new service if you participate in the research. But if you do not participate, there is no chance that your child will receive the new service. You only will

be able to get the service that the agency has traditionally offered." This approach leads to coerced rather than true consent, and managers should ensure that such practices are not
utilized in their agencies.

Client preferences (and consent to receive only certain services) may also raise issues when one treatment group primarily is
composed of clients who seek a specific treatment. These clients
may profit more from the treatment simply because they believe
in it (the power of positive expectations). Although an evaluator
could compare the treatment results of this group with individuals who agreed to be randomly assigned to treatment, the group
of "self-selectors" could differ on traits other than treatment motivation. It is helpful, however, to know whether individuals who
seek a specific treatment are more likely than others to profit from
that service, even when real intervention differences cannot be
clearly established. Agencies should first evaluate perceived impact of the intervention and then attempt to measure true impact.

Client Consent and Issues of Confidentiality

In most human service agencies, clients who agree to participate
in outcome studies are aware that their clinical records are confidential. They generally are comfortable when they learn that the
tools they complete will help staff in assessing their responses to
treatment. Clients may need assurances that their responses on
such tools likewise will be treated as confidential, particularly, for
example, when they are asked to complete satisfaction surveys in
which they may criticize agency staff.

The question is how an investigator can match pre- and post-
measures when the measures are gathered anonymously. One
common technique is to generate a code for each individual on
the basis of self-reported, personal characteristics that are stable
over time and to use the code on each tool that the client completes. The codes must have high variance and high stability. Examples of information that can be used to construct codes are: age,
gender, ethnicity, birth month, number of brothers, number of sisters, and family placement (only child, oldest, youngest, middle,
or other). Using such constructed codes, investigators are able to

correctly match about 75% of completed questionnaires. Usually about 3% of questionnaires are incorrectly matched and 22% are left unmatched.

A rather unique method of preserving client confidentiality is described by McGloin, Holcomb, and Main (1996) in a study of public school children. In this study, each participant received two numbered stickers and one blank sticker. One participant, for example, received two stickers numbered "E61" (E was the class code and 61 was randomly assigned) and one blank sticker. The participant was asked to place one "E61" sticker on the pretest interview form and the other "E61" sticker in an envelope. The participant then sealed the envelope with the blank sticker, signed his or her name across it, and returned the sealed envelope to the investigator. All envelopes then were placed in a large manila envelope and sealed under the signatures of two participants who served as witnesses. At the time of posttesting, the witnesses opened the large envelope and returned the individually sealed envelopes to each participant. The participants then placed their second numbered seal on the posttest form.

Purposeful Sampling and Attrition

Two issues that must be addressed in assessing service impact are sampling and the effects of attrition on evaluation efforts.

Purposeful Sampling

Although an agency can assess outcomes by selecting a random sample of clients who receive a specific service, it is more useful to employ purposeful sampling techniques that cull specific samples of clients from a larger group. In conducting outcome assessment, a researcher might select mental health clients who lived with an alcoholic father or a mentally ill mother and clients who experienced childhood sexual abuse. The researcher could perform outcome assessment or a follow-up study on a relatively small number of such clients who received a specific treatment, such as day or residential treatment (although, generally, 25 clients are considered the minimum). The researcher then could compare the findings to findings for 25 other clients who received the same intervention but who did not have the characteristics that were used in the purposeful sample. This approach provides a strong basis for outcome assessment.

Attrition

Attrition is an issue that must be considered in evaluation of service impact. Attrition may take different forms. A common form of attrition in human services is the failure of clients to complete treatment. About 50% of mental health clients discontinue psychotherapy or medication regimens prematurely. In one study, for example, only 27% of clients receiving mental health services remained in treatment at 6 weeks, and only about 6% remained at 15 weeks. Even greater percentages of clients fail to complete alcohol and substance abuse treatment programs. In some programs (such as services for individuals who are addicted and homeless), so few participants complete treatment that the programs are at risk of being terminated altogether. In the arena of child welfare services, the parents of many children withdraw them from day or residential treatment before treatment completion. In some cases, treatment services for children who are placed in foster or group homes are prematurely discontinued. Although there are methods to prevent premature withdrawal from treatment by some client populations, it is likely that evaluators will have considerably more pre- than posttest data and will have to ascertain whether clients who did not complete the intervention differ in some significant way from clients who did.

For example, when two treatment conditions (A and B) are compared it may be found that more African Americans than Caucasians failed to continue with A than with B. Further comparisons of the two interventions would require an analysis by race. Investigators may analyze this issue in different ways. One approach would be to remove African Americans from the analysis and compare only the results of Caucasians. Another approach would be to compare African Americans in B with the outcomes of Caucasians in A and B. If African Americans and Caucasians do not differ on outcome measures in B, investigators may conclude that B is not subject to the effects of race regardless of whether B achieves results that are inferior or superior to A. If, however, there is a sufficient number of African Americans remaining in A to compare their outcomes with Caucasians, the effects of race also can be determined for A. If the two racial groups do not differ, investigators may conclude that although more African Americans failed to continue with A, those who remained achieved results similar to those of Caucasians. If the outcomes of the remaining African Americans in A are poorer than the outcomes for Caucasians, it may be concluded that A achieves superior results for Caucasians and African Americans are more likely to terminate treatment early in A. Depending on the results of this type of analysis, a clinic may be required to determine which intervention it will offer to clients: the intervention in which more clients remain but make fewer gains or the intervention in which many clients drop from treatment but the clients who remain make greater gains. This problem can be avoided to some extent by assessing case status at intervals, a process called concurrent measurement.

Attrition also occurs when clients who complete an intervention fail to respond to requests for information. This type of attrition is a particularly serious problem when there is no comparison or control group or when responding clients in the intervention group differ from responding clients in the control or comparison group. As an example, only 40% of the clients in each group may respond to requests for information: the 40% in the treatment group who are making the greatest gains and the 40% in the comparison or the control group who are making the fewest gains. Because of the attrition in responses, it would appear that the treatment had an effect when that conclusion may not be correct. More often, there will be a higher number of responses from clients who experienced their treatment as successful and far fewer responses from clients who perceived their treatment as unsuccessful. In these cases, there will be an overestimation of perceived treatment effects when there is no comparison group and an overestimation of real effects when the treatment group is compared to a nontreatment control. This result is less likely if subjects participated in several different treatment conditions, unless one intervention was of no perceived or real help at all.

To further illustrate the impact of attrition, a range of possible scenarios might emerge from a program that evaluates its job-training program by comparing outcomes for clients who receive training and clients who do not:

1. Respondents from the training group report higher wages than respondents who did not receive the training. A high percentage of clients with less formal education and who make less money in both groups—the training and no-training groups—fail to return the survey. If an equal number of such clients in each group fail to respond, attrition will not affect the evaluation results. If the numbers of nonrespondents is large, however, the effects of training will be overestimated because low wage earners in both conditions will have been eliminated.

2. A larger number of clients with low education and lower wages in the no-training group than in the training group fail to respond to the request for information. If the number of such clients is so large that only high wage earners remain in the comparison group, the training will appear to have no positive effect on wages.

3. Clients who received the training, have low wages, and are dissatisfied with the training they received return a greater number of surveys (as an expression of their dissatisfaction) and an equal number of high and low wage earners in the no-training group return surveys. In this situation, the effects of the intervention will not only be negated but the intervention will appear to have a detrimental effect.

4. Clients in the no-training group know that the training was withheld from them. Clients with higher wages are proud of their accomplishments, having made significant achieve-

ments without the benefit of training, and they return a greater number of surveys. In this case, it will appear that the training was detrimental and that nontrainees earn higher wages.

5. High numbers of completed questionnaires are received from respondents in the training group who have high wages and are proud of their accomplishments and from respondents in the no-training group who have low wages and are angry because they were denied training. The training will appear effective even though it may not be.

Clients' failure to complete treatment and to return follow-up surveys are major obstacles to program evaluation. These attrition problems can be addressed by measuring proximal outcomes during treatment (concurrent measurement) and conducting evaluations with small samples so that a variety of contact procedures can be used to maximize the return rate.

Assessing the Level of Real Impact

Managers unfamiliar with findings from outcome research may be surprised to learn that measured intervention effects tend to be quite small. They should not expect large differences between treated and untreated groups. Even the best of outcome research cannot relate much of the variation on outcome measures among individuals to intervention effects.

Use of Statistical Significance and Effect Size

For many years, outcome researchers were satisfied with the results of their research when the differences between the mean gain scores (or D scores) of the experimental and the control group had a low probability of occurring by chance when conventional levels of statistical probability were used. Typically, the difference between the mean D scores of the treated group and the untreated group is considered "real," or unlikely to have occurred by chance, if the probability of the difference occurring by chance is less than 6 out of 100. Such methodologies, however, leave two key questions unanswered. First, how much of the variation in gain scores between individuals in two groups can be attributed to the effects of treatment? Second, how large is the difference between the groups (between-group variation) in comparison to the normal variation within an untreated group (within-group variation)?

Answers to the first question require reporting the correlation of the dependent variable (or the outcome D scores) with the independent variable of treatment versus nontreatment or control. D scores are ranked in ascending order with treatment ranked as "1" and control ranked as "0." In many published studies in which the difference between the intervention and control group mean gain scores was considered "real" rather than by chance, the correlation coefficient (r) was relatively low. For example, Haase and his colleagues (1982) reported that the median r reported in research in the *Journal of Counseling Psychology* for the years 1970 to 1972 was around 0.30. In some reported studies, however, the r was as low as 0.10, which meant that only 0.01% (the correlation squared) of the variation between individuals could be attributed to treatment effects. Although treatment did create "real" gains, the gains were so small that those attributed to the intervention were negligible. In other words, most of the change scores had very little to do with the effects of the intervention. An intervention must be powerful to influence client variability on an outcome measure when samples are small. When samples are quite large, there can be a statistically significant difference between a treatment and a control or a comparison group (that is, it is highly unlikely that the difference is due to chance). However, even in these cases the intervention can account for very little of the variation between subjects. The difference is real but relatively meaningless.

Sensitized to this issue, outcome researchers began to include in their reports of treatment effectiveness the correlation between the outcome measure and the intervention condition, called the "effect size" (Cohen, 1988). The use of r cannot answer the second question posed above (how large the difference is between the groups compared to the normal variation within an untreated group) because it gives no information about the magnitude of change reflected in gain scores. As a result, the use of other measures of effect size (*ES*) has been recommended. Perhaps the most widely used measure today is the Glass *ES* (1981) in which the difference between the treatment and control group means is divided by the control group's standard deviation. Using this formula, an *ES* of 0.50 is obtained when the difference between the means of the two groups is half the size of the control group's standard deviation (*SD*). As an example of *ES* in studies of children's mental health treatment, a recent meta-analysis (a statistical procedure in which effect sizes are summed and averaged across published studies) suggested that the average *ES* for psychotherapy of children, using the Glass method for calculating *ES* is 0.54 (Weisz et al., 1995). Such an *ES* would be considered a "medium" effect (Cohen 1988).

Larger effect sizes now are associated with more meaningful results. Just as earlier investigators were satisfied with statistical significance, many outcome researchers are now satisfied with finding large effect sizes. The *ES* has replaced the level of statistical significance as the basis for value judgments about outcome research.

Difficulties in Interpreting Intervention Effect Size

Mental health investigators who have reviewed a number of outcome studies may conclude, like Weisz and colleagues (1995, p. 450), that the "overall mean effect of therapy was positive and highly significant." When investigators use the term "significant," they mean that the effect size is significantly different from zero (which would mean that there is no relationship between treatment and outcome). Researchers, however, may go one step further and state, for example, that "psychotherapy with young people produces positive effects of respectable magnitude" (Weisz et al. 1995, p. 460). To the layperson, "magnitude" implies "large" and suggests that the outcome measures used in treatment effectiveness studies reveal "large" adjustment gains in treated groups.

However, interpretation of findings can be difficult. When there is a clear understanding of the measuring instruments that are used in a study, the evaluator may be able to interpret findings in a meaningful way. For example, if the IQ of individuals in a treated group went up 7.5 points (a Glass ES of 0.50 in IQ tests with a standard deviation of 15), some judgments could be made about the meaningfulness of this finding. Unfortunately, it is more difficult to interpret measures of treatment outcomes than IQ measures. For example, how should a Glass ES of 0.50 be interpreted when the treated group's mean D score is three points more than the mean D score of the untreated group on a child behavior checklist and the standard deviation of the untreated group is six?

Interpretation of findings also can be difficult when using r as a measure of ES. Difficulties arise even with an r of 1.00 (which would mean that 100% of the variance between children can be attributed to the treatment effect) or when every child in the treated group has a gain (or D score) larger that the largest gain score of any participant in the control group. The ability of most standardized outcome measures to reflect meaningful treatment gains in these situations is questionable. As an example, the mean pretest score on a child behavior checklist of both a treated and untreated group may be 10 scale points above the highest scale score considered to be in the range of normal behavior. After treatment, the treated group mean score may decrease to 7 points above the highest normal scale score, and the untreated group mean score may remain at 10 points above the highest scale score of the normal range. Every child in the treated group may be found to have a decreased posttreatment scale score, and every child in the untreated group may be found to have identical post-treatment scale scores (a mean D score of zero for the control group). The ES, using r, would be 1.00 (which has never been achieved in any study).

Difficulties in Interpreting Gains

Is a change in several scale points on a measure of child psychopathology of value in the real world? How much change in scale points is needed before the change is meaningful? Regardless of the measure used, *ES* does not touch on these questions. A value judgment must be made regardless of the *ES*. For example, would child care workers who work with children who hit other children 10 times daily be happy with evaluation results that show that a treatment reduces the hitting behavior to only 7 times daily? Many would say that a 30% decrease in hitting behavior is meaningful. Some child care workers may value a treatment that results in a reduction in hitting behavior because they would be required to intervene less often. Other child care workers may value the treatment if there is no relapse following its termination or if the continued use has a cumulative effect. Administrative staff may value the treatment if it is relatively cheap, easily administered, and its effects are permanent. Nevertheless, even if the treatment is valued by these groups, children who experience these improvements will continue to need residential treatment because of the overall high degree of aggressive behavior.

Even more complicated is the question of whether different values should be placed on identical gain scores made by children with different initial scale scores. Is a five-scale point gain made by a child with extremely deviant scores, for example, similar to a five-scale point gain made by a child with moderately high scale scores? *ES* can be important when the measures employed to assess change reflect interpretable and/or meaningful change. An investigation that reports a small ES but employs a meaningful outcome measure, would produce findings that are preferable to an investigation that reports a large ES but uses a less meaningful outcome measure. However, assessing the meaningfulness of change in a client is a judgment call that must rely on real world factors, such as the opinions of others. For children, the opinions of their teachers, parents, and others in their lives are key. For example, if a child is referred for mental health services following inappropriate behavior in school, parents are likely to be satisfied with services when the child's teachers report that he is displaying more age-appropriate behavior or when they receive fewer complaints about their child from the school principal.

Measurement in Outcome Research

Regardless of *ES* size, outcome investigators rarely make value judgments in written reports of their findings. They typically report the amount of intervention-produced change on client measures of functioning and leave the reader to decide the actual effectiveness of an intervention. For example, some professionals may believe that a mental health intervention is effective only when client scores on objective measures of dysfunction change from the abnormal range to the normal range. Other professionals consider an intervention effective only when a significant number of clients become less dysfunctional. However, employing either of these criteria can be problematic. Both criteria assume that measuring instruments are available that can reliably identify clients or their family members as either dysfunctional or functional. These criteria assume high discriminate validity in current measuring instruments (that is, the ability to discriminate between individuals with and without a disorder) and a low number of false positives (clients who score above a critical cutoff score for dysfunction who actually are not dysfunctional) and false negatives (clients who score below the critical cut off score but who actually are dysfunctional).

Some years ago, Waskow and Parloff (1975) imagined a dialogue between a clinical researcher and a research consultant. The conversation focused on ensuring that an agency used a broad representation of measures concerning content and choice. In the course of discussion, the researchers gave practically no attention to issues of methodology of measurement. Similar dialogues are taking place today. The managed care literature makes it appear that many standardized tools with acceptable reliability and validity are readily available or can be produced quickly and that agencies can easily administer them to treated and untreated groups.

Instruments that are useful in outcome research must meet criteria similar to those identified by the National Institute for Mental Health (1986): acceptable levels of reliability and validity, ease of administration, and brevity. In reality, many published scales and standardized interview schedules have poor discriminate validity, and few are brief. In fact, Hodges (1993, p. 63) states that the "task of documenting the psychometric soundness of structured interviews has not been taken seriously;" "there has been limited study of the psychometric properties of symptom scales;" and most symptom scales and structured interviews are "labor intensive and costly to the researcher as well as time consuming and tedious for the children and parents." The best available children's symptom rating scales are the Child Behavior Check List (CBCL) (a child behavior rating scale used by mental health outcome researchers that takes about 10 minutes to complete or about 30 minutes to computer score) (Achenbach, 1991) and the Devereux Scales of Mental Disorders, formerly the Devereux Child Behavior Rating Scales. These instruments reliably classify about 60% to 70% of children (which is 10% to 20% above the chance level) in their standardization studies.

Laboratory Versus Real World Findings

Very few studies of intervention effectiveness have been conducted by staff whose primary place of employment is a human services agency. Few studies have considered the effects of treatment as it is practiced in actual child and adolescent clinical settings. Instead, studies have reported on laboratory interventions conducted by professors and their graduate students in university or medical school clinics. Findings about interventions delivered outside of real-world settings may reveal little about the effectiveness of agency-based interventions.

As an example, two practicing school psychologists submitted an article describing their findings to the *Journal of Adolescent Research,* an article which this author reviewed. The study was well designed and took more than three years to complete. Slightly more than 200 children were involved in the study, and there was insignificant attrition (resulting in 194 pre-post pairs). Children were matched on relevant nuisance variables and randomly assigned to two group treatment conditions and one nongroup treatment condition. In one group treatment condition, children were enrolled in a 10-session (50 minutes per session) group counseling protocol for raising self-esteem. Eight groups used this protocol. Sixty-six children completed these groups, with seven to nine children in each group. In the second group treatment condition, children were enrolled in a 10-session (50 minute per session) group of self-structured counseling. Children selected activities that they believed would raise their self-esteem and identified topics for group discussion. The third group (65 children) received no group counseling services for enhancing self-esteem, but many received individual counseling because school staff and parents were not agreeable to the children going without services.

Each of the two school psychologists led an equal number of both groups in order to control for therapist effects. If they had not used this approach (and, instead, one therapist had led the protocol-structured groups and the other the self-structured groups), differences between the two groups could have been the result of therapist variables rather than the interventions. Based on a variety of distal outcome measures (such as changes on a self-esteem measure and in teacher and parent ratings), the greatest gains were reported for the self-structured groups, followed by the protocol-structured groups, and individual counseling a distant third. (However, it should be noted that the outcome measures were selected to examine the impact of group counseling on specific behaviors associated with self-esteem, and the individual counseling that the third group of children received focused on a variety of problems that were not directly assessed by the outcome measures employed.) College students who were unaware of the groups to which the children were assigned administered and scored the pre- and posttreatment outcome measures. This approach is referred to as "blind" scoring and provides a control for experimenter bias often overlooked in many studies on intervention effectiveness. The reliability of the student scoring was assessed and found to be acceptable.

The sophistication of this study, particularly because it was done in a human service setting by human service staff, was impressive. This author, as a reviewer, could not recommend publication of the study, however, because it was apparent that the two investigators developed a growing preference for the self-structured approach as they became more skilled in its use. They found the self-structured approach more enjoyable to deliver, reported that the children seemed more involved in the group process, and stated that the children posed fewer discipline problems during group sessions. The investigators could not control for their increasing enthusiasm for the approach. To adequately control for therapist enthusiasm, therapists who were equally enthusiastic about the use of the structured protocol would have been needed. The author recommended that the investigators rewrite their article for a practice journal, including the research methodology and research findings, but also describing in greater detail how the children were helped to structure their groups and clarifying that their growing preference for these groups may have contributed to the outcome findings.

Outcome findings in the real world do not necessarily result in clearly interpretable findings. The two investigators perceived the self-structured group as more effective and demonstrated that the children derived significant benefit from this type of group. Academic researchers may claim that the observed group differences resulted more from differences in therapist enthusiasm than from differences in therapeutic procedure. However, real-world evaluators are less concerned about this possibility. Like clients, parents, and managed care reviewers, their primary concern is whether clients make improvement. When programs demonstrate that clients prosper from services regardless of the reasons, referral sources will recommend those services to clients. More importantly, agencies that evaluate service effectiveness are more likely to improve programs deemed effective, even when many of the factors that contribute to program effectiveness remain unknown.

When client change is the result of interest and enthusiasm of the staff who employ an intervention rather than the specifics of the intervention itself, less will be made of this fact in the real world of human services. In fact, two factors unique to the protocol may be the interest and the enthusiasm that a service protocol generates, making it impossible to separate these factors from other service features. A number of studies have demonstrated that clients in treatment and placebo conditions (that is, simulated rather than actual treatment such as a sugar pill instead of actual medication or individual attention rather than cognitive-behavioral therapy) can make progress. These findings suggest that the specific procedures that define a treatment may be less important in alleviating certain conditions than was previously recognized.

Statistical Procedures

Not all managers will be familiar with the tools that may be used to determine whether the findings of outcome studies are statistically significant. There are some simple tools that managers can use to determine the probability that the observed differences between the intervention and control or comparison groups occurred by chance. Although managers may hire consultants, it is preferable that they first become familiar with nonparametric statistical procedures. Unlike parametric procedures, nonparametric procedures do not assume that scores on outcome measures are distributed normally (and in most situations, they will not be). The procedures can be done by hand and do not require sophisticated computer programs.

Nonparametric procedures include the Chi-Square technique, which is easy to understand and relatively easy to compute. Scores are assigned to levels, such as high scores and low scores, and the treatment and control groups are compared to determine if the percentage of scores in each level differs significantly from what would be normally expected. A manager can use the Chi-Square technique to determine whether there are more clients in the "high level" who received the intervention and more clients in the "low level" who received the control or comparison condition. As an example, the Chi-Square technique can be used to determine if significantly more single parents answer "yes" to a questionnaire item than do parents with a partner.

All outcome studies should examine effects by race, age, and socioeconomic status through studies of interaction effects. These studies are important because treatment effects can differ for subpopulations. Older African Americans, for example, may respond differently to treatment than younger African Americans, and African Americans as a group may differ from Caucasians on outcome variables. Treatment may differentially affect different subpopulations, even when the main effect of treatment is positive. Alternatively, treatment may have positive effects only with certain subgroups.

Statistical techniques called "analyses of variance" allow the comparison of mean outcome scores of different subgroups and make it possible to study interaction effects. A nonparametric analysis of variance technique that is relatively simple to apply is the Wald-Wolfowitz Runs Test. This test rank orders all clients on an outcome variable and applies a statistical test to determine if the ranks achieved by clients in the intervention group differ significantly from the ranks achieved by clients in the control or comparison group. This test and other popular nonparametric procedures are described in books on statistics, and a variety of specific procedures are described in books devoted exclusively to nonparametric statistical methods.

Investigators can determine relationships between variables by correlating them with one another through the use of easily learned correlation techniques. They cannot, however, make correlations among measures of client satisfaction, ratings of perceived improvement, and objective judgments of clinical change without employing analytic procedures that require a statistical background. In these cases, investigators will need the services of a consultant who is familiar with the "confirmatory factor-analysis model" (also called "structural equation modeling"), an objective method to evaluate a correlation matrix (that is, a group of correlations between variables), define hypotheses, and determine which hypothesis best fits the data.

Observational and Qualitative Research Methods

An assessment of service impact can be enriched through observational and qualitative research methods. Observational research (the direct observation of clients) and qualitative research (the analysis of data already contained in case records) can provide important information on service impact. "Post hoc" or retrospective studies of the records of closed cases constitute one form of qualitative research. No variables are manipulated by assigning clients to different intervention conditions. Instead, naturally occurring phenomena are explored in an effort to improve the understanding of intervention success and failure. Observational and qualitative research permit investigators to learn about the relationships between variables in the absence of experimental studies. Archeologists, astronomers, meteorologists, zoologists, and other scientific groups exclusively employ observational techniques and have learned much from them.

For example, there are many examples of observational and qualitative research in human services. Investigators may examine the records of children in day treatment or residential treatment centers to better understand treatment outcomes. They may review the records of children who seem to be making the least progress to determine whether these children appear to have similar characteristics that could account for their failure to make progress. An examination of the records of closed cases may reveal that children closest to academic grade level at the time of discharge did better at follow-up or that the best predictor of a child's placement in a residential treatment center, as opposed to a day treatment setting, was that a sibling had been placed out of the home. A study of outpatient records may indicate that poorer outcomes are reported by child guidance workers when three factors are present: the child has an alcoholic father, even when the father is no longer present in the home; the mother is depressed; and the child's family has multiple problems. In an educational setting, investigators may examine a classroom in which children failed to make improvements with a new curriculum and may learn that the teacher's instructional methods differ from those of the larger group of classrooms in which children profited from the new curriculum. In a health care setting, investigators may examine the atmosphere on various wards in a psychiatric hospital and find that ward atmosphere is related to patient status at discharge and that certain features of a milieu environment are related to patient improvement.

By using these techniques, researchers can obtain considerable information regarding clients' responses to interventions even when the reasons for the intervention effects cannot be determined. For example, by selecting subsets of clients from larger groups investigators may learn that some clients do not respond to a particular intervention as do other clients. Investigators might study the 10 children who had the highest number of restraints during a three-month period in a day or residential treatment and compare these children with the children who had the lowest number of restraints.

Observational and qualitative research methods allow investigators to look for a range of relationships. A finding of covariation between two events, however, will not mean that one event caused the other. Two events may vary together because of their relationship to a third variable. Women who experience multiple premature births may live a lifestyle that places them at risk for premature births. Smoking may be related to but not the cause of premature births. Smoking women may drink more alcohol than nonsmoking women, and alcohol use may be the cause of prematurity. As another example, older people have been found to have more auto accidents. Despite early assumptions that age and auto accidents had a cause-effect relationship, later studies demonstrated that older people drove more frequently on minor, as opposed to major, highways than did younger people, and that all age groups had significantly more accidents on minor highways. Finally, girls who are sexually abused may be found to respond less favorably to individual psychotherapy than girls with other histories, not because they were sexually abused but because they display fewer self-directed or self-determined behaviors.

Investigators may follow observational and qualitative research with experimental research. For example, a researcher may measure the level of clients' perceived self-determination and compare clients at different levels on outcome measures. In essence, clients at each level of self-determination would serve as a comparison group. Alternatively, a researcher may match clients on the levels of perceived self-determination and randomly assign them to two different treatment conditions. As a final example, investigators in a psychiatric hospital may randomly assign newly admitted hospital patients to two types of psychiatric wards and then examine outcomes.

Summary

Staff in the typical human service agency will be unable to perform outcome studies that will assess cause-and-effect relationships in all the services they offer, even when they have access to sophisticated information management systems. In the real world, agencies lack staff resources and time, sufficient willingness on the part of clients to participate in such studies, and a sufficient number of clients who can be appropriately matched and randomly assigned to treatment and control group conditions. Few clients can afford to wait for services that clients in the experimental group immediately receive. It is hoped that the current rhetoric about outcome measurement will wane as managed care professionals begin to realize that many human services agencies are not equipped to perform randomized design outcome research.

Nevertheless, agencies should evaluate program effectiveness in order to maintain program continuity, weed out programs perceived as ineffective from programs perceived as effective, and supply funding sources and clients with information about program effectiveness. Outcome assessment should be regularly performed, and whenever possible, assessment should include the use of a comparison group of clients who did not receive the intervention or who received another intervention. The closer the comparison group is to the intervention group, the more faith can be placed in the findings.

Chapter 7:
Tools to Assess Service Impact

In the two studies of parent effectiveness training discussed in Chapter 1, parents completed a questionnaire at the end of the training that asked them to rate their satisfaction with the services they received. Using what was essentially a crude client satisfaction survey, the vast majority of the parents in both programs reported that they were very satisfied with the program and felt that it had helped them to become better parents. In neither case, however, had the agency established program indicators by which parents were assessed, either before or after the training.

An indicator is a specific behavior that suggests the achievement of an outcome. For example, in a parent effectiveness training program an outcome may be that "parents will acquire more understanding of the causes of children's behavior," and an indicator might be the number (or percent) of parents who can identify two causes of children's defiant behavior after the completion of training. Outcome questionnaires (including self-administered surveys) are relatively useless without indicators. And for that reason, items in questionnaires should relate directly to defined indicators that indicate that outcomes have been achieved. In the parent effectiveness training programs an item on a questionnaire might ask parents whether they can name two causes of defiant behavior that they could not identify at the start of the program. Another item might ask whether parents had implemented a behavior management strategy described in the training program.

Typically, when clients complete surveys, they simply report whether they profited from participation in a program or service.

151

They are generally not asked to provide information that will assist the agency in assessing the effectiveness of a program in achieving change. For example, the surveys used in the parent training programs did not assist the agency in determining whether parents managed their children more effectively after they completed the training. The key outcome—whether the training program increased parenting effectiveness—was not evaluated. Parental satisfaction with the training provided inadequate information. It may have been that a group of parents who were provided with a room where they could meet informally to discuss their children's needs might have been equally satisfied with the assistance they received and might have achieved the same outcomes.

Surveys reveal that many agencies assess clients' satisfaction with services and do not use other outcome measures. A survey conducted by the Institute for Behavioral Health Care (1996) indicated that 93% of managed behavioral health care organizations used client satisfaction measures and ranked them as the most important indicators. The Health Care Financing Administration of the U.S. Department of Health and Human Services (Samen, 1996) supports the use of a client- or patient-directed, outcome-oriented approach. This approach, as opposed to the process and structures methodology described in the last chapter, focuses on client satisfaction and client rights (such as confidentially, privacy, dignity, and participation in care planning) in the context of quality assurance and performance improvement.

Although these views are sound, agencies must go several steps further in their outcome evaluation efforts. A 1995 survey of 74 psychiatric agencies indicated that although self-reports from clients were a frequent source of data for outcome studies, many organizations employed other measures (Trabin, Froeman, & Pollack, 1995). Intermediate care and public sector respondents, in particular, reported the use of observer ratings. Many respondents (other than managed care companies) reported the use of published outcome measures. A large number of respondents also reported using pre- and posttreatment and follow-up designs. Respondents listed about 45 different instruments, including a common core of general behavioral checklists and frequently used measures of depression and health status.

A number of tools may be used to assess service impact. Among them are client satisfaction surveys and outcome assessment measures such as staff ratings of client improvement, goal attainment scaling, measures of targeted behavior, and global adjustment scales (Mordock, 2000). In addition, agencies may use unobtrusive data to assess service impact. When an agency uses any tool or data, they must take into account certain logistical considerations to maximize implementation.

Client Satisfaction Surveys

Agencies should regularly gather formal client feedback about access, administrative efficiency, clinical quality, satisfaction with both frequency and length of treatment, and outcomes. As discussed earlier, three factors promote client well-being: clients feel that staff listen to them, they feel validated and respected, and they are given information. Satisfaction surveys should include questions about these three factors in addition to seeking information about clients' perceptions of outcomes. The agency should assess the relationship between client satisfaction and functional status and should analyze satisfaction by clients' race, sex, and primary language. Some organizations develop agency-wide consumer satisfaction surveys as an added component of efforts to determine the degree to which they are "family friendly." They use the results of client satisfaction surveys to improve the accessibility of services (issues with which consultants and consumer advisory boards can also provide assistance).

Client satisfaction surveys should be user-friendly. A well-designed client satisfaction survey contributes to the evaluation of services provided and to outcome assessment. For example, in the area of children's mental health treatment, DiMotta and Whaley (1996) used the client satisfaction and burden-of-care surveys from the Fort Bragg Demonstration Project (Bickman et al., 1995) to develop a psychometrically sound client satisfaction survey. This survey, which takes most people approximately five minutes to complete, measures a range of factors: satisfaction, convenience, improvement, parental burden, and family burden.

Client Satisfaction Survey Items

Satisfaction surveys should be directed at obtaining information about specific services and not simply clients' attitudes toward the larger agency. As discussed in Chapter 1, it is relatively meaningless to ask clients simply to assess the effects of clinic treatment, residential treatment, institutional care, foster home care, or special education (although a number of investigators do just that). Such research is, in effect, the equivalent of asking people if they like ice cream and not asking them about the flavors they prefer.

To enhance the effectiveness of client satisfaction surveys, agencies should include items that seek both factual and judgmental information. A judgmental item about a therapist, for example, would be "My social worker helped me," followed by the rating points, "A great deal," "Somewhat," and "Not at all." A factual item would be, "My social worker enrolled me in a parent-education group," followed by "yes" and "no." A judgmental item about a child's academic behavior would be "I would rate my child's current school adjustment as," followed by the rating points "Satisfactory," "Marginal," and "Unsatisfactory." A factual item about school functioning would be "Since discharge from treatment, my child has been suspended from school ___ times," with the parent completing the statement.

Client satisfaction surveys should address service delivery and service outcomes. Typical items from client satisfaction surveys regarding service delivery are in Figure 7.1. Typical items for seeking information about service outcomes are in Figure 7.2.

Client satisfaction has multiple dimensions. Clients may report a favorable outcome, but may also report that achieving the outcome required unnecessary effort or advocacy on their part, or subjected them to other unnecessary stresses. At the same time, different individuals completing satisfaction forms may view the client's progress differently. A parent, for example, may see a child as improved and his teachers or peers may see the child as unchanged.

Sampling a Subgroup for Study

When an agency has never undertaken a client satisfaction survey, its initial efforts should be simple. The agency should begin by collecting information from clients who currently receive agency services. The agency should survey clients in the latter stages of an intervention by asking them or, when the client is a child, their parents to complete a simple agency-developed rating scale. Because a high follow-up rate with a targeted population is preferable to a low follow-up rate with a total population, sampling a subgroup of clients currently enrolled in services is an excellent starting point.

Client satisfaction can be assessed by mailed surveys, telephone and in-person interviews, and focused discussion groups. A combination of mailed surveys and telephone follow-ups (estimated to cost between $20 and $40 per case for each survey point in time) maximizes survey return. The best return rate that the author has attained using only mailings (initial and follow-up) to current clients of an outpatient clinic was 60%.

Experience in surveying former clients suggests that return rates are particularly low for this group of clients, even when telephone follow-ups are used in conjunction with survey mailings. Generally, only 25% of former clients can be located. Mailings often are returned "address unknown," and telephones are disconnected, reflecting the mobility of many public sector clients. Leibrich (1994) has demonstrated that return rates in follow-up studies of former clients can be increased, but most agencies will be unable to undertake the search activities he describes unless they have special grant funding. His excellent suggestions, however, include the need to obtain advice from a range of individuals as to how to look for and approach different types of clients. In his searches, Leibrich utilized the client's last known address and information from family members, friends, church groups and informal governmental networks (including probation officers, as his research involved offenders). He reported that it takes longer to locate clients than is generally realized.

Using methods like those suggested by Leibrich, the staff of Astor Home for Children completed a follow-up study of clients who were treated in the agency's residential treatment center over a 20-year period. Staff achieved an 80% response rate, interviewing 356 clients of the 445 who had been treated over that time period. In a similar effort, staff at St. Francis Homes, Inc. achieved a 90% response rate, locating 592 clients of a total of 660 clients. Their follow-up research involved boys who had been discharged 2 to 5 years previously, whereas the discharge dates for many of the boys from Astor Home had been 10 and 20 years previously. These results illustrate that return rates can be maximized but that a number of factors may affect how successful such efforts will be.

The Meaningfulness of Measures of Client Satisfaction

It is not clear to what extent client satisfaction surveys provide helpful information for purposes of program evaluation. Early studies suggested that more than 90% of human services clients who returned completed customer satisfaction surveys (which did not include items to assess the presence of specific indicators) were satisfied with the services they received regardless of the type of services. When efforts were made to increase the number of clients who returned completed surveys, there was a somewhat lower satisfaction rate. This finding may be attributed to the likelihood that more satisfied clients tend to complete and return surveys with less prompting. Even in such cases, however, there were usually so few dissatisfied clients that further analysis of the data proved fruitless. Satisfaction also was high regardless of whether the situation that prompted services improved or worsened.

The author encountered a similar pattern when he attempted to determine if more experienced psychotherapists in mental health outpatient clinics had more satisfied clients than less experienced psychotherapists. Because the vast majority of clients who completed surveys were highly satisfied with the services and outcomes, it was not possible to undertake further analysis based on clinical experience. When the author attempted to develop a satisfaction survey that would "ferret out" lower levels of dissatisfaction, members of the agency's consumer advisory board advised against such an effort. Board members explained that many clients were reluctant to rate services negatively (even when the

---

Figure 7.1 Typical Items from Client Satisfaction Surveys

When your family first contacted the agency, were you seen promptly for intake and assessment?

Very promptly   Promptly   Somewhat promptly   Not promptly

During your first visit, did the counselor make every effort to select an appointment time that did not seriously interfere with your family's schedule of activities?

Yes, definitely   Yes, generally   No, not really   Definitely not

---

Did you understand the intervention plan that was developed for your child?

Very clearly   Somewhat clearly   Not very clearly   Not clearly

---

How responsive was your child's therapist to the questions or comments you had about your child's treatment?

Very responsive   Responsive   Moderately responsive   Not responsive

---

surveys were completed anonymously) because they knew that they might need clinic services in the future and feared past complaints might be held against them.

The relationship between client satisfaction and other measures of outcome has not consistently been found to be high. Some studies show moderate correlations of client and parent ratings of improvement and others show low correlations. For example, a follow-up study of children treated in a residential center (which used a relatively simple child-completed rating scale and a relatively complex clinician rating system) revealed a high positive correlation between child and clinician ratings of current adjustment. In other studies, adolescent perceptions of improvement correlated moderately high with ratings of symptom change. In contrast, other studies revealed that client ratings of improvement correlated poorly with adjustment ratings made by others. For example, studies of children with mental health problems suggested that parent satisfaction is unrelated to others' ratings of pathology change. Parent reports of perceived improvement appear to be more closely tied to ratings of satisfaction with services than to ratings of changes in symptoms. Similarly, studies show low to moderate correlations between therapist and client ratings of success.

In general, agreement among multiple informants on ratings of client improvement tends to be low to moderate. These research findings suggest that either perceptions differ among stakeholders or that the instruments that are used are unreliable. In any case, these findings emphasize the importance of using multiple measures and multiple informants (clients, spouses, parents, teachers, and trained interviewers) whenever possible.

Finally, it is important to recognize that studies show that interviews with clients have the lowest reliability of all sources of information because of the complexity of interactions between client and interviewer. Differences in interviewer style (including such factors as level of empathy), difficulties in communicating, and variation in respondents' moods at the time of the interview affect reliability. The reliability of client interviews will increase when questions are short and clear, terms are simple and unambiguous, and answers are primarily dichotomous rather than multiple choice.

The Development of Outcome Assessment Tools

General Principles in Developing Outcome Assessment Tools

The focus of outcome assessment must be the efficacy of treatment protocols for the specific types of clients who are served. For example, outcome assessment at an outpatient mental health center may focus on the effects of applying a specific mental health treatment protocol with children who display similar symptoms and have a similar background. A study may assess the effects of a self-monitoring and parent training program on children from ages 11 to 13, diagnosed with Attention Deficit Hyperactivity Dis-

Figure 7.2 Typical Items Seeking Information About Service Outcomes

Is your child making progress towards achievement of the objectives in the intervention plan?

Yes, definitely   Yes, generally   No, not really   Definitely not

Has your child achieved any of the objectives outlined in the treatment plan?

Yes, definitely   Yes, partially   No, not really   Definitely not

My problems got better during the period I was in treatment.

Strongly agree   Agree   Disagree   Strongly disagree

I stopped coming to the agency because I was satisfied with the progress I had made.

Strongly agree   Agree   Disagree   Strongly disagree

Members of our family now deal more effectively with our child.

Strongly agree   Agree   Disagree   Strongly disagree

order, and residing in single parent families with no community or extended family supports. Or an outcome study may assess the effects of a residential treatment program designed to assist aggressive, borderline adolescent clients who are freed for adoption to develop job-related social skills.

Outcome assessment tools that address the effects of specific interventions can be completed by clients (children and families) and consumers (teachers and other caretakers). Questions should be simple. Clients may be asked, "How much did the intervention help with the specific problems that brought you to this agency?" The client could check one of the following ratings: "Made the problems a lot better," "Made the problems somewhat better," "Made no difference," "Made the problems somewhat worse," or "Made the problems a lot worse." When agencies use a client-directed approach to outcome measurement, a client advisory committee and clients who complete the measures in pilot samples (if used) can be involved in reviewing the outcome measures. Simplicity in outcome questionnaires also facilitates data collection and management.

Steps in Developing Outcome Assessment Tools

When developing outcome assessment tools, agencies should clarify expected outcomes, involve staff in developing outcome measures, ensure management support, anticipate implementation obstacles, refine instruments and expand the outcome assessment process, and understand the larger context in which outcomes are measured.

Clarifying Expected Outcomes

In the initial stages of outcome assessment, an agency should clarify the outcomes expected for each service in terms of distal outcomes (the "client status variables" that define expected outcomes following the termination of services) and proximal outcomes ("case status variables" or "indicators" that address the extent to which a client has achieved specific objectives that will lead to an expected outcome). The following examples illustrate how a child welfare agency might define outcomes and indicators:

- A child welfare service is provided to families whose primary problem is unsuccessful resolution of family crises. The outcome of the services could be that the family better manages crises as treatment progresses and following discharge from the service. The agency could measure the parents' and child's ability to prevent new crises; their perceived skill in handling future crises; the family's perceived confidence in avoiding crises; and the parents' and children's ability to manage unavoidable crises.

- A child welfare service has the goal of improving a client's skill at advocating for himself in the community and making better use of community agencies. The agency could measure the client's "recovered personal efficacy and competence." An academic researcher might employ a formal measure to assess the client's improved sense of control over his environment, such as change scores on Rotter's measure of Internal Locus of Control. Real-world agencies are likely to find that a better approach is simply to ask the client and other informants to rate the client's progress in self-advocacy.

- A child welfare service is designed to foster general improvement in family functioning and the family's increased involvement in outside activities (sometimes referred to as "residential stability"). The agency could measure each family member's increased personal involvement in life-enhancing activities, including the frequency of social and leisure time activities and the intensity of social ties.

- A child welfare service has a goal that caregivers will take better care of the physical environment and display improved cooperation in child care. The agency could measure improvement in the two areas through home visits and ratings of caregivers on an agency-developed scale of household care and parental cooperativeness.

- A child welfare service is designed to reduce conflict and hostility between parents and their children. The agency could develop questionnaires that ask parents and children such questions as: Can you talk out disagreements with your parents (your child)? Can you resolve disputes with your parents (your child) without getting really angry? Does your child follow through on parental requests? Does your child hold conversation with parental figures?

- A child welfare service seeks to increase family cohesion and mutual support. The agency could measure the degree to which parents and children support each other's activities; the parents work together on issues confronting the family; the parents monitor their children's whereabouts; and parents show less symptoms of distress, such as better sleep, fewer somatic complaints, or better self-organization.

- A child welfare service has as a goal that a child remains stable or maintains social connections. The agency could assess stability and connectedness on such factors as: whether the child's unexcused school absences exceed the school average; whether the child continues to have a best friend; or whether the child visits his grandparents monthly.

Agencies should set absolute standards for clients, that is, an agreed-upon level of performance that each client is expected to reach. It is not enough to know that the average client made gains. Agencies should record the number and percentage of clients who reach the standard as well as the number of clients who demonstrate substantial improvement. It may be that every client makes some gains but no client reaches the standard. If the agency believes that achieving the standard is absolutely necessary for a client's successful functioning, it may be necessary to revise the program so that clients can reach the required standard.

In the context of an agency's total quality improvement effort, it can be expected that more clients will show gains at each subsequent evaluation. As an example of the need to put such expectations in place, a program director at a day treatment center developed a form to be completed by children with emotional disturbances. The form was excellent, using nonverbal cues to guide children's selection of responses. The children were asked to respond to such items as "My teacher likes me," "I understand the classroom rules," and "I know how to earn points for good behavior." No item elicited a 100% affirmative response. Only 60% of the children felt that their teacher liked them, and only 80% reported knowing all the classroom rules. The program director consulted the author about what would be reasonable percentages in response to such questions. For example, the director was uncertain whether a finding that 60% of the children believed that their teachers liked them was a low or a high figure for a group of children who were distrustful and disturbed. Absent a standard, the director felt he could not judge the meaningfulness of the children's answers. The author's response was that a standard made no difference because the goal should be that 100% of the children feel loved, know the rules, and understand how to earn points for good behavior. The director had established a starting point for comparisons of program effectiveness over time and was beginning to move toward the goal of total quality improvement, that is, the goal of zero defects.

Involving the Staff in Developing Outcome Goals

Staff, as well as clients and their families, should be involved in selecting meaningful outcomes. For example, the management staff at St. Francis Homes did a follow-up study on their clients, boys with conduct disorders who had been referred for residential treatment. At the time of the proposed follow-up, many clients had achieved adult status. Investigators consulted staff about the questions that clients should be asked to determine if they were functioning normally. Staff stated that clients should not only be "well adjusted" but should display behaviors that were targeted in their treatment goals; have strong family ties and play clear roles as family members; show no abusive behaviors toward others; engage in responsible behavior; be relatively satisfied with themselves; and have no contact with the justice system. Investigators developed a questionnaire that targeted each of these areas. The questionnaire was sent to parents for completion. Some examples of questions that were posed to parents about their sons were:

- Does he remember family occasions?

- How emotionally close is he?

- Does he pay his bill on time?

- Does what he says he is going to do?

- Is he mentally abusive of others?

- Does he cheat at games?

- Is he financially independent?

- Is he happy?

Parents rated each item on the questionnaire on a four-point scale: "never," "occasionally," "frequently," or "very frequently." Success of the scale was attributable to involvement of staff in its development. The agency makes the scale available to other investigators.

Ensuring Management Support

Without management support, very little activity in relation to program evaluation will take place. When management is supportive, staff can develop evaluation instruments, begin to use them once they have been refined, and improve the tools over time. In one case, top management staff in a comprehensive children's mental health and child welfare agency expressed an interest in evaluation. Management provided support for the development of two questionnaires to standardize the information collected by social workers who contacted families at regular intervals following each child's discharge (these forms are found in Appendices D and E). Although agency administrators were given the tools to review, these instruments have not been utilized to date. The interest of top management was never followed up with a commitment to implement program evaluation.

Anticipating Implementation Obstacles in Outcome Assessment

Agencies should anticipate that early efforts related to outcome questionnaires will be met with staff reluctance to use agency-imposed data collection instruments and client resistance to completing forms or interviews. Staff typically prefer to remain flexible when interviewing clients and initially reject the use of standardized data collection instruments. They need to see, first hand, the value in collecting standardized information about clients. When agencies initially ask staff to collect data from a small sample of clients and provide them with feedback about the findings, staff usually agree that the process produces information that previously was unavailable to them. For example, clinicians in one outpatient mental health clinic were unaware that regardless of diagnosis, children with an alcoholic parent who was absent from the home made less progress than did other children. This information became available when standardized data allowed clinicians to compare clinician ratings of children's status at discharge with background material. This information led to modifications in treatment delivery to single mothers with alcoholic ex-spouses.

Once staff members overcome their own resistance to standardized data collection techniques, client resistance usually disappears because staff ask questions in a less stilted and more relaxed manner. When clients are very resistant, members of the agency's consumer advisory board can be called on for help. Usually, advisory board members are happy to contact agency clients and explain how the information is helpful to consumers and contributes to the agency's ability to provide more useful services.

Refining Instruments and Expanding the Outcome Assessment Process.

Once an agency has designed and implemented an initial measurement tool, it should refine the instrument. The creation of a useful client-completed questionnaire is a developmental process as unproductive questions are replaced by more informative ones. As an example, when a child is placed in a specialized group within a larger program, parents and the child initially may be asked about the changes they believe can be attributed to the child's participation in the group. Through the ongoing development of the client-completed outcome questionnaire, items can be added, such as questions regarding the parents' and child's confidence in each intervention they received ("How confident are you that your child's participation in the group helped him to function better?" or "How confident are you that the family therapy sessions helped your family communicate more effectively about your child's problems?"). Additional items may seek parents' ratings of the severity of the child's symptoms, the extent of the child's developmental attainments, or may ask the family to assess burden-of-care issues before and after treatment and at follow-up intervals.

The final version of outcome questionnaires should cover multiple areas with a number of related items (including, for example, information about a child's problem behaviors; his or her developmental attainments; and his or her functioning in the home, the school, and the larger community). Questionnaires should be designed with decision-tree questions to maximize the information that is collected. For example, if an informant answers "yes" to a general question about alcoholism in the family, he or she should be asked a series of more specific questions about the issue (questions that would not be asked of an informant who answered "no" to that question). Outcome assessment can be extended to obtaining information from other informants. Standardized tools, such as Child Well-Being Scales (CWBS) or the Parent Outcome Interview (POI)—both of which are discussed later—can be used to provide a more comprehensive picture of outcomes. Increasing the length of the instrument also will enhance outcome assessment. The validity of an instrument (the ability to differentiate between groups) depends upon its reliability (the same score or ranking being given in repeated administrations). Reliability depends upon instrument length (that is, more items increase the chance of finding real differences between informants). As a result, validity also depends upon instrument length. When the number of related items in an outcome questionnaire is increased, the internal consistency reliability (clients giving the same response to similar but differently worded questions) also increases. At the same time, with increased internal consistency reliability, the within-group variation in scores decreases and the between-group effect size increases. Adding related questions to an outcome tool, as a result, allows an agency to use a smaller sample size and to lower evaluation costs.

Researchers recommend the use of multiple outcome measures. Because the measured outcomes of most interventions appear to be poor at best, the use of a variety of outcome measures (or a core battery of measures) will increase the chances of finding gains. However, most human services agencies will find the use of multidimensional measurements to be challenging because they lack staff resources and funds to engage in such projects.

Understanding the Larger Context in Which Outcomes Are Measured

Children may improve as a result of an intervention, but improvement may come at the expense of other aspects of their lives. If a family suffers economic hardship because of the costs of the intervention or they neglect another family member in their efforts to help the client, the positive effects on the client may be offset by other negative effects on the family. Unlike the knowledge base regarding the side effects in many medical treatments (for example, aspirin is known to relieve muscular aches and pains and reduce heart attacks but also to cause ulcers, bleeding, and immune failure), little is known about the side effects of human service interventions. Outcome assessment tools that focus on changes in the identified client are not likely to identify the negative effects of the intervention on others. Agencies should be aware of this limitation in outcome assessments.

At the same time, it may happen that a client does not achieve a specific objective but makes progress in other areas in response to the intervention. Agencies may attempt to assess these unanticipated outcomes. In a program in which a child is receiving services, parents may be asked, "What do you feel is the most important way that your child is doing better in school?" or "In what ways does your child's behavior need to improve?" Questions such as these items can be selected from the Parent Outcome Interview (Magura & Moses, 1986). Ultimately, clients, parents, and the children themselves must decide what was of help to them.

In some situations, the majority of clients will make small gains as a result of an intervention, but a small number of clients will do more poorly. In such cases, value judgments must be made. An agency may conclude that the detrimental effects of an intervention for a few clients outweigh the small positive effects for many clients. Agencies interpreting the results of outcome assessments must attempt to examine the total effects of treatment, using outcome assessment items that may provide information about the range of possible effects.

Types of Outcome Assessment Measures

There are four main types of outcome assessment measures: staff ratings of client improvement, goal attainment scaling, measures of targeted behaviors, and global adjustment scales.

Staff Ratings of Client Improvement

The simplest outcome measure is a staff-completed five or seven point scale of client improvement, with the point scale ranging from "much improved" to "much worse." The reliability of such scales can be established by employing clearly defined behavioral characteristics for each point on the scale, training staff to rate client improvement, and using the tool initially with a small group of clients. Once reliability is established, staff may rate each client's progress at discharge. Although outcome researchers appropriately have criticized staff judgments about client change (particularly in the absence of a control group), use of such measures nonetheless provides valuable information. Staff improvement ratings, as is the case with client-completed questionnaires, have proven fruitful in providing outcome information that is, in fact, more helpful in many cases than the information provided by standardized symptom or global functioning scales (discussed later). At the very least, involving staff in the development and use of a rating scale raises awareness about outcome assessment and its contribution to program development.

Goal Attainment Scaling

Although academic researchers utilize standardized measures of change (such as rating scales, observational schedules, and personality tests) to measure outcomes, agencies must assess real world outcomes. For example, if a child receives treatment for school phobia, the only successful outcome is return to school and an acceptable absentee rate over a designated time period. If the child does not return to school during or following treatment, improvement on an objective measure of anxiety is irrelevant. In other cases, such measures are highly relevant. If an agency has designed an intervention to decrease symptoms of anxiety in a group of children traumatized by sexual abuse, the outcomes to be measured will be decreases in anxiety-related behaviors. Such decreases could be assessed by determining (through self or caregiver reports) the frequency of nightmares, flashbacks, and other indicators of anxiety, and assessing the frequency of the indicators during treatment (proximal outcomes) and after treatment (distal outcomes). However, not all children in an intervention group will display the same symptoms of anxiety. Some children will have nightmares, others will have flashbacks, and still others will show regressed toilet functioning. As a result, the specific goals for each child in treatment will differ. One approach to assessment is to use symptom checklists, with the symptom change for each child in the group totaled, regardless of the specific symptoms that each group member displays.

The better approach is to combine individual changes into a group score through a process called Goal Attainment Scaling (GAS) (Seaberg & Gillespie, 1977; Kiresuk & Sherman, 1977). Developed in the late 1960s, GAS is a method that allows children with different goals to be treated as a group for statistical purposes. Although the GAS has fallen into relative disuse, it is a procedure that holds promise because it is in keeping with today's emphasis on client-specific goals. Currently, expected outcomes in most interventions are both client-specific and prenegotiated. For example, the Uniform Behavioral Record, developed in New York State for use by child welfare agencies, requires that intervention plans target specific and measurable objectives. The GAS allows an assessment of the extent to which clients attain predetermined intervention goals as established at the time that a service is initiated. In order to use the GAS in an outcome study, however, data must be gathered, tabulated, and analyzed.

Measures of Targeted Behaviors

When undertaking outcome assessment, an agency must decide what data to collect, establish a set of effective procedures for data collection, collect data from specific client groups, and overcome client resistance. Once those steps are completed, an agency may decide to use standardized measuring instruments to assess targeted behaviors. Many evaluators prefer to produce findings on the broad, general effects of interventions on clients. Measures of targeted behaviors, however, have proven to be far more useful than measures of broad effects. A meta-analysis of 150 outcome studies in mental health suggests that outcome measures that precisely match target problems (such as verbalization of self-derogatory remarks) yield a markedly larger mean effect size than do equally specific outcome measures that do not match target problems (such as internalized symptoms). In addition, outcome measures that are in the same broad domain as the target problem (such as internalized versus externalized or overcontrolled versus undercontrolled behaviors) yield a larger mean effect size than do outcome measures in a different broad domain than the target problem

In selecting outcome measures of targeted behaviors, it is essential that clinically sensitive measures be used. Effective measures of outcome assessment reflect not only changes following treatment but therapeutic changes during the course of an intervention. The six primary dimensions that can be measured are physical, emotional, mental/cognitive, social, life satisfaction, and life direction. Client improvement may occur in stages along any or all of these dimensions. For example, in response to mental health treatment, a child may initially show symptom reduction (less anxiety or depression); may shortly thereafter show improved behavioral control (less impulsivity); then may demonstrate improvement in relationship skills; and finally, may show improvement in academic and vocational functioning. At the same time, clients may make gains in certain targeted behaviors but not others. For example, an adolescent may show improvement in academic and vocational functioning but show no changes in symptomatology. This situation often occurs when a child is in a facility that adapts its instruction to the child's symptomatology. The child may continue to display symptoms of schizophrenia, but because both he and others have "learned to live with the symptoms," the child is able to advance developmentally.

Types of Standardized Measures of Targeted Behaviors

Standardized rating scales of targeted behaviors may be used in client self-reports of symptom reduction and subjective well-being, caregiver reports of functional improvement, and clinician ratings. Examples of self-report ratings using standardized scales are manifest anxiety scales, ego-strength scales, and depression scales. Standardized scales in caregiver reports may involve ratings of the child and of family functioning. An example is the Burden of Care Scale (Bickman et. al., 1995), which measures the stress a family experiences because of a child's problems. Another example is the Parenting Stress Index (Magura & Moses, 1986) which likewise measures parental variables. Clinicians may use standardized scales to assess changes in personality traits, such as neuroticism.

Requirements When Using Standardized Measures

An agency should take a number of steps when using standardized rating scales. First, the agency should carefully define the expected outcomes for clients with different prognoses who receive specific treatment protocols and should clearly state the prognosis for each client. Second, the agency should ensure that sufficient baseline data on important prognostic indicators are recorded for all clients so that only clients with similar prognoses are compared. Third, the agency should carefully select the instrument that will be used. Any standardized instrument should meet the criteria developed by the National Institute of Mental Health (1986). The agency should consult this source for detailed information about these criteria. The agency also should keep in mind that even when the statistical manual for a published scale provides fairly acceptable confidence limits for a reasonably valid cutoff score, the agency should not use standardized measures in its initial efforts to measure outcomes [although Pfeiffer's survey

(1995) indicates that child welfare agencies typically do]. The score may not apply to clients in all settings and, particularly, may not apply when the population under study differs from the population on which the measure was standardized.

Limitations of Measures of Targeted Behaviors

An agency should be aware that the constructs (the targeted behaviors) being measured may not be defined clearly enough to avoid rater-specific definitions and other problems. For example, in the area of clinician ratings, the lack of clarity in measured constructs is evident in the tendency of mental health clinicians in inpatient settings to rate standard case vignettes more severely than do clinicians in outpatient settings. In the area of children's symptom rating scales, constructs also may lack clear definition. On the Child Behavior Checklist (CBCL), for example, the cutoff score on the Total Scale Score is 63: children scoring above 63 are viewed as having symptoms of psychopathology and children who score below 63 are viewed as normal. In one psychiatric hospital, however, the mean CBCL score was well below 63 (Kazdin & Bass, 1988), suggesting that most children in the facility were normal. The scale clearly was not valid for this population. In other cases, children in more restrictive treatment settings (who would be considered more disturbed) have obtained lower CBCL scores than children in less restrictive treatment settings (who would be considered less disturbed).

Although symptom-rating scales can reflect changes resulting from an intervention, the meaning of the changes is not always clear. Very disturbed and moderately disturbed children may receive the same scale scores in the pathology range and other disturbed children receive scores in the normal range. Because of the inconsistencies in scale scores, evaluation often involves obtaining information from parents or children about their satisfaction with changes that psychometric tests reveal.

Staff in the same setting may view clients differently, and different informants may have different views of clients. In a mental health setting different informants may rate outcomes quite differently. Studies show that peers and children themselves (as opposed to other informants) are likely to report positive treatment effects on children with overcontrol problems. In contrast, teachers and trained observers are more likely to report positive treatment effects on children with under-control problems. Sophisticated methodologies have been developed to allow for the integration of ratings from multiple informants.

An Example of the Use of Different Standardized Measures of Targeted Behaviors

An agency may choose to use different standardized measures of targeted behavior to assess the program's impact on different subgroups of clients. As an example, an agency that seeks to evaluate the effects of alcohol and substance abuse services may choose two different types of measures. For patients who have acknowledged their abuse of substances, the agency might use the following targeted behavior measures: decrease in quantity of specific substances consumed per unit of time; decreases in peak density (percent of days or months drugs were used over certain periods of time); days of total abstinence from a specific substance or all substances; decreased rates of drug overdoses; decreased number of arrests or convictions for drug-related offenses or for all types of offenses; increased school attendance; self-reported improvement in health; and decreases in hospitalizations for related psychiatric conditions or for health-related conditions. Because youth who deny drug use rarely attend treatment programs voluntarily and often fail to profit when they do attend such programs, these outcome measures would not be appropriate with this group. More realistic measures of targeted behavior for adolescents who are mandated to attend substance abuse treatment group might be: increased participation in group discussions about the problems associated with being an adolescent; verbalized identification of stressors that create problems for the client; verbalized identification of coping strategies the client uses when faced with particular stressors; verbalization of healthy coping strategies the client can use when faced with stress; verbalized awareness of the impact of the client's behavior on others; and verbalization of previously denied conflicts.

Special Considerations on Mental Health Measures

It is important to note that in some cases, it is difficult to assess the importance of a measured change on targeted behaviors because the meaning of the change is not clear. In the mental health arena, it is usually difficult to assess the meaning of decreases in scores. When compared to scores on intelligence tests, scores on mental health instruments are more difficult to interpret for a number of reasons:

- Mental health measures are less reliable than measures of intelligence (the same rater may give different ratings on different occasions and different raters may give different ratings on the same occasion).

- Mental health measures generally are less valid measures than are measures of intelligence (that is, they have low correlations with other measures of personal adjustment and with referral for mental health services whereas IQ measures correlate highly with academic achievement).

- Mental health measures tend to be less stable measures than intelligence test scores. Repeated IQ testing over time results in very similar scores because intelligence is relatively stable, whereas repeated ratings of mental health symptoms over time results in dissimilar scores because behavior is not stable. Emotional adjustment is not an unstable trait, but emotional stability can wax and wane for some individuals over time. Longitudinal studies of individuals who are considered "normal" and individuals considered "disturbed" indicate that there is relatively little overlap between the two groups on measures of emotional adjustment. Many clients may improve as a result of treatment, but the majority of clients whose diagnoses fall within certain groups will be considered "disturbed" if they are evaluated thoroughly in later years. Mental health scales, by themselves, however, will not reflect the stability of the underlying condition.

- There is less understanding regarding the meaning of scale points on mental health measures than is the case with measures of intelligence.

- Generally, clients obtain mental health, child welfare and juvenile justice services when problems and distress are at unusually high levels. Over time, a client is not likely to feel as distressed, and as a result, subsequent ratings are likely to reflect the client's regression toward his average level of functioning regardless of the form of treatment he received or whether any treatment took place. This phenomenon, known as "regression toward the mean," makes it difficult to interpret any changes noted.

Global Adjustment Scales

Global assessment of functioning scales attempt to measure overall changes. Global assessments of functioning are relatively insensitive to certain changes, and for that reason, they are not recommended for assessing the effects of interventions that target specific behaviors. As examples of global functioning scales in the area of foster care, Magura and Moses (1986) developed two scales: the Child Well-Being Scales (CWBS) and the Parent Outcome Interview (POI). Each scale meets some of the criteria of the NIMH. The CWBS, although relatively brief, requires about 25 minutes for a trained social worker to complete. The POI requires a two-hour interview with the parent.

One measure of global changes in adults is the SF-36 Health Survey (also known as the Health Status Questionnaire) which may be administered to individuals 14 years or older. Consisting of 36 items (although alternate versions have 20 items and 12 items each), the scale yields scores on eight subscales: physical functioning, role limitations due to physical functioning, social functioning, bodily pain, general mental health, role limitations due to emotional problems, vitality, and general health perceptions. The scale has been adapted for computer administration and scoring, and is available from the Psychological Corporation.

In the area of mental health global functioning assessment, the Global Assessment of Functioning Scale (GAF), found in the Diagnostic and Statistical Manual of the American Psychiatric Association (DSM-IV), may be used to arrive at a score for global functioning on Axis V of DSM-IV. This scale, however, is too general to be of value with youth, and as a result, mental health investigators should use scales such as the Child and Adolescent Functional Assessment Scale (CAFAS) (Hodges, 1990) or the Social Adjustment Inventory for Children and Adolescents (SAICA) (Biederman et al., 1993). When assessing older adolescents, the Appropriate Adult Functioning Scale (AAF) (Burdsal et al., 1995), a measure of prosocial behavior, is also useful because although psychopathology may remain unchanged, prosocial behavior may increase. Appendix F contains information on the publishers of useful scales that may be used with children and adolescents. Information on additional instruments may be found in the catalogs of the major publishers of educational and psychological tests: American Guidance Services, the Psychological Corporation, and Western Psychological Associates.

Global functioning scales can be quite useful in assessing the progress that clients make. For example, in one study, 18 girls and 36 boys with obsessive-compulsive disorder (OCD) were treated with a five-week trial of clomipramine hydrochloride. Of these children, 10 received behavior therapy and 29 received individual psychotherapy. At follow-up two to seven years later, 70% of the children were still receiving medication. On a global assessment scale, 35 children were rated as significantly improved and 19 children were rated as unchanged or worse. Nevertheless, 43% of the children remained diagnosed as OCD, and another 46% displayed OCD features (subclinical OCD). Only three children were symptom-free. The global assessment scale revealed that children with a poor initial response to medication, who had a tic disorder as well as a diagnosis of OCD, and whose parents had an Axis I disorder were the least likely to show improvement at follow-up. Likewise, in another study, a global functioning scale revealed that adults who received 12 to 15 sessions of treatment for depression (involving interpersonal therapy, imipramine, and clinical management) had better outcomes than adults who received cognitive-behavioral therapy or a placebo combined with clinical management. When the researchers considered only depressive symptoms, the effects of different treatment conditions were not evident.

An Example: Assessment Tools in Child Welfare

There is now increased emphasis on outcomes in child welfare services. In some states, departments of social service fund foster care prevention programs based on milestones that take the form of concrete outcomes and specific performance targets leading to outcome achievement. Instead of small measurable differences between pre- and posttests, outcomes are expected to be verifiable accomplishments. As an example, a public child welfare agency may expect that an agency that it funds will be able to demonstrate that "90% of discharged children are still in their homes one year following their discharge from foster care." State agencies that fund child welfare services increasingly expect that outcome assessment will measure both effectiveness (the ratio of units of outcome to a standard unit defined in terms of maximum improvement or another standard of improvement) and efficiency (the ratio of units of outcome to units of program output or resource input).

As one example of efforts to develop child welfare outcome measures, the New York City Administration for Children's Services (ACS) and the Council on Family and Child Caring Agencies (COFCCA) have been working together to develop outcome measures for preventive services, measures that also would be useful in evaluating reunification services. Using the Magura and Moses Family Risk Scales (1986) as a basis for conceptualizing client service needs and client progress, a working group has drafted a set of scales to measure multiple areas of family functioning, including sobriety, domestic violence, and home management. The following areas have been identified for outcome assessment: motivation for parenting, physical need gratification, emotional need gratification, guidance and direction, supervision, discipline, treatment and management of the family's mental health needs, adult relationships, and use of community and family supports.

It is anticipated that the scales will be codified and integrated with existing recording tools (such as the Uniform Case Record and the Monthly Progress Reports).

Assessment of Service Impact through Use of Unobtrusive Data

The creative program evaluator does not rely solely on standardized and staff-developed measuring instruments. Behavioral changes also can be measured through unobtrusive data. In an early study demonstrating the value of unobtrusive measures in program evaluation, researchers assessed the effects of a community education program that stressed the value of the public library. Increased wear and tear on the library steps indicated that the library was being used more. Other examples of unobtrusive measures are reductions in alcohol- related accidents as a result of alcohol prevention programs; reductions in juvenile arrest rates as a result of increased recreational programming; and reductions in hospital admissions as a result of intensive home-based mental health services for high risk children.

A study of clinical records and other data that agencies typically collect (such as accident and illness reports, attendance records, paper use, and parent visits) can reveal relationships between variables that contribute to an understanding of client needs and intervention effects. A study at a residential treatment center, for example, revealed an interesting relationship between clinical ratings of outcome and parental visits. Children whose parents visited them during their first six months of placement had lower outcome ratings than other children. Children whose parents visited them during their last six months had higher outcome ratings than other children. Staff hypothesized that unstructured parental visits early in treatment (before families had changed the nature of their interactions with their children) could be detrimental to children's progress and visits after a period of treatment could enhance progress. This finding led to changes in visiting policy, with visits early in treatment structured around family therapy sessions.

Unobtrusive measures usually are less costly than other types of measures. A drug prevention program at a public school, for example, could sample 200 students, collecting and analyzing a brief self-report regarding their drug use at a cost of about $800. Alternatively, program staff could use unobtrusive data, examining refuse that has been collected at known after-school hangouts, at a cost of $80.

Logistical Considerations

Procedures and systems are needed to effectively implement objective measures of client change. Issues that warrant consideration are the use of computer and hand-scored forms, time and staff management, and use of data analysis software packages.

Computer and Hand-Scored Forms

An agency is likely to prefer to use forms that can be scanned for computer scoring. Unfortunately, only a few published scales have answer sheets that can be computer scored. The scales that can be computer scored are discussed below. When an agency develops its own forms, it should retain a vendor that specializes in creating computer-scanned forms.

There are four mental health instruments that may be used with adolescents and adults, which have answer sheets that can be scanned for computer scoring. The Beck Depression Inventory (the BDI-II) may be used with individuals 13 years and older. The Beck Hopelessness Scale, the Beck Anxiety Inventory, and the Beck Scale for Suicide Ideation may be used with individuals 17 years and older. These forms are available from the Psychological Corporation.

Mental health instruments for use with children that can be computer-scored are the Conner's Rating Scales-Revised, the Devereux Scales of Mental Disorders, and the Child Behavior Checklist.

Scales that can be administered and scored in groups are the Trauma Symptom Checklist (for use with children from 8 through 16 years) and the Substance Abuse Subtle Screening Inventory (for use with youth 12–18 years of age). These forms are available from the Psychological Corporation. In addition, a global measure for children that can be computer-scored is the Social Skills Rating System (SSRS), which is available from the American Guidance Service. This tool measures the positive social behaviors of cooperation, assertion, responsibility, empathy and self-control, and the problem behaviors of externalization, internalization, and hyperactivity. A scale that can be administered to parents on-screen or entered manually is the Parenting Stress Index Scales.

Scales for children and youth that can be rapidly hand scored are the Children's Depression Inventory (for children ages 7 through 17) which is written at a first grade reading level; and the Suicidal Ideation Questionnaire in two versions (a 30-item version for young people in grades 10 through 12 and a 15-item version for children in grades 7 through 9). Both forms are available from the Psychological Corporation.

Appendix F lists each of the tests and provides information as to how each can be obtained.

Time and Staff Management

Time considerations are important when an agency selects the tools that it will use. It should take no longer than 15 to 20 minutes for clients to complete instruments. Perhaps more challenging than the selection of a tool that requires limited time to complete, however, is the development of office procedures to ensure ease of administration.

Agencies should make modifications in office practices so that measurement tools are easily administered and scored. Certain logistical issues must be addressed when an agency has an evaluation program that includes the administration and scoring of instruments by computer, the comparison of scores to preprogrammed norms, and the printing of results. The agency should designate an office that can accommodate several clients who are scheduled to use computers to complete the instruments. Clerical staff should be trained to handle a range of duties: scheduling clients for instrument completion, distributing instruments to clients, escorting them to the testing room, ensuring that clients understand the task, collecting completed scales from clients, scoring the forms through a scanning system, printing out the results, and determining if any client data is missing. These additional responsibilities may pose particular challenges in small agencies in which one secretary often serves as the receptionist, maintains records, collects fees, handles billing and correspondence, and watches over children in the waiting room.

Other alternatives may be available. One out-patient mental health clinic (which collected the Child Behavior Checklist from schools on each child referred and administered the instrument to each parent) found that data entry took approximately 15 minutes per child and that only a few staff members were devoting the time needed to enter the scores into the computer system. The clinic solved the problem by assigning field placement students from nearby universities to complete this task.

With regard to the time and staff management issues related to the administration of instruments, Hunkeler, Westphal, and Williams (1996) offer the following guidance: agencies should double or triple the amount of training time for clerical and clinical staff originally estimated; they should ensure that the demonstration of any system using a scanner is thorough for all staff; and they should use commercially available software with reliable telephone support.

Use of Data Analysis Software Packages

Unless an agency opts to hire a consultant to manage the statistical analysis of data, the agency should assign one staff member in each service the responsibilities of analyzing and interpreting data, determining the statistical significance of treatment differences and treatment effect sizes, and generating written reports. This staff member will need access to the Statistical Analysis System or the Statistical Package for the Social Sciences. Data should be exported to simple, delineated text files for analysis using either of these data analysis packages. Response Information Services, an outcome vendor, markets a system that collects data in

Microsoft Access databases that are accessible by export to other systems through open database connectivity drivers.

The best approach, particularly for large service systems, is to fully integrate the outcome information system with the network's information management system. Integration will enable the system to have real-time access to integrated outcomes and to administrative and financial data. When data is integrated, cost-effectiveness statistics can be integrated, including statistics associated with studies of unit-of-service per unit-of change.

Summary

Instruments developed to assess the effects of an intervention should be tailored to the goals of each intervention the agency offers, and nonrevealing items should be replaced with revealing items as the agency gains experience in instrument use. By gathering, analyzing, and regularly reporting the results of evaluations on each intervention, the agency will enhance its quality improvement efforts and keep pace with other providers in a managed care environment. Outcome assessment requires that measuring instruments serve a self-monitoring or feedback function; be short and provide actionable information; measure the change in specifically targeted behaviors; include both global and specific measures; and include measures of positive functioning and stabilization.

Chapter 8:
• •
Determining Cost-Effectiveness

In any professional journal or book that addresses issues in managed care, articles stress the need to determine the cost-effectiveness of human services. Discussions about employing interventions that produce the greatest gains at the least cost imply that the relative merits of different human service interventions are well understood. In reality, few human service agencies have demonstrated the effectiveness of their services, and without such information, the cost-effectiveness of different interventions cannot be compared. Determinations of both service effectiveness and cost-effectiveness, however, are laden with value judgments. It may be that an agency will decide to provide an intervention that yields the "best" results in terms of client functioning even if it is less cost-effective than other interventions.

The Focus on Cost-Effectiveness

The recent emphasis on cost-effectiveness results from the intrusion of scientific management concepts into human services. Cost-effectiveness is tied to the emergence and growth of human services capitalism, increasingly managed professionals, and supply-side economics focused on competitiveness. This emphasis began in the middle of the 20th century when, as sociologist Neil Fligstein points out, accounting began to be embraced as a means of exerting control. Financial measures of performance based on profits replaced other measures of a company's status, such as good community relationships, a high-quality workforce, strong product development, a record of marketing innovation, and well-made and high quality products.

The role of financial measures as the determinant of power and resource allocation in an organization has continued to grow. Accounting has emerged as the only way to measure a company's success. Costs are seen as negatives and are considered as investments only when linked to an expected return. If costs lead only to "nonquantifiable goods" (which characterize the outcomes of human services and, typically, have far less clout than quantifiable outcomes), finance finds it difficult to certify those outcomes as valuable investments. At the same time, labor is viewed as a cost and the basis for potential savings. Better means cheaper, growth means reduction, productivity means discipline, and knowledge means regulation. Just as Taylor's assembly line controlled the output of manual laborers, financial concerns now control the output of professional staff.

Although the business of human service agencies is helping others, financial systems have begun to compete with "helping others." In some cases, a business focus is dominating thinking in the helping professions. Many managed care organizations, struggling to survive in the competitive marketplace, now operate under principles of cost containment rather than cost-effectiveness. The measure of success may be the number of clients turned away from a service rather than helped by it. The immediate casualties of this level of financial control are new ideas, new programs, and new combinations of service.

In the new financially controlled environment, managers of human service agencies (with missions of preventing, alleviating, and removing human suffering) should make every effort to keep financial concerns from dominating the organizational culture. Cost consciousness should be reflected in efforts to serve clients more efficiently and effectively, and the focus should be on the cost of services to clients, not simply the costs of services. Cost-effectiveness should be determined with regard to the specific service that will result in the best outcomes at the least cost, both to the client and to the provider.

Defining Cost-Effectiveness

The relative merits of different forms of interventions, in terms of effectiveness and cost-effectiveness, have yet to be established. Research in this regard is quite limited. Cost-effectiveness may be defined most meaningfully from the perspective of clients.

The Limited Research Demonstrating Cost-Effectiveness

Cost-effectiveness is not widely addressed in research. For example, in the field of mental health, academic researchers have demonstrated that many forms of psychotherapy produce measurable changes in clients. When they compare the relative merits of one therapy over another, however, they usually fail to find significant differences. In fact, groups of clients who receive placebo treatment often are found to make progress. Other research suggests that clients improve when they work with empathic and supportive therapists regardless of the intervention method employed. In some research, clients have reported as much progress in 6 sessions as they make in 12, 15, or 30 sessions, suggesting that "more" treatment is not better. In other research, clients have reported greater gains following more sessions, suggesting that more treatment is better.

At present, there are no well-designed comparisons of the results achieved through different programs (such as residential treatment or day treatment), through different lengths of participation in the same program, or through different staffing patterns. In many cases, services are so poorly defined that program comparisons cannot be made. Treatment foster care, for example, is practiced very differently in different settings, with many variations in staffing patterns, staff interactions with clients, and services provided. There also is little information that ties outcomes to the length of time that services are provided. For example, it is not clear whether one year of day treatment is better than eight months; how long it takes to provide an adult with gainful employment when he is affected by mental illness and is given training in social and pre-vocational skills; the number of young emotionally disturbed adults, enrolled in community college with the assistance of a mental health association program, who succeed in graduating; nor the length of time that treatment is needed to produce meaningful changes for children with severe anxiety disorders or for adults with moderate levels of depression. Finally, it is unclear to what extent variations in the staffing of human service programs effect outcomes. Must a certified elementary teacher have an advanced degree in special education to effectively work with a child who has special education needs? Is the best staff-to-student ratio one teacher and one teacher's aide to eight children who are emotionally disturbed? Can only a highly trained psychotherapist produce positive results with children who are depressed? How many childcare workers are needed to care for different groups of children? In the absence of this type of information, decisions cannot be made based on assessments of effectiveness or cost-effectiveness. They likely will continue to be made on the whims, beliefs, or pocketbooks of staff and funders.

At the same time, some of the research that has compared programs and concluded that certain ineffective programs suffer from methodological problems and raise concerns about reliance on their findings. For example, a recent large-scale study compared one community with a full range of mental health services with two communities with a limited range of services. Researchers reported that children receiving the full range of services made no more gains on standardized mental health instruments than did children who had access to a limited range of services. Children who had a number of outpatient treatment sessions made as many gains as did children who received more intensive services. The study was criticized on methodological grounds, but the researchers maintained that their findings (which suggested that community-based intensive mental health services are ineffective) were sound. Should policymakers accept such findings, they may conclude that day treatment centers, home-based crisis intervention services, therapeutic group and foster homes, and long-term outpatient treatment should be discontinued.

Similarly, policymakers could look to studies that suggest the inefficacy of substance abuse treatment. Many adults have been found to recover from addiction without treatment. Several studies of the effects of rehabilitation services have suggested that most clients fail to make progress in any form of treatment, in large part because they withdraw before treatment completion. The limitations on the understanding of substance abuse and its treatment, however, have not always been recognized. Particularly, the longer-term aspects of substance abuse treatment are not well understood. Outcome studies that follow clients for more than one month are rare, with the exception of studies of the longer-term outcomes for clients who participate in methadone maintenance programs. At the same time, some clients who are affected by substance abuse report progress only after multiple attempts to become engaged in treatment.

Finally, research on effectiveness and cost-effectiveness may fail to distinguish which programs are effective for whom. One recent study demonstrated that residential treatment for alcohol abuse was more effective than day treatment (in which fewer clients made gains and more clients discontinued treatment). Nonetheless, the researchers concluded that day treatment should be considered more cost-effective than residential treatment because a significant number of clients made progress in day treatment. It was not made clear that day treatment and residential programs are not designed to serve individuals with the same needs and should not be viewed as comparable treatments for the same client populations.

Cost-Effectiveness from the Client's Perspective

Some commentators, pointing out that cost-effectiveness has not been empirically demonstrated, contend that efforts should be made to determine the costs of equally effective treatments and deliver the interventions that are cheaper. This approach focuses on the delivery of the most cost-efficient services and ignores the fact that costs are not simply associated with delivering an intervention but extend to costs borne by the participants. For example, parents may be asked to pay $80 an hour for a 15-week family intervention designed to help their child recover from depression and regain feelings of self-worth and self-esteem. In order to receive this service, the parents may have to travel some distance with their child and give up evening activities that the family has enjoyed. If it appears that the child is likely to achieve the same gains in treatment that he would achieve through participation in a self-esteem group offered at the public school, the parents are unlikely to use the clinic services. Similarly, they may not choose clinic services even if no other treatment alternative is available because the expected gains are, at most, a decrease in the severity of only one or two of the child's numerous symptoms. If they believe that their child might benefit from nontreatment activities, such as sports, they may conclude that the efforts they must expend on clinical services are not worth the gains that could be realized. As this example illustrates, an intervention may produce real gains, but the magnitude of those gains may not be meaningful to the participants if they are outweighed by the time and effort involved in receiving the service.

Value judgments are involved in determining what constitutes a meaningful magnitude of difference as a result of an intervention. However, the magnitude is so small in some cases that it is difficult to make the case for cost-effectiveness. For example, if a service designed to increase the job skills of unemployed individuals results in participants making 10 cents an hour more than individuals who did not receive the service, it is doubtful that the program would be considered effective. Even if participants report high satisfaction with the program, it is not likely that they would have enrolled had they known that their incomes would increase to such a small extent. Similarly, clients are not likely to view as effective a cognitive intervention for disadvantaged children that requires children and parents to be extensively involved but produces only a few points increase in measured IQ. However, if the program produces an increase of 10 or more points, both clients and agency staff would probably consider the program effective.

True Cost and Cost-Effectiveness

Although the cost of providing a human service may be known, the true cost is usually unknown. True cost refers to the optimal staffing pattern and the optimal number of intervention sessions needed to achieve a desired result with a specific population—that is, the true cost of a "best practice." If a service is not a best practice, it is not possible to determine its true cost because the service can be provided in a variety of ways.

Cost-Effectiveness and Evolving Best Practices

Although true cost is tied to best practices, best practices themselves may evolve over time, and value judgments may be needed regarding the result that is most cost-effective. A model of foster care prevention, a diversion program called the Homebuilder's Model (Kinney, Haapala, & Booth, 1991), provides an example. The Homebuilder's Model demonstrated that the foster care placement of many children who are at immediate risk of placement can be prevented with intensive services. In the model, each social worker has a caseload of only two clients and provides six weeks of intensive, around-the-clock services, using a behavioral based treatment model. One measure of the cost-effectiveness of the program has been the comparison of the costs of foster care with the costs of the diversion program. Over time, agencies have modified the basic program model, using different staff ratios and different eligibility criteria, and they have achieved outcomes similar to the outcomes achieved under the original model. For example, program modifications have included caseloads of four families instead of two; serving families for four as opposed to six weeks; employing social workers with bachelor degrees instead of masters degrees; and using intervention practices that require less costly training of staff. When these changes have been implemented, agencies have realized further cost savings. Eventually, however, there is a point when increasing caseloads, lowering educational requirements for staff, and providing less training results in poor outcomes. Modifications can reach a point at which the cost-effectiveness of a program is undermined.

The decision regarding cost-effectiveness, however, requires a judgment call. Is it better to keep caseloads small and prevent 85% of children from entering foster care, or is it more cost-effective to increase caseload size, decrease the level of service, and prevent 60% of children from entering foster care? The decision may rest on the extent to which decisions are based on financial outcomes or on beliefs regarding what is best for clients. On the one hand, studies have demonstrated that remaining at home is better for most children, in which case financial concerns will not predominate. However, it is clear that some children profit from foster care placement as some families provide grossly inadequate care for their children and some children need the services offered by therapeutic foster care programs. It may not be in all children's best interests to attempt to prevent 85% of children from entering foster care. Policy views and value judgments necessarily will enter the cost-effectiveness equation.

True Cost in a Changing Marketplace

True cost, as defined in terms of a "best practice," may be difficult to determine because of changes in programs in response to changing market conditions. For example, in the early 1980s, staff at the New York State Office of Mental Health believed that the psychiatric hospitalization of children in crisis was not the best treatment method to resolve the problems that led to children's escalating symptoms and regressed behavior. In their view, hospitalization primarily provided a "holding place" where the child and the family obtained temporary relief from pressing problems. Although hospitalization offered medication and medication management, the staff believed that it was not an effective approach to helping the family better manage the child. Staff funded four demonstration programs in New York State in which the Homebuilders Model was used to divert children from psychiatric hospitalization. Statewide, there was a team of four social workers, each of whom had a caseload of two clients for a period of six weeks. The program was able to serve 64 clients each year, assuming continuous client flow. The budget for the program (which included a full-time supervisor and a part-time psychiatrist, funds for travel and client emergencies, and administrative overhead) was $300,00 per year.

As the program was implemented, there was not the continuous flow of clients (predicting the ability to service 64 clients) as anticipated. Because psychiatric emergencies occur on an irregular basis, there were times when clients could not be accepted into the program because social workers already had full caseloads, and there were other times when social workers received no referrals. In each of one program's first five years, an average of 55 clients (rather than 64) were served, and 85% of referred children (an average of 47 children each year) were diverted successfully from psychiatric hospitalization. The cost for each successful diversion during the program's first five years was $6,383. Had the children entered a hospital instead, the cost of each child's care would have been approximately $9,600 (the average cost per day of hospitalization of $800 times the average length of stay of 12 days). On the basis of financial savings alone, the diversion program saved $3,217 per child.

This information was shared with local managed care companies. Interestingly, the response of some companies was not to contract with the diversion program but to pressure hospitals (with whom they had long-standing relationships) to decrease children's length of stay by three days. Therefore, hospital stays became the more cost-efficient service. In response, one diversion program reduced costs by eliminating one staff position, reducing the supervisor position to part-time, and increasing caseloads by one client so that the program could potentially serve 72 clients each year. The cost cutting was possible because the changes were made after several years of program operation, and there had been little turnover in team staff and no turnover among supervisory or management staff. With these changes, the program served an average of 61 children and their families each year and maintained a diversion rate of 85%. The cost per successful diversion was reduced to $4,327, the cost of five days of hospitalization.

Despite this success, it became evident that managed care companies were further reducing the approved number of days of psychiatric hospitalization for children. In some parts of the country, only three days of psychiatric hospitalization were being authorized, with an emphasis on rapid stabilization with medication and discharge to outpatient care. In this atmosphere, diversion programs could not survive as caseloads would have to continue to increase and service time continue to decrease. Under such conditions, a diversion program could no longer be effective. As this example illustrates, a program that initially is cost-effective can lose that characteristic in a changing marketplace.

Tying Cost to Client Change

The true measure of cost-effectiveness can be determined in a variety of ways. In the above example, a comparison of hospital costs with diversion costs is a true measure of program cost-effectiveness only if outcomes are defined solely in terms of financial savings. The problems with this approach to cost-effectiveness are captured by a comment about the recent cost cutting practices of some managed care companies: "The most cost-effective way to serve a patient is to let him or her die." In effect, when cost-effectiveness is viewed only in financial terms, the optimal approach may be cost shifting, that is, shifting the cost of serving the client to the family who must pay funeral expenses.

Specific Client Outcomes

It is only when cost-effectiveness is defined in terms of client outcomes that true costs can be determined. In medicine, there is considerable data about the costs of best practices. Certain medical conditions require a specific treatment for a specific time period, results are predictable, and costs are relatively easy to determine. Because health outcomes can be reliably measured, cost comparisons of different interventions are possible. Cost-effectiveness ratios can be calculated, with the numerator and denominator of the ratio the reported differences between alternative interventions. The numerator of the ratio is the cost of an intervention minus the cost of an alternative intervention; the denominator is the effect of the intervention minus the effect of the alternative intervention.

Although "cure" is relatively clear in health care (although it, too, can be multifaceted), it is less clear in human services. Are equal outcomes achieved through psychiatric hospitalization and hospital diversions programs? Do the two programs result in equal gains in clients' mental health status? For children, are there equal improvements in their coping skills and equal decreases in their symptomology? Do parents of children in each program develop equally effective child management techniques? If outcomes for the programs are the same, the costs can be compared.

However, even assessing the exact cost of providing the intervention can be difficult because the costs of a service may vary while outcomes remain the same. Two seemingly similar children may be referred to the same service on a continuum of child and family services. One child may remain in the service for 6 months and the other for 18 months, and both children may achieve the same outcomes. At the same time, costs may reflect a failure to comply with the concept of "best practices." In foster care prevention and diversion programs, costs can be reduced by providing the service only to families who fit the client profile and are therefore most likely to profit from the service. If a program deploys resources to serve many needy families whose children do not meet the criteria of imminent risk and does not target services to families of children at imminent risk of placement, the program is not likely to prove cost-effective.

Broader Client Outcomes

When cost-effectiveness is considered in terms of client outcomes, there may be longer-term aspects of client outcomes. Hospital diversion services may result in the child's gains in the mental health arena so that the child uses fewer mental health services in the future or has need of fewer medical services because of a decrease in psychosomatic problems. However, these types of longer-term client outcomes are difficult to measure. From a logistical perspective, many families change their managed care providers, and managed care companies often change the mental health providers they use, as these organizations rise and fall in the managed care marketplace. Given these realities, managed care companies may have few immediate concerns about future costs, particularly if it is likely that the client will not remain enrolled in their programs.

The larger picture from a societal perspective involves a consideration of the total costs for "all payers for all persons." From this perspective, it is important to evaluate the effects of a service on admission rates to other services, such as the effect of hospital diversion on referrals for school counseling, special education, child welfare and juvenile justice services, and adult mental health services. The impact may be negative or positive. A broader negative societal impact can be seen in the developments in child welfare when in the 1980s, changes in policy forced many children's institutions and group homes to close. The result was a tenfold increase in children's admissions to psychiatric hospitals. From a more positive perspective, the delivery of a service may decrease the service needs of other clients. For example, one study of families whose children received mental health services revealed that the parents' need for mental health services for themselves decreased by almost 50% when their children received services. Unfortunately, an examination of the whole picture is difficult because of the failure to share data among agencies in the same and in different fields.

Cost Calculations and Outcomes

Costs should be associated with achieving specific service outcomes rather than providing the services themselves. The calculation of costs should take into account the costs of achieving clearly defined service outcomes, the relationship between costs and improved outcomes, and the range of cost elements that are relevant to the calculation.

Costs of Services Versus Cost of Achieving Outcomes

An agency should determine the cost of achieving clearly defined service outcomes. An agency might ask, "What is the actual cost of the services needed to achieve permanency for a child in foster care who is emotionally disturbed and tests as having low intelligence?" Framed in this manner, the cost of providing treatment foster care per child may be $35,000 per year. The question, however, should be "What is the cost of achieving permanency for a child in foster care who is emotionally disturbed and tests as having low intelligence?" When the question is framed in this way, the agency must consider outcome data. If the data reveal that only 50% of children in the program are successfully integrated into the community following discharge, the actual cost of successful service is $70,000 per child per year. In such a case, one-half of the costs of providing the service would have been spent in serving children who did not achieve the favorable outcome of permanency. Similarly, if only half of the children who receive residential treatment that costs $50,000 per child benefit from service (achieve positive outcomes), the true cost of achieving a favorable result is twice the actual cost of the services delivered, or $100,000 per successfully treated child. One-half of the funds would be spent on serving children who did not improve. For example, if a county refers 10 children to the center at a cost of $500,000, it would have spent $250,000 on ineffective services. As these examples illustrate, costs can be reduced by developing a profile of the child most likely to profit from a service and admitting only children who fit the profile to the program.

Calculating Cost-Effectiveness in Terms of Improved Outcomes

An agency may find that it must increase service costs to successfully treat more clients. Drawing on the example of the residential treatment center described above, it may be that the center successfully treats two-thirds (instead of one-half) of the children admitted. However, its service costs may increase to $60,000 per child to achieve this outcome. In such a case, the true cost of successful treatment would rise to $80,000 per child. If a county refers 10 children at a total cost of $600,000, the money spent on unsuccessful treatment would be reduced to $200,000. Would a county be willing to pay $10,000 more per child to achieve better outcomes for 16% more children? A county may well make such a decision, but there would likely be a limit on the extent to which it would incur further costs regardless of changes in outcomes.

A county may discover that another residential treatment center successfully treats three-fourths of its clients at a service cost of $70,000 per child, with a true cost of successfully treating each child of $87,500. In this case, a county that sends 10 children to this center would pay a total of $700,000; and of this amount, $175,000 would have been spent on the unsuccessful treatment of children. A county is not likely to spend an additional $10,000 more per child to achieve better outcomes for only 9% more children. At the very least, the county would not likely refer children to this center if the first center had available treatment beds, particularly if county funders focused only on the costs of care. Even if parents prefer the second institution to the first (because more children benefit), funders will prefer the first institution because both service and true costs are lower. The first center is more cost-effective than the second center even though its success rate is lower.

Similarly, from a cost-effectiveness perspective, a psychotherapist who charges $80 per session, sees each client for an average of 10 sessions, and helps three-quarters of her clients is preferable to a psychotherapist who charges $70 per session, sees each client for the same average number of sessions, but helps only one-half of her clients. The first therapist is more cost-effective. In this scenario, the first therapist would be paid $8,000 to treat 10 clients and, of this amount, $2,000 would be spent on the unsuccessful treatment of clients. The second therapist would be paid a total of $7,000 but $3,500 of this amount would be spent on unsuccessful treatment. In this case, a managed care company would save $1,500 for the additional $1,000 that is spent and more clients would be helped.

Cost-effectiveness, however, should not be the only factor that is taken into account in determining which service or which provider is preferable. For example, in the scenario with the two psychotherapists, the facts could be changed so that the amount of money spent on unsuccessful treatment is less for the less successful therapist than for the more successful therapist. The two therapists, for example, may each contract to serve managed care clients for $70 a session. One therapist sees clients for eight sessions and helps 50% of the clients. For 10 clients, this therapist would receive $5,600, and the cost of a successful outcome would be $1,120 per client ($5,600 divided by five). The second therapist sees clients for an average of 15 sessions and helps 80% of theclients. For 10 clients, the $10,500 would be received and the cost per successful outcome is $1,312 per client ($10,500 divided by 8).

In this scenario, the first therapist is more cost-effective because, although fewer people are helped, the low costs of successful treatment offset the costs of unsuccessful treatment. If a managed care company's chief motivation is cost savings, it will send clients to the first therapist. Most clients, if they are provided with information on both therapists and given a choice of provider, will choose the second therapist. In fact, if a managed care company is familiar with the results of outcome research, it will realize that the first therapist is performing at no better than chance levels of success, and it will question her therapeutic skills.

Cost Elements

A variety of cost elements must be taken into account in calculating the true cost of best practices.

Unit of Service Costs in Relation to True Cost

The cost of a unit of service is never the true cost. The unit cost, for example, of an hour of psychotherapy for a child at a mental health clinic may be $80 per hour (determined by dividing expenses by the number of billable treatment hours). It may take at least 10 one-hour sessions to achieve a favorable result in two-thirds of the children seen. In this clinic, the true cost of successfully treating a child is not $800 ($80 times 10). It is instead $800 multiplied by the cost of serving the one-third who did not profit from the 10-session psychotherapy and the children who prematurely withdrew from treatment.

By comparison, if another mental health clinic has a unit cost of $100 per hour but achieves success with 80% of its clients in the

10-session treatment protocol, that clinic will have a lower true cost of treatment. As this discussion suggests, true costs can be decreased when clients remain in treatment for the complete protocol and when a program admits only those clients who will respond favorably to the treatment. Additionally, true cost (as well as unit cost) will decrease when a program can increase billable hours without sacrificing outcomes (for example, in a mental health clinic, therapists schedule a greater number of clients or minimize the number of no-shows). It is important to note, however, that the field of human services is a long way from determining the true cost of most interventions.

Key Cost Elements

There are five major categories of cost when an agency changes from one intervention to another: direct costs (such as labor, equipment, and materials); overhead (such as rent, maintenance, and depreciation); induced costs (such as treatments added or avoided); indirect costs (such as lost wages or productivity); and incremental costs (costs per unit of outcome). Agencies that provide the same service may have different costs in any of these areas. A key cost element in the human services is labor, and as a result, labor costs should be carefully assessed. This assessment can be facilitated when staff maintain detailed logs of hours spent in planning and delivering each service and staff other than direct supervisors analyze time logs. Such information can allow investigators to determine the cost-effectiveness of different interventions provided in the same setting.

Cost-Benefit Factors

Whether a managed care company would prefer the first over the second residential treatment center, the first therapist over the second, or the first clinic over the second in the examples previously presented will depend on cost-benefit factors. A cost-benefit analysis places a monetary value on the benefit of an outcome. An analysis of cost-benefit factors is essential in determining true cost-effectiveness, but is rarely done because the analysis is complex.

The Financial Costs Associated with Unsuccessful Treatment

One key cost-benefit factor is the cost to society when clients do not receive treatment. Although this factor is difficult to calculate, greater efforts should be made to assess such costs. In most human service fields, cost-benefit research of this nature has not been undertaken. In some fields, preliminary work is underway. In the field of mental health, data is being gathered that demonstrates the relationship between psychotherapy and reduction of other medical costs for clients who are successfully treated.

In child welfare, cost-benefit factors have not been well examined. For example, it is clear that most children who are not successfully treated in residential treatment centers present significant financial demands on their families and communities upon their return. They may need special education or juvenile justice services; they may cause property or personal damage; and meeting their needs may generate additional costs for their parents. If a community refers children to a residential treatment center that has a 66% success rate, it will incur considerable expense in serving the 33% of children who were not successfully treated at the center. These children may need day treatment, private day schools, or special education classrooms in the public schools. Some of the children who have been unsuccessfully treated will remain in the residential treatment center or will be referred to a residential treatment center for older children. The costs associated with these services may far exceed the costs of sending children to a residential treatment center that achieves better outcomes at higher service costs.

Other cost-benefit factors from a financial perspective may be illustrated by returning to the example of the two therapists. The clients who were unsuccessfully treated by the first therapist may have lowered work productivity, with real costs associated with their poorer performance. If these work-related costs exceed the costs of the second therapist's treatment, a managed care company may prefer the second therapist. There may be costs associated with processing the complaints that unsuccessfully treated clients have about the first therapist as well as requests for changes in insurance coverage because of clients' dissatisfaction. If these administrative costs are higher than the costs of the second therapist's treatment, the managed care company again may prefer the second therapist. In both cases, the managed care company would obtain greater value, or more cost-benefit, for its money by using the second therapist.

The Cost-Benefit of Reducing Human Suffering

The value of a service should not be determined by examining financial costs alone. Another cost-benefit is the elimination of human suffering. From a financial perspective, a greater number of services may produce more favorable outcomes, but the costs may be unwarranted because the cost-benefit ratio is negligible. Nonetheless, from a humanistic viewpoint, the increased costs may be well justified. As an example, 15 sessions of outpatient psychotherapy (as opposed to 10 sessions) may enable a child with emotional problems to return to school and perform at an acceptable level but the gains from additional sessions may be of no financial value to the payer. However, from the child's perspective, the additional sessions may help reduce the child's achievement anxiety, raise his self-esteem, and strengthen the child's ability to make lasting friendships. The outcomes of a service clearly are value-laden, and in a managed care environment, human service agencies often will need to advocate for outcomes that enrich clients' lives.

Demonstrating Cost-Benefit

Cost-benefit may be demonstrated through research, although there are many challenges in this regard in the human services. Cost-benefit of human services also may be demonstrated from a community perspective.

Use of Research Designs

In an environment of reduced funds for many human service activities, agencies face pressures to immediately demonstrate their cost-effectiveness or risk reductions in funding. For example, a recent article in the *New York Times* stressed that child welfare prevention programs have not been subjected to "rigorous" scientific evaluation. Nevertheless, rigorous scientific evaluation cannot always take place in real world settings. How can control groups be established in studies of prevention programs? A scientist easily answers that at-risk families should be randomly assigned to prevention and non-prevention groups and comparisons of foster care placement rates should be made at various periods during and following the intervention. In many communities, however, when at-risk families are identified, the family court is involved and the judge orders that the family receive prevention services. No judge would ignore the needs of children at risk of foster care placement by supporting random assignment to a non-intervention control group. An alternative is the use of a comparison group, with an examination of foster care placement rates in communities that have and do not have prevention programs. Almost every county, however, provides some level of service designed to prevent foster care placement, and as a result, even counties that lack specific prevention programs may have relatively low rates of foster care placements. As a consequence, they would not be acceptable as a comparison group.

A third alternative is a cohort study in which the rates of foster care placement could be compared prior and subsequent to the initiation of prevention programs. This approach, however, could be criticized on several grounds. It could be argued that the prevention program was established because of increasing rates of foster care placement, and although the program might prevent a significant number of placements, the total number of children placed in foster care might remain stable. Scientists might take issue with the numerical manipulations that are needed when future placement rates are extrapolated from past rate increases and the current rates are compared with predicted rates. For example, if placement rates over a 5- or 10-year period increased exponentially, a future rate could be easily predicted. If placement rates climbed irregularly, however, predictions based on a -5 or 10-year average rate could produce an artificial figure that would make results difficult to interpret. Others may contend that prevention programs enable counties to identify more children in need of services, children who might have needed foster care placement in prior years, but were never identified. Because prevention programs now identify and serve these children, more children may be placed in foster care. As a result, placement rates may actually increase over past years.

Monroe County, New York, has tracked almost 2000 children for one year and three years following the closure of their cases and found that 95% of the children served through its prevention program had not been placed in foster care after one year and that 84% percent had not been placed after three years. The county, however, has not compared county placement rates before and after program implementation.

Assessment of Cost-Benefit from a Community Perspective

Critics of outcome research point out that effective programs do not view clients in artificial isolation from their environments but seek to support families through broad-based interventions, often in partnership with other agencies, that impact on entire populations. In this context, programs that seek to prevent foster care placements should not operate in isolation from other efforts to strengthen families. Examples of such broad-based efforts include the organization of tenants in communities where dangerously substandard housing conditions have forced large numbers of families and children into homelessness; provision of a range of positive socialization, athletic, and cultural activities for youth on evenings and weekends in neighborhoods plagued by gang violence; the organization of neighborhood watch and the development of police/community partnership programs in areas where the easy availability of drugs is a constant threat to family life; and the identification of census tracts with limited access to primary health care facilities with efforts to ensure that every child in those tracts is immunized. This approach views cost-benefit in terms of the value of enabling neighborhoods to be more conducive to healthy family life, block by block, school by school, and precinct by precinct, an approach that is more efficient than repairing families damaged by toxic environments one at a time.

Demonstration of the effectiveness of such an approach is a long-term project. Although proximal and distal goals can be stated in objective terms, quantification of achievements will involve a trial and error process. The process of demonstrating the achievement of long-range community building goals may be undermined by pressures to demonstrate immediate, short-term cost-effectiveness. For example, broad-based efforts can lead to lower foster care placements rates, but it will be necessary to convince funders that community mobilization is a necessary first step in placement prevention.

Staff Involvement in Assessing Cost-Effectiveness

In his book, *The Great Game of Business,* Jack Stack (1992) advises that all employees, regardless of their positions, be provided with financial information about the agency and receive training in interpreting financial data. Stack demonstrates that financial information can help each employee understand how his or her work fits within the organization and why he or she is important to company success. Each employee can provide feedback that can change the financial state of the organization in many ways. Stack's form of total quality improvement, called "open-book management," is based on the premise that "the more people know about the company, the better it will perform." He advises, as "an iron clad rule," that an agency "will always be more successful in business by sharing information with the people you work with than by keeping them in the dark." When financial information is closely guarded at the top or used to manage at a distance, employees will not support cost-effectiveness studies. On the other hand, when financial information is shared, it can promote mutual consultation and collaborative planning.

Outcome Management

An examination of cost-effectiveness requires outcome management, a process that differs from outcome assessment. Outcomes are tied to access (which relates to outcome management) and quality (which relates to outcome assessment). Outcome management recognizes the conditions of communities and families that influence outcomes in the real world, seeks to communicate to clients the risks and benefits of different follow-up services, and takes appropriate steps to compensate for the deficiencies in each discharge destination. For example, outcome management would recognize and respond to the fact that children who are discharged from residential treatment to communities with minimal mental health services or schools with insufficient special education services are likely to have higher rates of second admissions to residential treatment.

An agency can engage actively in outcome management by developing the services absent in the communities to which clients are discharged or by contracting with other providers to deliver such services. For example, in a community lacking mental heath services for children, child welfare agencies may join together to convince the Department of Social Services to support earlier discharges of children from foster care accompanied by longer aftercare services for children and their families. These efforts might include involving school systems or individual schools in developing services for certain children who are discharged from foster care. Such outcome management efforts can lead to long-term favorable results for children and families.

Summary

The cost-effectiveness of various interventions can be determined only by an examination of the outcomes achieved. If it is clear that clients achieve the same outcomes from services that differ in length, difficulty of implementation, or costs to deliver, it would easy to refer them to the most efficient service. However, the field of human services is a long way from being able to make such assessments. Human services still struggle to demonstrate that a clearly articulated intervention produces changes in a specific group of clients; to streamline service delivery so that it is most cost-efficient; to determine the costs of interventions; and to compare service costs with costs of interventions that achieve similar results with similar clients.

When an intervention is demonstrated to be the only intervention that achieves specific results with a specific group of clients, it is a "best practice" that should be utilized until another practice is proven to be more efficient or more effective. Many best practices require the expenditure of considerable funds, and the extent to which society values such results reflects the extent to which funds are provided for this purpose. Pearl Buck said, "A society should be judged by how it treats its weakest members." It is only when society holds that same view that sufficient funds, through taxes or contributions, will be made available to ensure best practices in human services.

Chapter 9:
•••••••••••••••••••••••••••••••••••••

Evaluation of Effectiveness: A Case Example

This chapter illustrates some of the principles discussed in previous chapters by describing an intervention model and discussing methods to evaluate the effectiveness of the program. The model involves the creation of a milieu program in a residential treatment center for emotionally disturbed children. The model was first applied at the Astor Home for Children in the early 1970s, and the agency has retained many of its features. Readers in the field of children's residential treatment may be interested in the model itself. However, readers who work in other human services can use the described evaluation methods, irrespective of the services they provide. Those readers who are only interested in the program evaluation should go directly to the section entitled "Monitoring Program Integrity."

The Milieu Model: The Theoretical Orientation

The philosophical orientation that guided milieu development at the Astor Home for Children Residential Treatment Center in the early 1970s was "developmental ego-supportive." A major postulate of this philosophy was that children referred for residential treatment display arrested ego development in certain areas of functioning, and that only by meeting earlier unmet needs can the children become "unstuck" from these arrested levels and

207

move into more advanced levels of development. The staff who planned the program were influenced by Abraham Maslow (1954, 1971), particularly his theory of need hierarchies and his belief that although unmet needs inhibited personality development, emotional growth would follow if those needs were met. Maslow's theories suggested that ego-development was achieved by providing experiences that met the child's needs at the arrested level of development. Once these needs were sufficiently met, the natural "push" for growth and hierarchal differentiation (first postulated by Heinz Werner, an organismic-developmental psychologist) would move the child to the next higher level of development. Like most ego-theorists, the program planners believed that ego growth best occurs within meaningful relationships with caregivers, including child care staff and parents.

In the planning process, emphasis was placed on the creation of environments in which children were "pushed" through structured relationships to develop new adaptive skills, especially improved interpersonal social behavior. Attention was given to carefully planned day-to-day programming designed to increase developmental attainments. Specific emphasis was placed on the developmental imbalances displayed by children in residential treatment and the therapeutic needs that result from those imbalances.

The Milieu Model: Implementation

The milieu program in the residential treatment center was implemented at the same time that Astor Home for Children was implementing a catchment-area service model to improve family services. In the context of this catchment-area model, the residential program began to admit whenever possible more children from the Bronx where the agency already operated two group homes. Services were developed in the Northeast Bronx to better serve children who resided in the residential center and in the group homes. By the mid-1970s, the agency had established a social service office, a number of foster homes, two more group homes, a school consultation service, and an outpatient clinic. Shortly thereafter, the agency established a day treatment center and a prevention program. The social service center was designed to provide a "homey" place for family treatment services for the parents of children being served in the residential treatment center and a place where parents could meet in support groups or informally for a brief respite and companionship.

The key programmatic elements of the milieu approach were family grouping, unrestricted home visiting, developmental assessments, the development of specific milieus, a focus on developmental attainments, a career ladder in child care, recreational programming, the fostering of relationships with "special children," and relationship and companionship therapy.

Family Grouping

Based on the theoretical orientation that child and family growth occurs as a result of guided relationships, the new model changed the overall milieu design so that children no longer were assigned to living units by age. The center was divided into independent living units (living groups) of nine children, a feature designed to contribute to feelings of intimacy. This approach was termed family grouping.

Prior to the model's implementation, children had been assigned to living groups by age and, whenever possible, staff were assigned to work with the age groups with whom they were most experienced. Therapists whose interests and skills in treating psychopathology matched children's presenting diagnoses were assigned to individual children. Until 1968, one of three part-time psychiatrists, accompanied by therapists, made regular morning rounds to the living units to learn about significant events that affected the children. In 1968, the "rounds" process was replaced with the "treatment team concept." Teams composed of the professionals who worked closely with each child began to meet regularly and participate in quarterly formal meetings led by one of the psychiatrists. A study undertaken shortly after this change (which today would be considered a quality assurance study) revealed that a higher number of treatment recommendations were implemented under the "team" as opposed to the "rounds" approach.

When children were placed in living units by age, they were regularly moved from unit to unit as they grew older or when new children were admitted. This approach was typical of institutional practices at that time. For example, if a 12-year-old child was discharged and a 6-year-old was admitted to a unit already at capacity, as many as a half-dozen children could be moved from one age unit to the next to accommodate the 6-year-old's admission. Such continual changes disrupted children's and parents' ongoing relationships with staff. They also disrupted the milieu as the movement of children among groups caused considerable unrest. The changed social structure that resulted from the addition of a new child to a living group caused temporary loss of group control, and because changes often occurred in more than one group, temporary loss of program control often occurred following each new admission. Under this system, the child's individual therapist remained with the child throughout the child's stay, and consequently, the therapist also had to relate to different child care staff each time the child was moved. At the same time, child care workers had to relate to many different therapists whose theoretical orientations varied widely and who held a variety of clinical viewpoints. In this situation, it was difficult to develop an integrated milieu treatment philosophy.

The staff who planned the new approach were aware of the wealth of data that supports the view that changes in behavior and attitude occur within consistent, positive relationships. They predicted that children would improve to a greater extent if they had ongoing relationships with consistent caregivers and that child care workers would be more apt to heed clinical advice if given in the context of an ongoing interpersonal relationship with a specific clinician. These principles suggested that children should remain in a single living group throughout their stays, and that clinicians should be assigned to specific living groups.

The concept of placing younger and older children of different sexes in the same unit (and assigning new admissions to the unit where there was a vacancy) met with considerable resistance. Only the social work staff initially favored the idea. They tended to see the negatives identified by other staff as positives. For example, they understood the concern that many of the older children who entered the residential treatment center had bullied and sexually molested younger siblings at home, but they saw family grouping as an opportunity to develop treatment plans to address this issue within the milieu. Social workers also saw family grouping as providing an opportunity for therapists, child care workers, and families to relate consistently to one another. One benefit identified was that child care workers may be less susceptible to the "adoption syndrome" so prevalent in residential settings where they become allied with the child against "irresponsible" parents and, often, against the social workers whom child care staff see as allied with the parents.

Eventually, child care workers and therapists supported family grouping. Child care workers realized that family grouping would allow them to work consistently with a small group of parents around discipline and child management issues, and that it presented an opportunity to assume a more meaningful role. Clinicians saw family grouping as an opportunity to broaden their role. The position of "team clinical coordinator," for example, was created.

At the same time, social workers became more integral members of the treatment teams. To some extent, their roles increased because of the catchment model that the agency was implementing. Social workers previously had served families in a number of geographical regions, and some social workers were serving families of children in all the age-groupings. The catchment model resulted in most of the children in the residential center being admitted from the Bronx rather than all five boroughs of New York City. With this change, social workers' assignments could be limited to the families of children in only two living groups.

One compromise was made because so few girls were referred for treatment. The living unit of the oldest group of girls (ages 10–12) was maintained, but the girls spent planned time visiting and socializing with children in the other units, serving as "big sisters" to younger children and, especially, to children in the youngest, mixed-sex unit.

Although the program planners considered having each child remain with the same teacher throughout his or her stay, they ultimately rejected this idea because the school program (comprising special education classrooms operated by the New York City Public Schools) was inadequately funded funding to obtain the wide range of curriculum materials each classroom would need to educate children at widely varying grade levels. It was possible, however, to ensure that each child had only one teacher in a year's time, and the educational program was patterned after psychoeducational models that stressed relationship building and conflict resolution. Teachers also agreed to consider keeping children in their classrooms for an additional year when children remained longer than one year in treatment and the treatment team felt that academic progress was primarily the result of the teacher-child relationship. Interestingly, many teachers felt validated by this plan as they had wanted to keep some children in their classrooms but never felt comfortable making such a request.

Unrestricted Home Visits

Prior to the 1970s, Astor Home for Children policy allowed a child to visit his family at home only when the child "earned" such visits. Newly admitted children had very few visits home, although the agency did allow parents to visit their children at the center and provided bus transportation for families. If a child who had been at the center for some period of time had behaved relatively well during the week, the treatment team might authorize weekend visits home toward the end of that week. The practice of granting home visits at the end of each week resulted in considerable behavioral disruption. All children constantly questioned staff about their chances for an upcoming visit. Some easily discouraged children believed they would never earn a visit and their behavior became worse as their anxiety mounted, and other children became disruptive when told they could not visit home. In some cases, staff believed that children's behavior worsened as the week progressed to avoid going home, a theory that was usually incorrect. Staff also felt concerned about children who earned home visits but who could not visit because of their families' problems. They wondered how to motivate children in the future when the children knew that home visits would not be possible. Child care staff also saw home visits as a motivator of behavior change. However, they argued that permitting children to have home visits regardless of their behavior would remove a major motivator for self-control.

At that time, staff knew little about the effects of brief separations. When children did "earn" a weekend visit, they often were difficult to control upon return. Staff questioned the wisdom of home visits for these children. Social workers were challenged on the quality of the family services that they were providing. For example, when social workers would report that a child was relatively well managed during a visit home, the staff would dismiss the report with questions such as, "Did you make a home visit during the weekend or are you relying solely on the parent's report?" Clinical staff often held strongly to the view that home visits were undoing the positive effects of treatment and should be prohibited for "problematic" children, and some treatment team members became pitted against the social worker and the family.

These issues led to staff training sessions on attachment and loss and the effects of brief separations on children. Training focused on how home visits can arouse unfulfilled expectations, how prolonged absence can lead to fantasies of abandonment by family, and how the disappointment the child feels upon returning to the center can be reflected in angry misbehavior. It also addressed the belief that disturbed children could make meaningful developmental changes simply by having their anticipation of a home visit realized. The training was combined with discussions about the developing philosophy of relationship building with caregivers, including parents.

The outcome of this work was an abandonment of the home visit policy. A new policy was put into place that whenever possible, all children were to go home every weekend regardless of their behavior. The new policy permitted exceptions only upon full team assessment and only for parental reasons. Parents, rather than staff, were to convey the decision not to have a home visit, preferably in family therapy sessions. Social workers were delighted by the policy change. The new policy allowed parents to have their child home more often, practice new child management practices, and discuss these practices with their social worker. The new policy also avoided problems related to strained attachments between parents and child as a result of the child's prolonged absence. Finally, with the new policy, the problems created by last-minute scheduling of family sessions before and after home visits were eliminated.

Developmental Assessment

Coinciding with the changes relating to family grouping and home visits, staff participated in a number of seminars on developmental issues. Clinicians began to realize that therapies were differentially effective with children at different developmental levels and began to work together on alternative therapeutic approaches rather than debating the relative merits of their individual theoretical orientations. This work led to a shift in diagnostic emphasis. Instead of looking at psychopathology with its emphasis on reality testing, personality description, and diagnostic classification, assessment focused on examining developmental attainments, including defenses against anxiety and developmental imbalances.

To guide their assessments, the agency provided clinicians with a written manual that contained a simplified version of Anna Freud's Developmental Profile and Jean Piaget's stages of cognitive development. The manual outlined five areas of development (object-relatedness, ego-control, socialization, psychosexual, and cognitive); the behaviors displayed by normal children at each of four age stages within each of these five areas; and the behaviors that characterized the functioning of children whose development was arrested in each of the age stages within each area. As examples, the manual described how a 2-year-old boy at the anal level of psychosexual development might be overly preoccupied with his feces, whereas an 8- or 9-year-old arrested at the anal level might be preoccupied with nose picking, smelling, pulling down other children's pants or smacking them on the rear end, "mooning" others, and using predominately anal curse words. When anxious, the child might engage in anal masturbation, and when very angry, he might smear his feces. With such information, clinicians began to make assessments based on a formalized developmental framework and develop specific recommendations for the child's treatment based upon developmental attainments rather than on behavioral symptoms. Child care staff began to complete checklists at regular intervals to record children's progress in developmental areas.

Developmentally Organized Milieus

The most significant change, but also the most difficult to implement and maintain, was the creation of uniquely different therapeutic milieus. Several milieu therapies had to be developed because of the different needs of children arrested at each of four general age stages of emotional development. A milieu therapy is a specialized interpersonal environment that is postulated to meet a child's stage-related developmental needs. Table 9.1, developed by a staff psychologist at Astor Home for Children, identifies components of milieus thought to optimize the development of children arrested at each of the four general stages of emotional development.

The model involves four uniquely different milieus, which could be used together in a living group. Because both family and age groupings can include children arrested at different levels regardless of their chronological ages, multiple milieus are often needed. Each milieu provides a specific set of experiences designed to foster a child's growth throughout the program. With the new program in place, the treatment plan for each child included an individualized "milieu" or a "specific attitude" about the child's needs and how to consistently respond to those needs.

In practice, it was found that significantly large numbers of children were arrested at the two earliest developmental levels and that almost no children who were admitted to the center were at the highest developmental level. The few children who progressed to the third or fourth developmental levels often went to outside schools, spent time with volunteers in the community, and participated in community-sponsored programs, such as the boy scouts or little league baseball.

Table 9.1 Developmental Levels and Treatment Environments

Stage of Emotional Development	Optimal Learning Conditions	Teaching Techniques	Milieu Treatment Implications	Milieu Techniques
Age 0 –1 Years The child feels and behaves like an impulsive, demanding infant.	Give maximum gratification and loving acceptance with minimal demands. Create a desire for the teacher's approval and a feeling of success.	Concrete rewards. Ample supplies. Visual objects. Teacher demonstrations. Rote learning. Avoidance of general discussions.	Meet needs unreservedly, lovingly, and consistently. Do not demand self-denial or sharing. Provide a permanent one-to-one relationship. Rely on staff and do not allow visits with unfamiliar people.	Offer maternal gifts in abundance. Use food as a highly personal and pleasurable experience (special dishes and feeding). Use cuddling and touching. Involve extra staff so that the maximum individual attention can be given. Have child care workers remain with the same children.
Age 1 –3 Years The child both defies and clings to adults, is often unreasonable, and shows poor self-control.	Provide highly structured environment for external support so that rules can be learned. Avoid inconsistency.	Order and routine. Few distractions. Simple directions. Short, definite tasks. Labeling and sorting. Emphasis on norms.	Utilize approval and disapproval by a loved person to assist child in gaining internal controls. Reassure without overprotection and use external support of controls without letting the child control the environment. Avoid punishment, impatience, and criticism.	When the loved person is absent, use group and institution rules as firm guidelines. Tolerate food fads and provide sweets freely. Provide a great deal of individual, free, recreational activity leading to physical mastery, such as bike riding and roller-skating. Use well-controlled paint and clay activities.

Age 3–6 Years

The child seeks pleasure rather than achievement and will control behavior to please a liked caregiver.	Maximize opportunity for independent self-assertion. Promote autonomy rather than enforced compliance. Promote relationships with caregivers for approval.	Discovery method. Individual activities. Free discussion. Exploration to provide sensual gratifications for eyes, ears, and hands. Experience in all modalities—music, games, and storytelling.	Provide explanation and reassurance. Accept masturbation within limits. Do not accept peer sex play. Allow freedom and encourage initiative. Continue to use approval and disapproval by loved person with further demands for self-control. Start using shame for destructive or unethical behavior; and use logic to aid control.	Recognize that child has relatively little need for mothering but needs close contact with adults of both sexes. Tolerate overemotional attitudes toward adults. Use fantasy play and storytelling. Encourage individual creative projects. Make use of trips and provide opportunities for new experiences.

Age 6–10 Years

The child is interested in mastering skills and making friends.	Opportunity to achieve in accordance with internalized aims, interests, and values.	Group projects. Learning about the environment. Mastery of skills with practical applications. Use of peer competition and peer approval.	Have realistic expectations. Provide compensatory experiences and skills. Give opportunities for practical achievement. Teach moral attitudes. Accept delay and frustration. Expect self-sacrifice.	Create high status for educational progress through admiration, interest, modeling. Foster other ego skills and talents, particularly in the poorest school achievers. De-emphasize athletic process unless it is the child's sole asset. Make real jobs available. Reward contributions to group living. Offer discussion. Focus on use of rationality and empathy as techniques for forming character and resolving conflicts.

Staff were trained on the components of milieus thought to optimize the development of children arrested at each of the four general stages of emotional development. The training involved audio taped presentations, seminars, team meetings, supervisory sessions, and daily team planning sessions. Staff also helped parents to relate to their children in keeping with these concepts. Some of the social workers, who had the primary responsibility for family services, began to conceptualize some of the problems that parents experienced in terms of developmental imbalances and designed their interventions accordingly.

To implement the four milieus, the Residence Director and the Director of Group Living (the key players in the model's implementation) invested considerable effort "behind the scenes." Some child care workers were not able to create each of the milieus by virtue of their personalities or ingrained beliefs. For example, some child care workers were unable to provide the "cuddling and physical attention" needed by a child arrested at the first level. Other child care workers felt the need to continue to "mother" children who had progressed to the third level when such nurturing was no longer needed. To minimize the effects of staff attitudes and preferences, the Director of Group Living and the group living supervisors (who had varying levels of commitment to the model) determined the developmental level of each child and the strengths and weaknesses of each child care worker. With this knowledge, they made treatment-related accommodations in scheduling and unit assignments.

Because the majority of children were at the two lowest developmental levels, general principles for managing children at these levels were continually reviewed with staff. These principles were culled from the literature on ego-impaired children. Because children at the lowest developmental level rarely show impulse control, the following principles were applied to their milieu:

- Protect and rescue the child from situations when the child is frightened, which is almost any time the child loses control and attacks another child.

- Ensure that there are no experiences when the child will lose face.

- Provide predictable restraints and prohibitions.

- Limit punishment, and when the child is disciplined, make statements such as "I want to help you control yourself" when using the controlling techniques.

- Help the child with frustrations by clarifying the ambiguity and uncertainty the child experiences.

- Expand the horizons of "do's" to offset the many "don'ts" experienced by the child.

- Expand the child's concrete skills.

- Support the child's defenses and reinforce use of more mature defenses.

Children at the second development stage have variable control, and the following principles were applied to their milieu:

- Make efforts to enable the child to please a cared-for adult.

- Expand the notion of good behavior to include notions broader than that of simple obedience.

- Help the child to feel admired for ego achievements.

- Provide opportunities for the child to be admired for behaviors other than compliance so that the child begins to feel that he or she wants to do what the caring adult wishes.

- Help the child develop trust in good impulses and the ability to control or mitigate bad or aggressive impulses.

- Set prohibitions that are protective rather than punitive or humiliating.

- Reinforce the child's sustaining fictions (beliefs that the child holds that are not necessarily true but maintain the sense of well being) and reaffirming past positive relationships.

The characteristics of children in the first developmental stage (no control) and in the second developmental stage (variable control) that led to these principles will not be described here. As emphasized in Chapter 2, however, a complete description of the children (and families as appropriate) is a requisite for meaningful program evaluation.

A Focus on Developmental Attainments

When children were no longer grouped by age and went home more often, staff identified many previously unobserved needs and modified individual treatment plans and unit and classroom behavior management plans accordingly. Behavior modification systems were employed in the school and the living units; an ego-supportive and psychodynamic approach was used in group therapy; and behavior management programs were modified to monitor and reward developmental attainments rather than impulse control and symptom improvement. Staff observed that symptom improvement was difficult to monitor because as a child moves from one developmental level to another, he displays different symptoms at the new developmental level. After an extensive review of the literature, staff concluded that developmental adaptive traits were better long range predictors than symptomatic traits.

A focus on developmental attainments may be challenging because as a child progresses up the developmental ladder, his behavior can appear to worsen. Often, the new behaviors create more difficult management problems for caregivers. Without a developmental framework, for example, staff may find it difficult to interpret new behaviors as indicators of growth when a child progresses from anal interests to obsessive interest in the opposite sex. Even when a developmental model is employed, it may be difficult to reach a consensus about change. Clinical experience suggests that advancements in emotional development can be reflected in a child's responses to personality testing before they are seen in actual behavior. The program instituted regular charting, monitoring, rewarding of developmental attainments, and periodic psychological assessment to keep the focus on development rather than on symptoms.

A Career Ladder in Child Care

Another major change was the establishment of a career ladder in the child care department. Career movement up the ladder required, in part, that child care workers demonstrate in writing and orally their understanding of different child development theories and their relationship to the stated philosophy of milieu treatment. Clinical staff assisted child care staff in obtaining the necessary knowledge for advancement by providing training material and audio tapes on a range of issues, including ego development and developmental assessment.

Recreational Programming

Initially, the program established a small division within the child care department to develop recreational programming. The staff created a developmental approach to recreational assessment and planned the major recreational activities that child care staff provided for children. Following the identification of each child's level of development by the treatment team, staff used a recreational assessment to identify the child's specific recreational needs and the developmentally appropriate recreational activities that would meet these needs. The agency subsequently established a recreation department.

Fostering Relationships with "Special Children"

Enhancement of the relationships between child care workers and children was a specific focus of the program. Prior to the implementation of the milieu approach, child care coverage consisted of one worker per living group; three shifts of workers between 7 A.M. and 9 P.M.; and two night workers who circulated from group to group while the children slept. If any situation required additional staff coverage, members of the Daughters of Charity who lived on-site would assist child care workers.

Each child care worker's schedule was for a seven-day period, with rotations so that each staff member periodically had a weekend off. One child care worker awoke the children in the morning, served them breakfast in the unit, prepared them for and then accompanied them to school, stayed with children who were ill, and intervened in crises that occurred when children's loss of control in the classroom required their temporary removal. A second child care worker provided noon and afternoon coverage, and a third child care worker covered the evening hours. Shift schedules overlapped, and child care workers could attend department, unit staff, and team meetings and receive group and individual supervision. Each staff member rotated among each of the three shifts.

The children quickly learned the staff coverage schedule and anxiously awaited the shift when their favorite child care worker would come on duty. Child and staff favoritism was a topic that constantly surfaced at unit staff and team meetings, as well as in supervision and informal discussion with clinical staff. Some child care workers were concerned by their own fondness for particular youngsters, feeling that their favoritism was unfair to the other children. Others were proud of the individual relationships they had formed with specific children in spite of the jealousies that other children displayed.

Program planners decided to capitalize on this natural phenomenon and maximize special relationships. Rather than feeling guilty for their favoritism, child care workers were encouraged to develop and sustain individual relationships with children, but in a structured way. Because the group size was usually nine children, each child care worker was asked to develop relationships with three children as "special children." The child care worker would relate to these three children in greater depth than the other children in the unit. Child care staff initially rejected this proposal, claiming that they could not devote their time to three children when nine children needed their attention. However, it was relatively easy to demonstrate that child care workers already related differently to their current favorites. Although they spent equal time with all children, the quality of their relationships with their favorites was different. It also was pointed out that if the three child care workers actually worked "equally" with all nine children, no really meaningful relationships would develop. Assigning all children to "special relationships" was an effort to ensure that each child had quality relationship time and could feel special. As concrete examples, a child care worker, after ensuring that all nine children were in bed, might read a bedtime story to one or more of three "special" children; a child care worker might stand next to and talk with one of his "special" children while supervising the bathroom routines of all nine children; or a child care worker might walk next to one of his "special" children while the group hikes or sleep in the tent of one of her children on an overnight camping trip.

Relationship Therapy and Companionship Therapy

In planning the new approach, a number of child care workers expressed the view that they could enhance their relationships with children and more easily manage children's behaviors if they could spend individual time with children. They believed that individual time with children would facilitate the quick resolution of the frustrating stage when children are ambivalently attached to the child care worker and strongly express both love and hate when reprimanded or ignored. Like other centers where naturally occurring relationships are fostered, staff had supported relationships between children and housekeeping, clerical, and maintenance staff, but other than the "special children" approach, the agency had never established a structured approach to such relationships. These considerations led to the development of two additional modalities of individual treatment: relationship therapy and companionship therapy.

Relationship therapy involves an individual relationship between an adult and a child where the child's emotional need for an attachment is met by a caring but firm adult. When this modality was added to the agency's program, time was scheduled in a play therapy room so that the child care worker could focus on fostering his relationship with the child. The relationship building process, modeled on the work of Alpert (1957), was regularly supervised by a trained psychotherapist to ensure that the focus remained upon relationship building, help the child care worker understand and manage particular behaviors that arose within the relationship, both within the therapy room and the living unit, and to help the worker understand and manage his feelings about the child.

Companionship therapy involves a one-to-one relationship of an adult with a child who has low self-esteem and relatively few same-sex adult role models with whom to identify. Its use followed from research findings that children with emotional problems made developmental improvements when he or she spent individual time with a caring adult under the supervision of clinical staff. At Astor Home for Children, both the support staff and community volunteers provided companionship therapy to children at the two highest levels of emotional development.

Summary

In summary, Astor Home for Children made nine major programmatic changes based on the theoretical model that contributed to milieu development: assigning children to mixed-age living groups, called "family groups," rather than to equal age groups; unrestricted home visits; a developmental approach to both initial and ongoing assessments and monitoring growth through assessment of developmental attainments; the implementation of four therapeutic milieus that were designed to meet developmental needs and "push" the child to the next stage of emotional development; creation of behavior modification programs that emphasized rewarding developmental attainments and task mastery; creation of a career ladder in the child care department based partially on written and oral demonstration of child development knowledge; selection of a small group of child care workers to create recreational assessments and design recreational activities in keeping with the learning and milieu needs identified at each developmental stage outlined in the model; assigning child care workers to relate more intensively to "special" children within their living unit and ensuring that each child was "special" to one child care worker; and the addition of two new individual treatment modalities to the treatment program—relationship and companionship therapy.

Monitoring Program Integrity

When staff do not experience the energy draining problems associated with meeting accreditation standards and work in an agency where interventions flow from a clearly articulated and operationalized treatment model, they generally have no trouble conceptualizing meaningful quality assurance studies. The purpose of quality assurance is to ensure treatment integrity. In assessing the milieu program just described, quality assurance would seek answers to such questions as: Are assessments focused on developmental issues? Is the milieu plan for a child being implemented correctly? Are the treatment team recommendations being followed? Do staff-child interactions reinforce the child's defenses? Are the workers relating differently to their three "special children?"

The importance of quality assurance in milieu therapies is emphasized by Rabkin, Weinberger, and Klein (1966, p. 282) who write:

> There is no magic in the words "therapeutic milieu," but there can be much seductive magical thinking following its initial creation. Such thinking assumes that the therapeutic milieu is self-perpetuating; that it can maintain a constant strength without continual surveillance; and that it can automatically mend a gap created by the loss of significant people.

Consequently, Astor can use the observational and coding techniques delineated by Paul (1991) to assess whether children at assessed developmental levels are receiving the appropriate services. For example, is a child diagnosed as emotionally arrested at between 2 and 3 years old receiving the optimal learning, teaching, and milieu techniques designed for a child at her assessed developmental level? Are staff tolerating food fads and encouraging high levels of gross motor activity? Is punishment kept to a minimum?

An assessment may reveal that a child is at a developmental level where growth will result if the child engages in pleasurable activities, experiences minimal frustration, and has a strong relationship with a caregiver. A child at this level should be participating in a recreational program in which the recreational activities are not contingent upon acceptable behavior; initial activities require the development of a new and simple skill, such as record playing, tumbling, simple card games, well-known table games, crayoning, and storytelling; the activities require no extra help or support; waiting and taking turns is minimized; there is no element of danger; demands regarding impulse control are minimal; participation in group games involves only high-powered "It" roles, such as "red-light, green-light," "Simon says," or "statues," and food and rhythm are involved whenever possible. The recreational programming for the child would not achieve the appropriate objectives if evaluation indicates that the child was expected to participate in treasure or scavenger hunts, relay races requiring concentration, dodge ball, or hide-and-seek; or if the child was periodically deprived of participation following disruptive or aggressive behavior. Should these elements be found, it may be that the recreational staff has "forgotten" that the child is at a level in which such activities are not appropriate, a condition sometimes referred to as treatment plan amnesia. On a larger level, if an ongoing analysis reveals increased restraints during evening recreational activities, further study might reveal that the evening staff has "forgotten" the objectives of the model and has lapsed into delivering inappropriate recreational activities. This type of "forgetting" is sometimes referred to as model amnesia.

An Evaluation of Proximal Outcomes

For each of the nine programmatic elements of the model, there were specific proximal outcomes. As the following discussion indicates, an agency could evaluate the achievement of these outcomes in a variety of ways. Some of the outcomes were assessed by Astor Home for Children, and some were not.

Family Grouping

A range of positive and negative outcomes associated with family grouping were predicted. Staff who favored family grouping predicted that it would result in a number of positive outcomes. Specifically, they postulated that family grouping would, in order of importance:

- Enhance the child's and, to some extent, the parent's relationships with caregivers.

- Improve milieu stability throughout the program as fewer children would be moving to new groups with each new admission.

- Produce a wider range of treatment team recommendations.

- Produce more meaningful communications between clinicians and child care workers.

- Enhance the social worker's effectiveness as a treatment team member.

Staff who opposed family grouping predicted a range of negative outcomes. They believed that family grouping would result in:

- More bullying of younger by older children.

- More sexual acting out in the living units.

- Greater difficulty in delivering appropriate recreational activity in the living units.

- Greater difficulty with transitions because as a result of the wider age range in each living group, older children would make the transition more quickly than younger children.

- Greater difficulty finding unit staff who could effectively work with children across a wide age range.

All of the predicted positive changes could be assessed in a variety of ways, depending upon available information. One approach would be a staff opinion questionnaire that asked about each of the predicted outcomes. Other measures also could be used. If, as predicted by supporters of family grouping, the relationships between children and caregivers improved and relationship improvement was considered the major prerequisite for change, it would be important to identify the other improvements that were realized. Lengths of stay might have shortened; discharge prognoses might have become more favorable; developmental advancement might have proceeded more quickly; the number of parental complaints might have decreased; or child and parental consumer satisfaction surveys might reveal increased levels of program satisfaction or satisfaction with program staff. For example, parents might make more phone calls to the living groups, not only to speak to their child but to talk with the child care workers, or might communicate to child care workers through letters.

Astor Home for Children examined only length of stay. The agency utilized a comparison group of children admitted prior to the model and found that the average length of stay of children treated under the new model was shorter than children admitted in the three years prior to the model's implementation. These measures could not be examined because, at the time, parental complaints, phone calls, and letters were not logged consistently, nor were consumer satisfaction surveys utilized.

The second positive predicted outcome, increased milieu stability, could be assessed by examining critical incidents or daily logs before and after each new admission. The number of crisis interventions or time-out room placements, the extent to which restraints were used, accident reports, and staff turnover rates could be analyzed. Staff reports indicated that after the model was fully implemented, newly admitted children caused temporary disruption only in the group to which they were admitted. New admissions no longer precipitated total center disruption. An analysis of time-out room placements supported staff reports as there was a significant decrease in the use of the time-out room by all living groups after new admissions to the center. Staff also reported that treatment team time, which formerly was focused to a great extent on reaching a consensus as to which children would be least affected by required transfers to older groups, was now spent on other issues.

An evaluation of the third positive predicted outcome (wider range of treatment team recommendations) could be accomplished through a clinical record review of a sample of cases before and after the full implementation of family grouping. An evaluation of the fourth predicted positive outcome (more meaningful communications between clinical and child care staff) could be undertaken through a staff questionnaire; a review of department staff meeting minutes to determine the extent of meeting time devoted to discussion of interdepartmental friction, or an analysis of the number and type of interdepartmental memos exchanged before and after the change in grouping. An evaluation of the fifth predicted positive outcome (enhanced social worker effectiveness as a member of the treatment team) could be conducted through an assessment of the extent to which treatment plans were more family-oriented. Specifically, the analysis could determine whether there were recommendations in the child's treatment plan regarding visits or whether plans had been made for parents to discuss discipline strategies with child care workers. The Astor Home for Children did not evaluate these outcomes.

It also would be important to assess the presence or absence of the predicted negative effects of family grouping. An analysis of staff logs or incident reports could reveal whether bullying of younger by older children or sexual acting out (the first two predicted negative outcomes) occurred more frequently in family grouping than in age grouping. It may be that the evaluation would reveal that the incidence of either behavior increased in some living groups but decreased program-wide. Should this finding emerge, a more detailed study could be undertaken of the children in each living group who bully or sexually molest others (a maximum variation sample) to determine if their relationships with their victims differ in some significant way.

Greater difficulty in providing recreational activities in the living units as a result of the wider age range in each living group (the third predicted negative outcome) could be assessed through staff interviews, child satisfaction surveys, or incident reports. Evaluation of this outcome would not be necessary if, along with a change to family grouping, there was also a change in recreational programming. In fact, such concurrent changes occurred at Astor Home for Children. Child care workers were assigned to activities rather than to living groups for certain periods during the day which were designated as recreational, and children were assigned to activities by developmental level. Staff reports indicated that the majority of child care workers were pleased by the new program direction.

Difficulty in transitions (the fourth predicted negative outcome) could be assessed by an analysis of critical incidents occurring during transition periods. At Astor Home for Children, this anticipated problem did not materialize because the children who were older and more accomplished in each living unit began to help the younger children prepare for transitions. The final anticipated negative outcome (greater difficulty finding unit staff who could effectively work with children across a wide age range) likewise did not materialize. The change in the delivery of recreational activities partially addressed the anticipated skill deficiencies among the wide age range of children in each living group. In addition, staff began to clearly understand the developmental needs of the children and to recognize that most children fell into the lowest two developmental levels. It became apparent that children who varied in age by as much as six years could profit from the same recreational activity.

Unrestricted Home Visits

The agency expected that a number of changes would result from unrestricted as opposed to "earned" home visits (or visits contingent upon improved behavior). The following positive outcomes, in order of importance, were predicted:

- Fewer feelings of abandonment by and less interpersonal distance between parents and children.

- More frequently scheduled family therapy sessions.

- Less disruption throughout the milieu at the end of each week (Thursday and Friday).

- Shorter lengths of stay.

- Greater social work satisfaction with service delivery scheduling.

- Greater parental satisfaction with the program (although it was recognized that parents who expected respite from their child may show lower levels of short-term satisfaction).

Several potential negative effects also were identified:

- More program-wide disruption on Sunday evenings and Monday mornings.

- A higher level of overall disruption throughout the program because a major motivator for change (earned home visits) would no longer be available.

- Increased lengths of stay because of two factors: increased time away from the program would dilute the program's effectiveness (children would receive less than the maximum treatment dose); and more time would be spent in the presence of pathological parents, which would increase the opportunity for negative parental influences on the child.

- Because the length of stay was limited by some funding sources, less of an opportunity for the child to improve during time-limited treatment.

The presence of increased attachment and decreased emotional distance between parent and child (the first and most important predicted positive outcome) could be assessed in a number of ways. Social workers could ask parents and children about their current relationships. Chart reviews of social workers' progress notes could be conducted to determine whether social workers' notes reflected the predicted positive changes. Staff psychologists could review children's responses to psychological tests to assess whether they reflected changes in their relationships with their parents. Psychotherapists could assess these feelings in ongoing therapy sessions.

The frequency of family therapy sessions (the second predicted positive outcome) could be assessed before and after the implementation of the model. A chart analysis did reveal an increased number of family therapy sessions with children who were treated under the model compared to children enrolled in previous years. However, a criterion sampling study was not performed. The extent to which lengths of stay were shortened (the fourth predicted positive outcome) could also be examined, with an in-depth study made of children who exceeded the expected length of stay (criterion sampling) to determine whether home visits differed in some way for this subgroup of children. As previously noted, length of stay was shorter for the group of children treated under the new model, but any or all of the program components could have contributed to this finding.

If not obvious from general observation, staff, incident, or accident reports could be analyzed to determine whether there was either a decrease in disruptions on Thursdays and Fridays (one of the predicted positive outcomes) or an increase in disruptions on Sunday evenings and Monday mornings (one of the predicted negative outcomes). Another evaluative approach would be to examine staff absences. During these periods, if child care workers frequently called in sick or if "on call staff" were reluctant to report to duty, it would be likely that these days of the week were particularly troublesome. If disruption was common during these time periods, child satisfaction surveys might reveal decreases in children's feelings of being "safe." The agency did conduct an analysis of time-out room placements and found, as predicted, a decrease in room use. However, child satisfaction surveys were not in use at the agency at the time so they could not be examined.

Greater satisfaction on the part of social workers and parents (two predicted positive outcomes) could be assessed through the use of satisfaction questionnaires. Although client satisfaction surveys were not in use at the agency at the time the model was implemented, the agency did conduct an analysis of social work department meeting notes. A comparison of these notes during and after the model's implementation indicated increased social worker satisfaction with scheduling and greater parental satisfaction.

The final two predicted negative outcomes (related to increased length of stay and inability to maximize limited lengths of stay) are laden with value judgments. Both concerns assume that residential treatment requires a seven-day-a-week service in an out-of-home setting. There is no research evidence that demonstrates the maximum dose of residential treatment, and, consequently, residential treatment could just as well take the form of a five-day-a-week service. These negative predictions also suggest that only staff efforts are treatment and that children's home visits over weekends mean that no treatment is taking place. However, home visits could be viewed as an opportunity for parents, as partners in the treatment of the child, to practice newly learned skills of child management.

In actual practice, unlimited home visiting did not occur. Home visits took place only when social work staff believed that the visits would be helpful to children and parents. Home visits were restricted if it appeared that the family was not ready for the child's visits home. Because many parents had serious problems themselves, they often were not able to make rapid changes in their child management skills, and it was not expected that children in residential treatment would quickly become more manageable. Far more home visits took place during children's second year of residential treatment. This practice was consistent with the agency's previous findings that home visits during the child's first year of treatment were associated with more negative outcomes for children and home visits during the second year of treatment were associated with more positive child outcomes.

Developmental Assessment

The contribution of developmental assessments to program enhancement can be evaluated in several ways. The agency could ask child care and educational staff and parents to evaluate the meaningfulness of developmental reports. Using a case record review, the agency could determine the number of recommendations based on developmental assessments that staff actually implemented (comparing current and older clinical records). Alternatively, the agency could survey referral agencies about the helpfulness of developmental assessments (although it is likely that few agencies would respond).

To evaluate whether developmental assessments identify each child's developmental imbalances and unique conflicts, the agency could maintain a sample of written reports separate from children's clinical records. The findings and recommendations of the assessments could be presented verbally at the initial planning meetings for children, but the written assessments could be kept confidential from staff. After children have been in treatment for several months, the assessments could be retrieved, identifying information deleted, and the child care and educational staff asked to identify which assessment belonged to which of the children with whom they worked closely. If staff are unable to identify the child for whom each assessment was developed at well above a chance level, the assessments would be worthless, even if the recommendations were helpful. This component of the model was not formally evaluated.

Developmentally Organized Milieus

Unique therapeutic milieus were the heart of the ego supportive and developmental model. Milieus were designed to meet the needs of children whose development was arrested at one of four developmental stages, although, as noted earlier, most children were arrested at the first two stages of emotional development. One method of measuring the perceived impact of the model, and the first step in quality assurance efforts, would be simply to ask staff if they know what they are doing. If staff are unable to verbalize how the model works, they cannot apply it to their work with children. The daily presence of the model in child care workers' minds can be assessed by asking staff to describe treatment plans for individual children. Although written procedures and developmentally-based individual treatment plans will have stated what child care workers are to do, if staff have not committed the procedures or plans to memory, the result is obvious. No further evaluation would be necessary.

If this step reveals that staff understand the model, the second stage of quality assurance efforts is to assess whether the model is being correctly implemented. Using stratified purposeful sampling, children at each of the four developmental levels could be observed as they participate in milieu activities. If observations indicate that the model is being correctly implemented, the third stage in quality assurance efforts is to assess whether implementation is ongoing. Only when it is clear that the model is being implemented throughout children's stays in residential treatment can the fourth stage of quality assurance be implemented: an assessment of the perceived effectiveness of the program.

The perceived effectiveness of the model could be assessed through parent and child satisfaction surveys that include questions about the milieu programs and, particularly, questions about their relationships with program staff and their satisfaction with outcomes. High scores on satisfaction surveys suggest perceptions of program effectiveness. Other aspects of program effectiveness also could be assessed. For example, if it is found that children's relationships with their parents improve, clinical staff could administer a measure of attachment or reexamine psychological tests that were administered as part of treatment planning for evidence of changes in the child's attachment to parents. If children are assessed with personality tests at admission and again at discharge, they can be scored for level of object-relatedness and the levels can be compared. If children show more object-relatedness at discharge, evidence other than staff and client opinion would suggest that program goals have been met. This type of data provides a type of construct validity for the model.

Construct validity, or the degree to which a measure relates to theoretically similar measures, can be established with other data. For example, several investigators have demonstrated that as children become more attached, their fantasies become less distant and include more human images. A child initially may fantasize living in outer space surrounded by monsters; later in treatment, the child may have predominant fantasies of living in the wild with frightening wolves that are eventually befriended; and at discharge, the child may fantasize belonging to a gang or playing on a baseball team and hitting lots of home runs. These fantasies may be expressed in children's drawings throughout treatment, and the drawings may be compared. Similarly, children's creative stories can be analyzed.

Once it is established that most children's relationships have improved, the agency can compare confirming and disconfirming cases to further clarify the treatment process. Confirming cases would be children whose developmental progress was in keeping with predicted changes in all areas. Disconfirming cases would be children whose relationships improved but who remained arrested in other developmental areas or children whose relationships remained arrested but who made developmental advancements in other areas. Astor Home for Children did not perform these evaluations. The agency conducted a retrospective study of clinical records, however, revealing that later hospitalizations of children were better predicted by the Rorschach Test for object-relatedness than by staff judgment (Tuber, 1983).

Revision of the Behavior Modification Program

Although child care staff typically are aware of children's responses to major changes in a behavior modification system, children themselves are key informants about the effectiveness of the program. Children, for example, can be asked about the role of the rewards that follow developmental attainments. If their answers reflect a lack of awareness of the relationship between rewards and developmental attainments, the behavioral modification system is not maximally effective. At discharge, client satisfaction questionnaires can include items such as "How much do you think the reward system used in your living group helped you to make progress?" or a question that asks the child to rank various treatment components, including rewards for developmental attainments, from "most helpful" to "least helpful." Astor Home for Children did not use such surveys at the time the model was implemented.

The Child Care Career Ladder

Opinion surveys can be used to assess child care career ladders. As an example, clinicians can be asked to evaluate the degree to which child care workers demonstrate child development knowledge in their daily work: Do child care workers use such knowledge in their discussions at unit staff meetings? Do they communicate with other staff about developmental issues? Do they convey developmental knowledge in their meetings with parents? Similarly, parents can be asked (either formally or informally) what they learned from child care workers. Specifically, they can be asked whether child care workers helped them learn how to set more realistic goals for their children, how to help their children with their developmental conflicts, how to play more appropriately with their children, and how to assist their children in selecting appropriate leisure time activities. This component was not assessed by the agency.

Recreational Programming

Staff and client opinion can be used to assess the perceived quality of recreational programming. Questions may include: Do child care staff believe that more appropriate recreational activities are now being provided? Do children who participated in both systems have more fun since the model was implemented? Do all children report having fun? Do children report making better use of their free time? Do children report playing with other children or playing alone for longer periods of time? Do parents report that their children play better with peers or that their children play alone for longer periods of time? Do parents have more fun with their children?

Following the implementation of recreational programming, clinical staff reported that child care staff offered a greater variety of recreational and leisure time activities. Activities more closely related to children's emotional and developmental needs replaced such activities as dodge ball, basketball, baseball, touch football, and capture the flag (which are more appropriate for normally functioning children). Competitive games were replaced by walks in the woods, camping trips, group singing, plays, group swims, collage making, aerobic exercises, tumbling, and dance. In addition, child care staff introduced simple indoor and outdoor games (such as hide-and-seek or leap frog), and although "sophisticated" street children initially resisted them, they later played them with relish. They also used simple relay races for children who were developmentally ready for some level of competition.

Special Children

As described earlier, each of the three child care workers assigned to a living group were asked to develop a special relationship with three children and with their parents, so that all nine children would be "special" to one staff member. Following implementation of this program component, staff reported that children quickly learned to wait for the special attention they would receive from their "special" child care worker and that the disruptions that previously had been associated with children's complaints about "favoritism" vanished.

The effectiveness of this component could be assessed through questions to children: Which child care worker do you like the best? Which child care worker likes you the best? Questions could be posed to parents, therapists, and teachers regarding which child care workers the child talks most about most during visits home, in therapy, and in the classroom. Psychologists can examine the results of sentence completion tests or create tests with items such as: "In the afternoons, I like myself best when the child care worker I am with is_____;" "At bedtime, the staff member I want to read me a story is _____;" or "When I am hurt on the playground, I want _____ to help me."

Relationship Therapy and Companionship Therapy

Relationship therapy (a child's individual time with a child care worker) can be evaluated with the same methods that are used to evaluate the "special children" component of the model. However, the evaluation of companionship therapy requires a somewhat different approach. Because this therapy is usually delivered by a community volunteer who may become important to the child but who is not the child's main affectional bond, the companion's name is unlikely to appear in response to items on a sentence completion test. As a result, evaluation should involve staff members who are asked to provide information about the value of the companionship experience. Does the child talk about the companion? Does the child boast or brag about new skills learned from the companion? Is the child more willing to try new things or does he feel less frustrated by failure following visits with the companion? Additional evaluation methods for companionship therapy are provided by Goodman (1972).

Distal Outcomes

The ultimate test of a program's effectiveness is whether clients achieve distal outcomes. Some human service providers are satisfied when distal outcomes are achieved by the end of the intervention. For example, in job training programs, the distal outcome is typically employment. Rarely do programs examine whether trainees are still employed several years later. In the health care arena, providers generally are satisfied when patients report feeling better. By contrast, mental health professionals are not satisfied solely with outcomes at the completion of treatment. They want to examine outcomes at regular follow-up intervals, although research with some groups of clients suggests that follow-up findings add little to information obtained at the end of treatment. Providers of mental health services want to know if interventions made clients stronger or better able to handle future stressors. Likewise, agencies that provide children's services are not satisfied simply to report that, under certain intervention conditions, children improve or improve faster. Do children treated under one model fare better than children treated under a different model? Do improvements last?

When Astor Home for Children implemented the new model, the decision was made to apply the program with children then in treatment and with all newly admitted children. This decision was based on a strong belief in the model and on practical limitations. The agency had performed two follow-up studies during the years that the traditional program was in place. In the second follow up study, the agency had located 365 out of 447 children, and the agency considered comparing the follow-up findings of this group of children (all of whom had completed the traditional program) with findings for children treated under the new model.

However, this design was problematic. First, the traditionally treated group of children were older than the group treated with the new model, and the children's state of adjustment at follow up would be confounded by length of time since discharge, age stage difficulties, and other life experiences. Next, although children from the second follow-up study could be matched with children treated under the model on age, IQ, length of time since discharge, and other nuisance variables, the agency could not assume that the two groups of children returned to the same community atmospheres. Some communities had fragmented service systems, and other communities had developed a more complete range of community mental health services for children.

Although enthusiastic about the model, the staff knew that few treatment models can exert a powerful lasting influence in the face of serious future obstacles. The two earlier follow-up studies had revealed that post-discharge factors, primarily community supports, were more important than past treatment factors in the child's current adjustment. Many children who had achieved their proximal goals returned to communities with almost no resources or social supports, and their adjustment was found to be negatively affected. Other children who were less well adjusted at discharge returned to communities with a full array of services and social supports and were rated as better adjusted at follow-up. In fact, as the agency implemented outcome management efforts, the residential treatment center began to admit children primarily from the Bronx where an array of community services had been developed. These developments created some of the postdischarge differences that undermined a comparison of the earlier, traditionally treated group and the group treated under the new model. Because there was not an adequate comparison group, the agency concluded that a follow-up study was not cost-effective. Such a study would have been expensive and would have revealed little about distal outcomes.

Summary

Although Astor Home for Children performed some evaluative procedures on the milieu model, it did not systematically perform all of procedures discussed in this chapter. Had staff done so, some of the unplanned institutional drift that took place in the program over the years might have been prevented. When planned program changes are proven effective, the results should be recorded in a program profile, as discussed in Chapter 1; written procedures should be developed; and every effort should be made to develop quality assurance procedures that will help to ensure program continuation.

Quality assurance procedures were initially conceived as methods of ensuring compliance with standards imposed by accrediting and licensing bodies. However, as time passed, professionals in the field came to realize that such procedures can help ensure service delivery integrity. Quality assurance can be used to ensure that clearly articulated services, perceived by staff and consumers as efficient and effective, continue to be delivered in the same format and manner as they were delivered when first evaluated.

Any suggested improvements in efficient and effective services should be subjected to close scrutiny. Whenever possible, clients should be matched on relevant nuisance variables and randomly assigned to new and traditional services. In this way, the progress and outcomes of the two groups can be compared and truly meaningful decisions can be made about program enhancement. When this approach is not practical, as was the case with the milieu model, a comparison group should be constructed. Clients served during the years immediately preceding the new model can serve as a comparison group. Although a comparison group was used to assess the relative effectiveness of the milieu model on proximal goal achievement, the group was not appropriate for use as a comparison group for distal outcomes following discharge.

Meaningful program evaluation cannot take place in a vacuum. Management staff must be intimately involved in the design, implementation, and analysis of outcome assessments. Correct program implementation is essential to evaluation and, like ensuring the continuation of efficient and effective programs, is a management function. The active management of outcome achievement requires an agency to develop best practices; continually deliver best practices as designed; and prevent best practices from being reinvented or changed capriciously (although refinement can be expected). Without these systems, the outcomes that are achieved will be fleeting. Outcome assessment and outcome management are important for continued client success.

References

Achenbach, T. M. (1991). *Manual for the Child Behavior Checklist and 1991 profile.* Burlington: University of Vermont.

Alexander, F. (1956). *Psychoanalysis and psychotherapy: Developments in theory, technique and training.* New York: W. W. Norton.

Alpert, A. (1957). A special therapeutic technique for certain developmental disorders in pre-latency children. *American Journal of Orthopsychiatry, 27,* 256–270.

American Managed Behavioral Healthcare Association and National Association of State Mental Health Programs. (1995). Public mental health systems, Medicaid re-structuring and managed behavioral healthcare. *Behavioral Healthcare Tomorrow, 4,* 63–69.

Bickman, L. (1996). A managed continuum of care: More is not always better. *American Psychologist, 51,* 678–701.

Bickman, L. (1997). Resolving issues raised by the Fort Bragg Evaluation. *American Psychologist, 52,* 562–565.

Bickman, L., Guthrie, P. R., Foster, E. M., Lambert, E. W., Summerfelt, W. T., Breda, C. S., & Heflinger, C. A. (1995). *Managed care in mental health: The Fort Bragg Experiment.* New York: Plenum.

Biederman, J., Faraone, S.V., & Chen, W. J. (1993). Social adjustment inventory for children and adolescents: Concurrent validity in ADHD children. *Journal of the American Academy of Child and Adolescent Psychiatry, 32,* 1959–1064.

Burdsal, C., Force, R., Klingsporn, M., & Jackson, D. (1995). Refinements in the measurement of appropriate adult functioning. *Residential Treatment for Children and Youth, 12,* 65–83.

Cohen, J. (1988). Things I have learned (so far). In A. E. Kazdin (Ed.), *Methodological issues & strategies in clinical research* (pp. 315–333). Washington, DC: American Psychological Association.

DiMotta, R. & Whaley, A. (1996, October). *Development of a questionnaire to assess client satisfaction at the Astor Child Guidance Center.* Paper presented at the Sixth Annual Virginia Beach Conference on Children and Adolescents with Emotional and Behavioral Disorders, Virginia Beach, VA.

Dougherty, D., & Bowman, E. H. (1995). The effects of organizational downsizing on product development. *California Management Review, 37*, 2844.

Dubin, M. D. (1995). Grasping capitation. In G. L. Zieman (Ed.), *The complete capitation handbook* (pp. 29–35). Tiburon, CA: CentraLynk.

Eber, L., & Nelson, M. (1997). School-based wrap around planning: Integrating services for students with emotional and behavioral needs. *American Journal of Orthopsychiatry, 67*, 385–395.

Freeman, M. A. (1995). Eleven types of risks and their antidotes. In G. L. Zieman (Ed.), *The complete capitation handbook* (pp. 37-42). Tiburon, CA: CentraLynk.

Fulcher, L. C. (1991). Teamwork in residential care. In J. Beker & Z. Eisikovitz (Eds.), *Knowledge utilization in residential child and youth care practice* (pp. 213–236). Washington, DC: Child Welfare League of America.

Glass, G.V., McGaw, B., & Smith, M. L. (1981). *Meta-analysis in social research.* Beverly Hills, CA: Sage.

Goodman, G. (1972). *Companionship therapy.* San Francisco: Jossey-Bass.

Grossman, J., & Tierney, J. R. (1993). The fallibility of comparison groups. *Evaluation Review, 17*, 556–571.

Haase, R. F., Waechter, D. M., & Soloman, G. S. (1982). How significant is a significant difference? Average effect size of research in counseling psychology. *Journal of Counseling Psychology, 29*, 58–65.

Hodges, K. (1990). *The child and adolescent functional assessment scale (CAFAS).* Unpublished manuscript. Ann Arbor, Michigan.

Hodges, K. (1993). Structured interviews for assessing children. *Journal of Child Psychology and Psychiatry, 34*, 49–68.

Hunkeler, E. M., Westphal, J., & Williams, M. (1996). Computer assisted patient evaluation systems: Advice from the trenches. *Behavioral Health Care Tomorrow, 5*, 73–75.

Institute for Behavioral Health Care. (1996). *Performance indicators in behavioral healthcare.* Portola Valley, CA: Institute for Behavioral Health Care.

Kazdin, K. E., & Bass, D. (1988). Parent, teacher, and hospital staff evaluation of severely disturbed children. *American Hournal of Orthopsychiatry, 58*, 512–523.

Keller, R. A., Cicchinelli, L. F., & Gardner, D. M. (1989). Characteristics of child abuse treatment programs. *Child Abuse & Neglect, 21,* 354–361.

Kinney, J., Haapala, D., & Booth, C. (1991). *Keeping families together: The homebuilders model.* New York: Aldine de Gruyter.

Kiresuk, T. J., & Sherman, R. E. (1977). A reply to the critique of goal attainment scaling. *Social Work Research & Abstracts, 13,* 9–11.

Leibrich, J. (1994). Improving the success rate in follow-up studies with former offenders. *Evaluation Review, 18,* 613–626.

Magura, S., & Moses, B. S. (1986). *Outcome measures for child welfare services: Theory and applications.* Washington, DC: Child Welfare League of America.

Maslow, A. H. (1954). *Motivation and personality.* New York: Harper & Row.

Maslow, A. H. (1971). *The farther reaches of human nature.* New York: Viking Press.

McGloin, J., Holcomb, S., & Main, D. S. (1996). Making anonymous pre-post tests using subjected generated information. *Evaluation Review, 20,* 724–736.

Miller, S., Rotheram-Borus, J., Piacentini, J., et al. (1992). *Successful negotiation acting positively: A brief cognitive behavioral family therapy manual for adolescent suicide attempters and their families.* New York: Department of Psychiatry, Columbia University.

Moos, R. H. (1974). *Evaluating treatment environments.* New York: Wiley.

Mordock, J. B. (1996). The road to survival revisited: Organizational adaptation to the managed care environment. *Child Welfare, 75,* 195–218.

Mordock, J. B. (1997). *Preparing for managed care in children's services: A guide for mental health, juvenile justice and special education professionals.* Providence, RI: Manisses Communica-tions Group.

Mordock, J. B. (1998). Preparing for managed care in residential treatment. *Residential Treatment for Children and Youth, 15,* 55–68.

Mordock, J. B. (1999a). Current practices in public child welfare. In S. Wernet (Ed.), *Managed care in the human services* (pp. 53–73). Chicago: Lyceum.

Mordock, J. B. (1999b). *Selecting treatment interventions: A casebook for clinical practice in child and adolescent managed mental health* (2nd ed.). Providence, RI: Manisses Communications Group.

Mordock, J. B. (2000). Outcome assessment: Suggestions for agency practice. *Child Welfare, 77,* 689-710.

Mordock, J. B. (in press). A model of milieu treatment: Implementation and factors contributing to "drift" from the model over a 30-year period. *Residential Treatment for Children and Youth.*

National Institute for Mental Health. (1986). *Assessing mental health treatment outcome measurement techniques.* DHHS Pub. No. (ADM)86-1301. Washington, DC: U.S. Government Printing Office.

Osborne, D., & Gaebler, Y. (1993). *Reinventing government.* New York: Plume.

Paul, G. L. (Ed.). (1986). *Assessment in residential treatment settings.* Champaign, IL: Research Press.

Pfeiffer, S. I. (1995). *American Association of Children's Residential Centers: Treatment outcomes assessment survey.* Alexandria, VA: American Association of Children's Residential Centers.

Phillips, E. L., Phillips, E. A., Fixsen, D. L., & Wolf, M. M. (1974). *The teaching-family handbook.* Lawrence, KS: University Printing Service.

Rabkin, L., Weinberger, G., & Klein, A. (1966). What made Allen run? The process of communication in residential treatment. *Journal of the American Academy of Child Psychiatry, 5,* 272–283.

Rogers, E. M. (1983). *The diffusion of innovation.* New York: Free Press.

Samen, J. (1996, June 27). *Health Care Financing Administration, Partial hospital team meeting.*

Seaberg, J. R., & Gillespie, D. F. (1977). Goal attainment scaling: A critique. *Social Work Research & Abstracts, 13,* 4–8.

Stack, J. (with B. Burlingham). (1992). *The great game of business.* New York: Currency-Doubleday.

Taylor, F. W. (1911). *The principles of scientific management.* New York: Harper and Brothers.

Trabin, T., Freeman, M. A., & Pallak, M. (1995). *Inside outcomes: The national review of behavioral healthcare outcome programs.* Tiburon, CA: CentraLynk.

Tuber, S. B. (1983). Children's Rorschach scores as predictors of later adjustment. *Journal of Consulting and Clinical Psychology, 51,* 379-385.

United Way of America. (1996). *Measuring program outcomes: A practical approach.* Alexandria, VA: United Way of America.

Wagner, M. M. (1995). Outcomes for youths with serious emotional disturbance in secondary school and early adulthood. *The Future of Children, 5,* 90-112.

Wagner, M. M., & Blackorby, J. (1996). Transition from high school to work or college: How special education students fare. *The Future of Children, 6,* 103-120.

Waskow, I. E., & Parloff, M. B. (1975). *Psychotherapy change measures. Report of the Clinical Research Branch (NIMH) Outcome Measures Project.* DHEW Publication No. (ADM)74-120. Washington, DC: U. S. Government Printing Office.

Weisz, J. R., Weiss, B., Han, S. S., Granger, D. A., & Morton, T. (1995). Effects of psychotherapy with children and adolescents revisited: A meta-analysis of treatment outcome studies. *Psychological Bulletin, 117,* 450-468.

Appendix A
Minimum Data Set for Children in Foster Care

_____ 1. Give the numbers of all the factors that were associated with the child's placement in care.

a. Parental alcohol abuse
b. Parental substance abuse
c. Parent's death
d. Parent's incarceration
e. Parent's health problems
f. Parent abused or neglected child
g. Parent's mental health problems

_____ 2. Family structure from which the child was removed for the current foster care episode.

a. Married biological parents
b. Married step parents
c. Father biological parent
d. Mother biological parent
e. Unmarried couple
f. Father step parent
g. Mother step parent

Biological mother:
h. Not divorced
i. Divorced

Biological father
j. Not divorced
k. Divorced

3. Year of birth of child's first caregiver _____

4. Year of birth of child's second caregiver (if applicable)
_____

_____ 5. Family structure of the foster family.

a. Married couple
b. Unmarried couple
c. Single female
d. Single male

249

_____ 5B. Write the numbers of all that apply.

        a. With natural children present
        b. With adopted children present
        c. With step children present
        d. With relative children present
        e. With other foster children present

_____ 6. Year of birth of current foster parent(s).

_____ 7. Race of foster parents.

        a. White   e. Native American
        b. Black   f. Other
        c. Hispanic   g. Unknown
        d. Asian

_____ 8. Placed child has been adopted.

        a. Yes   b. No

9. Child's age when adoption was legalized _____

10. Date of first removal from home _____

11. Total number of removals from the home _____

12. Date of last removal from the home _____

13. Computer generated date when "last removal date" went into the system _____

14. Date of placement in current foster care setting _____

15. Number of previous placement settings during the current removal episode _____

____ 16. Current removal was:

    a. Voluntary
    b. Court ordered
    c. Not yet determined

____ 17. Placement setting in which the child is currently living:

    a. Preadoptive home
    b. Kinship foster family home
    c. Nonrelative foster family home
    d. Therapeutic foster care
    e. Family treatment home (mental health program)
    f. Regular child care institution
    g. Residential treatment center (Department of Social
       Services funded)
    h. Residential treatment facility (mental health program)
    i. Supervised independent living
    j. Trial home visit

____ 18. Legal guardian type:

    a. Undetermined   g. Client
    b. Co-guardian   h. Public administrator or official
    c. Birth parent   i. Other relative
    d. Adoptive parent   j. Relationship unknown
    e. Sibling
    f. Non-relative has legal
       rights of guardian

19. Financial responsible party: _____

20. Guardian's legal relationship to child: _____

Last Name: _____

First Name: _____

Address: _____

City: _____

State: _____

Zip Code: _____

Phone: _____

Appendix B

Child and Family Survey Following Intensive Home-Based Treatment Services

BACKGROUND

Patient's name: _____

Birth date: _____

Age: Years _____   Months _____

Date of admission: _____

Date of discharge: _____

No. of treatment sessions: _____

   With patient _____   With parents _____

Child adopted: Yes _____   No _____   Age adopted: _____

Did time of admission correspond with any family member or family's anniversary date, such as a birthday, death, or auto accident?

_____ Yes _____ No

Describe: _____

_____

_____

Patient lives with: (check only one)

_____ Both biological or adoptive parents

_____ Single mother

_____ Single mother and partner

_____ Single father

_____ Single father and partner

_____ Mother and stepfather

_____ Father and stepmother

_____ Divides time between separated parents

_____ Divides time between divorced parents

_____ Grandparent with parent visits

_____ Grandparent without natural parent contact

_____ Other relation with parent present
       Relative: _____

_____ Other relation without parent present
       Relative: _____

_____ Non-family setting
       Type: _____   Name: _____

_____ Relatives living in family home
       Name: _____

Educational Placement:

_____ Regular class in age appropriate grade

_____ Regular class, but behind at least one grade

_____ Special class in public school for students with disabilities

       Give condition: _____

       Special education center: _____

       Day treatment program: _____

Child has history of prior mental health treatment?   Yes   No

List treatments: _____

_____

_____

Child has history of prior out-of-home-placements?   Yes   No

List placements: _____

_____

_____

• •

1. Presenting symptoms which led to referral for treatment: _____

_____

_____

2. Situational factors which contributed to referral for treatment: ___

_____

_____

3. Other conditions (Check all that apply):

_____ Death of family member
_____ Marital discord
_____ Parental sexual dysfunction
_____ Marital change
_____ Child visiting non-custodial parent
_____ Mother not living at home
_____ Other parental mental health problems
_____ Inadequate housing
_____ Health problems
_____ Recent relocation

_____ Financial problems
_____ Employment problems or changes
_____ Physical abuse of children
_____ Neglect of children
_____ Other family members placed or moved away
_____ Social isolation
_____ Addition of new person to family unit
_____ Criminal activity
_____ Custody dispute or placement
_____ Runaway
_____ Abuse of alcohol
_____ Abuse of drugs
_____ Domineering father figure
_____ Domineering mother figure
_____ Pregnancy   Who: _____
_____ Venereal disease
_____ Other   Specify: _____

5. Child's strengths: _____

_____

_____

6. Child cooperative with treatment process? _____ Yes _____ No

   Both parents equally cooperative?   _____ Yes   _____ No

   _____ Mother more   _____ Father more

7. Clinician rated outcome from termination form: _____

_____

_____

8. Treatment contracting?   _____ Yes _____ No

   Individual child contract utilized?   _____ Yes   _____ No

   Summarize contract:_____

   _____

   _____

   Parent contract utilized?   _____ Yes   _____ No

   Summarize contract:_____

   _____

   _____

9. Verbal therapies?   _____ Yes _____ No

   a) Individual patient counseling
   b) Parent counseling (check one)
       ___ Maternal caretaker
       ___ Paternal caretaker
       ___ Both caretakers together
   c) Family therapy

10. Behavior modification procedures?   _____ Yes   _____ No

    a) Patient contract with therapist, with therapist supplying
       reinforcers?

       _____ Yes _____ No

    b) Patient contract with therapist, with parents supplying
       reinforcers?

       _____ Yes _____ No

    c) Patient/family contract, with therapist supplying reinforcers?

       _____ Yes _____ No

d) Patient/family contract, with family supplying reinforcers?

_____ Yes _____ No

Describe behavior modification procedures including reinforcers: _____

_____

_____

Did therapist report that these procedures worked? As originally structured?

_____ Yes _____ No

With slight modification?   _____ Yes _____ No
After much trial and error work?   _____ Yes _____ No
Never worked, procedures dropped? _____ Yes _____ No

11. Cognitive therapies employed

a) Anger management training with patient? _____ Yes _____ No

b) Anger management training with parent? _____ Yes _____ No

c) Identification of specific stressors with patient and listing of ways to cope with each specific stressor?

_____ Yes _____ No

d) Identification of specific stressors with parent(s) and listing of ways to cope with each stressor?

_____ Yes _____ No

_____ Mother   _____ Father   _____ Both parents

e) Relaxation training? _____ Yes   _____ No

f) Guided imagery? _____ Yes   _____ No
   Describe: _____

12. Parent training provided (check all that apply)

_____ Training in specific symptom management
_____ Training in general disciplinary procedures
_____ Training in specific disciplinary techniques
_____ Training and support of limit setting
_____ Training in value of medications as adjunct to treatment
_____ Training parents in household management
_____ Training family to work together on household tasks

Describe: _____

_____

_____

13. Communication skills training received:
_____ Listening skills of patient
_____ Listening skills of (circle)

    Mother   Father   Both parents

_____ Teaching "I" messages to (circle)

    Patient   Father   Mother   Siblings

_____ Role playing techniques

Describe: _____

_____

_____

14. Problem solving skills taught:

_____ Conflict resolution
_____ Mediation skills
_____ Role playing techniques
_____ Concrete problem solving for problems unique to family

Describe: _____

_____

15. Helped family members move from isolation:

_____ Increased contact of family with school

_____ Increased family involvement in community activities:

Patient   Father   Mother   Siblings

_____ Helped family members obtain needed community resources

Patient   Father   Mother   Siblings

_____ Helped family members obtain needed employment (circle)

Patient   Father   Mother   Siblings

Describe: _____

_____

_____

16. Helped family members to develop recreational outlets:

_____ Encouraged family events

_____ Facilitated family members participation in community recreational activities (circle):

Patient   Mother   Father   Siblings   Whole family

_____ Therapist participated in recreational outings (circle):

With patient   With whole family

Describe: _____

_____

_____

17. Linking to other service providers? _____ Yes   _____ No

Summarize linking activities: _____

_____

_____

18. Supplementary funds employed? _____ Yes _____ No

Describe fund use: _____

_____

_____

19. Changes in family structure or in organization of family space?

_____ Yes _____ No

Describe: _____

_____

_____

20. Helped parents improve their marital relationship? ___Yes ___ No

21. Provided concrete services, such as driving child to school or parent
    to shopping?

_____ Yes _____ No

Describe: _____

_____

_____

22. Specific outcomes:
_____ Child's symptoms which led to admission no longer present
_____ Child's symptoms which led to admission decreased in
       intensity
_____ Child developed more adaptive behaviors

Describe: _____

_____

_____

_____ Family learned to manage child's symptoms better
_____ Family made structural changes to adapt to child
_____ Parent(s) learned to cooperate together in child's behalf
_____ Sibling(s) became either more cooperative or more
      supportive of patient
_____ Schools made adaptations to child
_____ Child effectively linked to supportive services

23. List other changes in child or family:_____

_____

_____

Appendix C
....

Case Review: Reasons for Treatment Failure

Client's name: _____ Age:_____ Sex: _____

Modalities of treatment attempted:

_____ Child in individual therapy   Date initiated _____
_____ Family therapy   Date initiated _____
_____ Parent counseling   Date initiated _____
_____ Group therapy   Date initiated _____
_____ Medication from clinic MD   Date prescribed _____
_____ Medication from other MD   Date prescribed _____
_____ Case management/linking   Date initiated _____

Salient Situational Factors: _____

_____

_____

Response to treatment limited by primary caretaker:

_____ Involved with alcohol
_____ Involved with drugs
_____ Denies involvement with drugs/alcohol
_____ Abusive
_____ Neglectful
_____ Intellectually limited
_____ Clinically depressed
_____ Severely mentally ill
_____ Denies seriousness of adult's problems which limits
        involvement with treatment plans

Response to treatment limited by marital conflict:

_____ Caretakers will not work together cooperatively
_____ Caretakers involved in non-family activities which limit time available
_____ Caretakers openly antagonistic or abusive
_____ Battering situation

Response to treatment limited by child's:

_____ Denial of problem
_____ Unrealistic view of caretakers
_____ Limited intellectual ability
_____ Serious psychopathology

Family participation primarily due to:

_____ CPS or other agency requirements
_____ Need for help during crisis
_____ Need for someone to hear complaints or feelings about child or agency

Unsuccessful plans attempted:

_____ Revision of the treatment plan
_____ Increase in the frequency of treatment sessions
_____ Decrease in the frequency of treatment sessions
_____ Change in the modality of treatment
_____ Evaluation for medication therapy
_____ Referral for psychiatric evaluation
_____ Referral for psychological evaluation
_____ Referral for neurological evaluation
_____ Referral of parents for own treatment
_____ Termination of services by clinician

Child's psychopathology required alternative level of care but:

_____ Parents would not accept
_____ School system would not classify child
_____ School system would not change educational placement
_____ Department of Social Services would not place child
_____ Intensive Case Management Unit would not accept child

Appendix D
Follow-Up Questionnaire
Caregiver Interview

Child's name _____ Child's birth date _____

Program: _____

Interviewer(s) _____

Date(s) of interview _____

Name of person interviewed _____

Relationship to child (check):

_____ Father		_____ Foster Mother	
_____ Mother		_____ Group Home Worker	
_____ Stepfather		_____ Teacher	
_____ Stepmother		_____ Childcare Worker	
_____ Foster Father		_____ Other	

Dates in program: _____ to _____

Child discharged to: _____

Child's residence at time of admission (check):

_____ With Parent(s)	_____ DFY Fac.
_____ Foster Home	_____ Family Treatment Home
_____ Relatives	_____ With Adult Friends
_____ Group Home	_____ With Peers
_____ RTC	_____ Alone
_____ RTF Child Care Inst.	_____ Homeless
_____ Res. School	_____ Other

265

Gender of child (check): _____ Male   _____ Female

Race of child (check):

_____ White   _____ Asian

_____ African American   _____ Native American

_____ Hispanic   _____ South Asian

_____ Biracial   _____ Other

Home address of child at time of admission:_____

_____

_____

Presenting symptoms of child at time of admission (from record):

_____

_____

_____

Progress made in treatment (from record):

_____ Much improved   _____ Worse

_____ Improved   _____ Much worse

_____ Same

Child's current living situation(check):

_____ With Parent(s)   _____ DFY Fac.

_____ Foster Home   _____ Family Treatment Home

_____ Relatives   _____ With Adult Friends

_____ Group Home   _____ With Peers

_____ RTC   _____ Alone

_____ RTF Child Care Inst. _____ Homeless

_____ Res. School   _____ Other

Address of child's current residence:_____

_____

_____

Address of child's permanent residence: _____

_____

_____

Places child has lived since discharge from program: _____

_____

_____

Number of family moves since child's discharge: _____

Has your child received therapeutic or counseling services since discharge from our program?

_____ Yes _____ No

    If yes, these services are delivered by (check):

_____ School   _____ Hospital

_____ Clinic   _____ Drug Rehab Program

_____ Day Treatment   _____ Residential Treatment

_____ Private Provider   _____ Other

Is your child currently enrolled in school?

_____ Yes _____ No   What grade? _____

_____ Public school regular class

_____ Public school regular class with support services
    (inclusion)

_____ Resource room services

_____ Public school special education class with main-
    streaming

_____ Self Contained special education class (circle one):
    1-6-1,   1-8-1,   1-10-1, 1-15-1, 1-12 or 1-15

_____ Alternative education center

_____ Day treatment program
_____ Private day school
_____ Residential school
_____ Other

How do you feel your child is doing in school (check one)?
_____ Very good
_____ Good
_____ Acceptable
_____ Marginal
_____ Awful

Explain: _____

_____

_____

Have you been approached by the school because of any
behavioral problems of your child?

_____ Yes _____ No

Explain: _____

_____

_____

Have you been approached by the school because of academic
problems of your child?

_____ Yes _____ No

Explain: _____

_____

_____

Since discharge from our program, has your child ever been suspended from school?

_____ Yes _____ No

If yes, how many times? _____

What was the longest period? _____

Is your child ever truant from school?

_____ Yes _____ No

If yes, how many times? _____

What was the longest period? _____

Explain: _____

_____

_____

Describe your child's interests, hobbies, leisure time activities, and recreational pursuits: _____

_____

_____

Is your child in any organized sports? _____ Yes _____ No

If yes, check one:

_____ Little, Junior, or American League Baseball

_____ CYO or PAL Basketball

_____ Township or Travel Soccer League

_____ Pop-Warner Football

_____ Hockey League

_____ School sponsored athletics

_____ Activity: _____

_____ Other: _____

How many good friends his/her own age does your child have? ___

How many hours per week does your child spend with friends? ___

Do you feel that your child's friends are good influences on your child?

_____ Yes _____ No

Explain: _____

_____

_____

Has your child been in trouble with the police or courts?

_____ Yes _____ No

If yes, how often? _____

Explain the circumstances: _____

_____

_____

Describe any instances of stealing since your child was discharged from our program:_____

_____

_____

Describe any instances of serious physical aggression since your child was discharged from our program:_____

_____

_____

Do you think your child uses alcohol or drugs?

     _____ Yes _____ No

     Alcohol _____   Drugs _____   Both _____

     Explain: _____

     _____

     _____

How often does he or she use:

     Alcohol _____   Drugs _____?

Is alcohol or drug use affecting his or her school work?

     _____ Yes _____ No

Is alcohol or drug use affecting his or her relationships with family or friends?

     _____ Yes _____ No

     Explain: _____

     _____

     _____

How does your child obtain his or her spending money? _____

_____

_____

Do you feel that the services offered by our program contributed to your child's ability to function better at home?

     _____ Yes _____ No

     In the community?   _____ Yes   _____ No

At school?   _____ Yes   _____ No

With friends?   _____ Yes   _____ No

Over all, the services your child received at our program:
_____ Helped greatly
_____ Helped
_____ Had no effect
_____ Made the situation worse

Compared to how your child functioned prior to receiving our services, your child is now doing:
_____ Better
_____ About the same
_____ Worse

Overall, do you see your child as currently able to handle his/her life satisfactorily?

_____ Yes   _____ No   _____ Not Sure

Do you or your child have any positive memories about our services?

_____

_____

_____

Any negative memories? _____

_____

_____

Comments: _____

_____

_____

Appendix E

Follow-up Questionnaire
Child Interview

Child's name: _____ Child's birth date: _____

Sex: _____ Male   _____ Female

Race: _____

Interviewer's name: _____

Interview date: _____

Tell me about your hobbies and interests: _____

_____

_____

Are you in school? _____ Yes   _____ No

If no, explain: _____

_____

_____

Do you receive special education services? _____ Yes   _____ No

Describe: _____

_____

_____

Have you ever been suspended from school? _____ Yes _____ No

How many times? _____

What was the longest period? _____

Explain: _____

_____

_____

Do you have any problems in school? _____ Yes _____ No

Explain: _____

_____

_____

Do you ever stay home from school simply because you do not want
to go?

_____ Yes   _____ No

Explain: _____

_____

_____

How many good friends your own age do you have? _____

What do you and your friends do together? _____

_____

_____

Have you ever been involved with the police or the court?

_____ Yes _____ No

Explain:_____

_____

_____

Do you remember anything about the services you received at our program?_____

_____

_____

What problems did you work on at our program with your therapist?

_____

_____

_____

What problems did you work on at our program with your family?

_____

_____

_____

How are these problems now? _____

_____

_____

_____

Appendix F
Selected Instruments

Appropriate Adult Functioning Scales (for boys with disruptive behavior disorders). St. Francis Academy Inc., Box 1340, Salina, KS 67401; Telephone: 913/825-0541.

Beck Depression Inventory and the Children's Depression Inventory (ages 8–13). Both available from the Psychological Corporation, Harcourt Brace Jovanovich, Inc.

Bene-Anthony Family Relations Test. Available from the National Foundation for Educational Research, The Mere, Upton Park, Slough, Bucks, United Kingdom.

Burden of Care Questionnaire. Available from the Vanderbilt Center for Social Policy, Vanderbilt University, Nashville, TN.

Checklist of Adolescent Problem Situations. Available from Timothy A. Cavell, Department of Psychology, Texas A&M University, College Station, TX 77843-4235.

Child Behavior Checklist, Attention Deficit Disorders Evaluation Scale, the Conners' Parent Scale, and Teacher Rating Scale (children's scales). Available from Hawthorne Educational Services, 800 Gray Oak Drive, Columbia, MO 65201. (Information 314/874-1710; Orders only 800/542-1673).

Child Well-Being Scales. Available from CWLA Press, P.O. Box 2019, Annapolis Jct., MD 20701-2019; 800/407-6273 or 301/617-7825; or www.cwla.org/pubs.

Child Sexual Behavior Inventory. Available from The Mayo Clinic, Section of Psychology, Rochester, MN 55905. Telephone: 507/284-2511.

Child Dissociative Checklist. Available from Frank W. Putman, M.D., Unit on Dissociative Disorders, National Institute of Mental Health, Bethesda, MD.

CRS-Revised and DSMD. Available from the Psychological Corporation. Ego Strength Scale (composed of items taken from the Minnesota Multiphasic Personality Inventory). Available from the Psychological Corporation.

Global Level of Functioning Scale and the Child Assessment Schedule. Available from Dr, Jay Hodges, Eastern Michigan University, Department of Psychology, 537 Mark Jefferson, Ypsilanti, MI 48197.

Piers-Harris Children's Self Concept Scale. Available from Western Psychological Services, 122031 Wilshire Blvd., Los Angeles, CA 90025.

Helping Alliance Questionnaire. Available in Luborsky, L. (1985). Therapist success and its determinants. *Archives of General Psychiatry, 42,* 602–611.

Parent Satisfaction with Treatment Scale. (developed by R. Dimotta and A.Whaley). Available from the Astor Child Guidance Clinic, 750 Tilden Street, Bronx, NY.

The SF 36 (a health questionnaire). Available from the Psychological Coorporation. Also see Ware, J. E. & Sherbourne, C. D. (1992). The MOS 36-item short form health survey (SF-36): I. Conceptual framework and item selection. *Medical Care, 30,* 473–483.

About the Author

Between 1983 and 1997, John B. Mordock directed the Astor Home for Children's outpatient mental health programs in Dutchess County, New York. Services under his direction included day treatment for children and adolescents; school-based counseling; 24-hour hospital and foster-care diversion services; intensive case management; and outpatient clinics with specialized teams that served sexually-abused children, youth with substance abuse problems, the Family Court, PINS diversion, and families where domestic violence had resulted in supervised visitation with children. Dr. Mordock was associated with the Astor Home and Child Guidance Centers for a total of 28 years.

He has published close to 100 papers in professional journals, many of which are devoted to program evaluation issues and practices. He is a Fellow of the American Psychological Association and a Diplomat of the American Board of Professional Psychology. His books include: *Counseling the Defiant Child; Crisis Counseling of Children and Adolescents* (an expansion of the life-space interview concept developed by Fritz Rydl); *Ego Impaired Children Grow-Up: A Follow-Up of Children in Residential Treatment; Selecting Treatment Interventions: A Casebook for Clinical Practice in Child and Adolescent Managed Mental Health* (which discusses the process of assessment, goal planning, and modality selection in children's services); *Custody Evaluations: A Clinician's Guide to Interviewing and Report Writing;* and *Preparing for Managed Care in Children's Services: A Guide for Mental Health, Child Welfare, Juvenile Justice and Special Education Professionals.* He is the only full-time, practicing professional to write a textbook, *The Other Children: An Introduction to Exceptionality,* that has been used by several hundred universities.

Dr. Mordock's professional experiences have been greatly enriched by having been a birthparent, a foster parent, a single parent, and currently, a stepparent.